MACMILLAN/McGRAW-HILL

GRADE 4

TESTING PROGRAM

MATHEMATICS IN ACTION

Teacher's Manual

Chapter Tests
- Forms A and B, Multiple-Choice
- Form C, Free-Response

Cumulative Tests

End-Year Test

BLACKLINE MASTERS & TEACHER'S MANUAL

MACMILLAN/McGRAW-HILL SCHOOL PUBLISHING COMPANY
New York   Chicago   Columbus

MACMILLAN/McGRAW-HILL SCHOOL DIVISION
866 THIRD AVENUE NEW YORK, NEW YORK 10022

Printed in the United States of America

ISBN 0-02-108675-3

9 8 7 6 5 4 3 2 1

CONTENTS

INTRODUCTION TM1

DESCRIPTION OF THE TESTS TM1

DESCRIPTION OF THE COMPUTER MANAGEMENT SYSTEM (CMS) TM2

PROCEDURES FOR ADMINISTRATION TM2

EVALUATION, PRESCRIPTION, AND RETEACHING TM3

CONVERSION TABLE FOR SCORING TESTS TM5

SCORING CHARTS AND PRESCRIPTION TABLES TM7–TM38

Chapter 1	• Scoring Chart	TM7
	Prescription Table	TM8
Chapter 2	• Scoring Chart	TM9
	Prescription Table	TM10
Chapter 3	• Scoring Chart	TM11
	Prescription Table	TM12
Chapter 4	• Scoring Chart	TM13
	Prescription Table	TM14
Chapter 5	• Scoring Chart	TM15
	Prescription Table	TM16
Chapter 6	• Scoring Chart	TM17
	Prescription Table	TM18
Chapter 7	• Scoring Chart	TM19
	Prescription Table	TM20
Chapter 8	• Scoring Chart	TM21
	Prescription Table	TM22
Chapter 9	• Scoring Chart	TM23
	Prescription Table	TM24
Chapter 10	• Scoring Chart	TM25
	Prescription Table	TM26
Chapter 11	• Scoring Chart	TM27
	Prescription Table	TM28
Chapter 12	• Scoring Chart	TM29
	Prescription Table	TM30
Cumulative 1	• Scoring Chart	TM31
Cumulative 2	• Scoring Chart	TM33
Cumulative 3	• Scoring Chart	TM35
End-Year	• Scoring Chart	TM37

STUDENT PROFILE CHART TM39

CLASS PROFILE CHART TM41

SAMPLE CMS ANSWER FORMS TM43

TEST ANSWER SHEET TM47

CONTENTS
(continued)

TESTS 1–106

Chapter 1 Test   • Form A 1
     • Form B 3
     • Form C 5

Chapter 2 Test   • Form A 7
     • Form B 11
     • Form C 15

Chapter 3 Test   • Form A 19
     • Form B 21
     • Form C 23

Chapter 4 Test   • Form A 25
     • Form B 29
     • Form C 33

Chapter 5 Test   • Form A 37
     • Form B 41
     • Form C 45

Chapter 6 Test   • Form A 49
     • Form B 51
     • Form C 53

Chapter 7 Test   • Form A 55
     • Form B 57
     • Form C 59

Chapter 8 Test   • Form A 61
     • Form B 65
     • Form C 69

Chapter 9 Test   • Form A 73
     • Form B 75
     • Form C 77

Chapter 10 Test   • Form A 79
     • Form B 81
     • Form C 83

Chapter 11 Test   • Form A 85
     • Form B 87
     • Form C 89

Chapter 12 Test   • Form A 91
     • Form B 93
     • Form C 95

Cumulative 1 Test 97

Cumulative 2 Test 101

Cumulative 3 Test 105

End-Year Test 109

ANSWER KEYS TM49–TM106

INTRODUCTION

This book contains a Teacher's Manual and a complete series of blackline masters for tests to accompany *Macmillan/McGraw-Hill MATHEMATICS IN ACTION,* Grade 4. The tests themselves follow this Teacher's Manual, which contains a variety of materials for use in administering and scoring the tests, record keeping, and reteaching.

DESCRIPTION OF THE TESTS

Chapter Tests. The Chapter Tests measure student progress on individual chapter objectives. These tests are available in three forms: Form A, Form B, and Form C, all of which test the same chapter objectives and have the same number of items. Any of the three forms may be used as a pretest, as a posttest, or for retesting.

Form A and Form B are multiple-choice tests that are parallel in length and content. In Form C the content of Form A is duplicated but in a free-response format; that is, students write in the correct responses to the items. Occasionally items on the Form C tests require students to select the best answer. These selection items include estimation skills for which a wide range of answers is possible or skills for which a truly open-ended item would be less appropriate. By using both the multiple-choice and the free-response formats, the teacher may help ensure that students get practice in taking standardized tests and have an opportunity to demonstrate higher level thinking skills than might otherwise be possible.

The three forms of Chapter Tests offer the teacher several means of assessing students' understanding of the material. A teacher may choose to use only one of the tests provided or may use Form A as a pretest and Form B as a posttest. Additionally Form A may be used as the principal test with Form B as a make-up test. Form C may be chosen as an advanced test or in place of Form A.

Each Chapter Test is designed to be scored by objective and by total test. In general the items on the Chapter Tests are sequenced in random order. There are, however, two exceptions: items that refer to a table, graph, or other stimulus are grouped; and problem-solving items are grouped at the end of the test. In the Chapter Tests, the computation items are separated from problem-solving items by a double line and a stop sign. This distinction is made so that, if the teacher chooses, students may use calculators for the problem-solving section of the test. The integration of calculators into the learning and testing processes is intended to enhance not replace computational skills. The use of calculators for these items is optional; calculators are not required to solve any of these problems. Students may use estimation, mental math, or paper and pencil if the teacher decides not to allow calculators.

Cumulative Tests and End-Year Test. The Cumulative Tests and End-Year Test are comprehensive multiple-choice tests that measure student progress on skills and concepts covered from the beginning of the year. Since these tests are cumulative, they measure all or most objectives from previous chapters, but with a greater emphasis on objectives from the most recently taught chapters.

The Cumulative Tests are designed to follow the conclusion of instruction for Chapters 3, 6, and 9, respectively. The End-Year Test may be administered after completing the last chapter of the textbook.

The Cumulative Tests and the End-Year Test are designed to be scored by strand and by total test. The items on these tests are sequenced in random order within strands, with the problem-solving strand always at the end of the test.

As on the Chapter Tests, the computation and problem-solving items of the Cumulative Tests and End-Year Test are separated by a stop sign and a double line. At the teacher's discretion, students may use calculators for the problem-solving section.

DESCRIPTION OF THE COMPUTER MANAGEMENT SYSTEM (CMS)

The Computer Management System, or CMS, is designed to help teachers manage and coordinate student progress. The CMS will:

- quickly and automatically score multiple-choice Chapter Tests (Form A and Form B), Cumulative Tests, and the End-Year Test;

- generate and print a variety of useful reports;

- organize testing information in a number of ways to help monitor student progress; and

- prescribe learning activities based on students' test results.

Answer Forms. Facsimiles of the CMS answer forms are provided for reference on pages TM43–TM46. Each facsimile of a CMS answer form is labeled for use with one of the appropriate optical mark readers listed below:

- Chatsworth OMR 1000 and 2000;

- True Data Micro Mark I and Micro Mark II;

- Scantron Model 1200 or 1300 Optical Mark Reader; and

- NCS Sentry 3000 Scanner.

In addition to the CMS answer forms, a practice answer sheet is provided on page TM47. You may wish to duplicate and distribute this sheet to give to students for practice in responding to test questions by filling in answer bubbles. The sheet can be scored quickly by hand.

PROCEDURES FOR ADMINISTRATION

The tests are not timed. In most cases the Chapter Tests may be administered in one sitting. The Cumulative Tests may be administered in one or two sittings. For the End-Year Test, which contains 75 items, the number of sittings will depend on the needs of the students.

For the multiple-choice tests, students may mark their answers on CMS cards (if you are using the Computer Management System), on copies of the generic answer sheet provided on page TM47, on the test page, or on a separate sheet of paper. Responses to the free-response Form C Chapter Tests should be marked directly on the test or on a separate sheet of paper.

A critical requirement in criterion-referenced testing is that students understand exactly what they are expected to do. To administer the test efficiently, the teacher should become familiar with the directions in this manual and with the test items before giving the test. During the test the teacher should closely monitor the students to make sure that each student is following the directions, is working on the appropriate task, and is indicating his or her responses correctly.

The students' performance on the tests will more accurately reflect their abilities if the students are comfortable. Therefore physical aspects of the testing environment such as lighting, ventilation, and temperature should be controlled to maximize the comfort of the students. Effort should also be made to minimize distractions such as noise or activities that draw students' attention from the test.

EVALUATION, PRESCRIPTION, AND RETEACHING

The Chapter Tests, the Cumulative Tests, and the End-Year Test provide an indication of each student's general mathematical achievement. Performance on the Chapter Tests is reported by objective, while the Cumulative and End-Year Tests are reported by strand. Scores on these tests may indicate if a student has mastered one or more of the mathematical areas tested. The test scores, therefore, can be used to plan further activities, whether for reteaching or for enrichment.

In conjunction with a program of periodic testing, continuous informal assessment of the student's performance during various mathematical activities will add important information to the assessment of mathematical competence and achievement.

After the tests have been administered, teachers may wish to record student scores on the Scoring and Profile Charts and use the other teacher resource materials provided in this Teacher's Manual. Methods for scoring the tests and descriptions for using these materials follow.

Scoring Charts

There is a Scoring Chart for each test. It is designed to be copied for each student in the class and used to record the student's performance. The Scoring Charts for the Chapter Tests may be used for Form A, Form B, or Form C.

The Chapter Test Scoring Charts are organized by objective and list the criterion score for each objective. The Scoring Charts for the Cumulative Tests and End-Year Test are organized by strand and list the criterion score for each strand. The criterion is based on a minimum of 75 percent correct responses. School districts and individuals using this program may decide to adopt this criterion or may modify or replace it as they see fit.

Scoring the Chapter Tests. After correcting a student's test, mark each incorrect item by placing an X over the item number on the appropriate Scoring Chart. Count the number of correct responses for each objective and note it in the appropriate column. Add the number of correct responses for each objective to determine the total test score and note it in the appropriate space. Compare the student's performance to the recommended criterion scores. Use the Conversion Table to find the total percent correct. Students who do not attain the criterion score for each objective may need further instruction. To identify appropriate reteaching (or enrichment) activities, refer to the Prescription Table, located on the reverse side of the Scoring Chart for each chapter.

Scoring the Cumulative Tests and the End-Year Test. Count the number of correct responses for each strand and note it in the appropriate column on the appropriate Scoring Chart. Add the strand scores to determine the total test score and note it in the appropriate space. Compare the student's performance to the recommended criterion scores. Use the Conversion Table to find the total percent correct.

Conversion Table

The Conversion Table on pages TM5–TM6 is provided as an aid for converting raw test scores to percentage scores. To use the Conversion Table, find the column that indicates the total number of items on the test. Then find the row that matches the number of items a particular student answered correctly. The percentage that is given in this row of the appropriate column is the percent correct. For example, a student who completed 25 items correctly on a test with a total of 33 items answered 76 percent of the questions correctly. The overall percent correct should reflect a student's performance on the entire test.

Prescription Tables

The Prescription Tables provide an easy-to-use reference to many of the follow-up activities that are available as part of the *Macmillan/McGraw-Hill MATHEMATICS IN ACTION* program. There is one Prescription Table for each Chapter Test. The Prescription Tables can be used in conjunction with Form A, Form B, or Form C test results as reported on the Scoring Charts. The Prescription Tables refer to the following materials:

- *Pupil Edition Pages* for Lessons, Extra Practice, and Practice Plus that address basic, average, and challenge levels of the tested skills;

- *Teacher's Edition Pages* for alternative strategies for reteaching the tested skills; and

- *Teacher's Resource Center,* containing lessons for reteaching specific skills and practice pages.

The teacher may wish to select reteaching activities to use with students who have not achieved the criterion score for specific objectives. After completing the reteaching activities, students may be retested using an alternate form of the Chapter Test.

Student Profile Chart

Student scores on the Chapter Tests, the Cumulative Tests, and the End-Year Test may be recorded on the individual Student Profile Chart, which provides the teacher with a cumulative record of each student's performance during the year.

Teachers may use this information to identify groups of students in need of help with a particular skill or may identify skills with which all students may need additional help.

To use the Student Profile Chart, make one copy of the chart for each student. For each test there is a row on the chart. The number of items in each test is provided. There is space to write the number of items the student answered correctly on the test. In addition there is a place to indicate the total percent correct for each test. Space is also provided for comments on the student's progress.

Class Profile Chart

The Class Profile Chart is designed to show the overall scores achieved by all students in the class during the year.

Copies of this chart may be made as needed. Each student's name can be entered on one of the lines. Then the overall percent correct can be entered for each test that each student takes.

Answer Keys

Answer Keys for all tests are located at the back of this book, beginning on page TM49. For the Form C Chapter Tests, some items may have more than one possible correct answer; sample correct responses are given. A range of acceptable responses is given for those estimation items in which the method of estimation is not specified. This range is based on the methods of estimation that are taught in the Pupil's Edition of the textbook.

CONVERSION TABLE FOR SCORING TESTS

Directions: To convert raw test scores into percentage scores, find the column that indicates the total number of items on the test. Then find the row that matches the number of items that the student answered correctly. The intersection of the two rows gives the percent correct.

Total Number Correct	Total Number of Items on the Test			
	25	33	50	75
1	4%	3%	2%	1%
2	8%	6%	4%	3%
3	12%	9%	6%	4%
4	16%	12%	8%	5%
5	20%	15%	10%	7%
6	24%	18%	12%	8%
7	28%	21%	14%	9%
8	32%	24%	16%	11%
9	36%	27%	18%	12%
10	40%	30%	20%	13%
11	44%	33%	22%	15%
12	48%	36%	24%	16%
13	52%	39%	26%	17%
14	56%	42%	28%	19%
15	60%	45%	30%	20%
16	64%	48%	32%	21%
17	68%	52%	34%	23%
18	72%	55%	36%	24%
19	76%	58%	38%	25%
20	80%	61%	40%	27%
21	84%	64%	42%	28%
22	88%	67%	44%	29%
23	92%	70%	46%	31%
24	96%	73%	48%	32%
25	100%	76%	50%	33%

(continued on next page)

MACMILLAN / McGRAW-HILL

CONVERSION TABLE FOR SCORING TESTS
(continued)

Total Number Correct	Total Number of Items on the Test			Total Number Correct	Total Number of Items on the Test
	33	50	75		75
26	79%	52%	35%	51	68%
27	82%	54%	36%	52	69%
28	85%	56%	37%	53	71%
29	88%	58%	39%	54	72%
30	91%	60%	40%	55	73%
31	94%	62%	41%	56	75%
32	97%	64%	43%	57	76%
33	100%	66%	44%	58	77%
34		68%	45%	59	79%
35		70%	47%	60	80%
36		72%	48%	61	81%
37		74%	49%	62	83%
38		76%	51%	63	84%
39		78%	52%	64	85%
40		80%	53%	65	87%
41		82%	55%	66	88%
42		84%	56%	67	89%
43		86%	57%	68	91%
44		88%	59%	69	92%
45		90%	60%	70	93%
46		92%	61%	71	95%
47		94%	63%	72	96%
48		96%	64%	73	97%
49		98%	65%	74	99%
50		100%	67%	75	100%

MACMILLAN / McGRAW-HILL

Macmillan/McGraw-Hill, MATHEMATICS IN ACTION
Grade 4

SCORING CHART
Grade 4, Chapter 1

____ Form A   ____ Form B   ____ Form C

Student _____ Date _____

Directions: For each item that is answered incorrectly, cross out the item number. Then record the number of correct responses in the appropriate Student Score column. If the student has not met the Criterion Score for an objective, circle the student's score. Recommended assignments are listed in the Prescription Table on the next page.

Objective	Item Numbers	Criterion Score	Student Score
A. Read and write whole numbers to millions	1 7 12 15	3/4	/4
B. Write money amounts from pictures and word names, and make change for dollar amounts up to $20	4 6 14 16	3/4	/4
C. Compare and order whole numbers, including money amounts	3 8 10 13	3/4	/4
D. Round numbers to the nearest 10, 100, or 1,000, and money amounts to the nearest $.10, $1, $10	2 5 9 11	3/4	/4
E. Interpret and display data in a table	17 18 19 20	3/4	/4
F. Solve problems including those that involve number sense	21 22 23 24 25	4/5	/5
Total Test Score		19/25	/25
Total Percent Correct			%

MACMILLAN / McGRAW-HILL

PRESCRIPTION TABLE
Grade 4, Chapter 1

Objective	PUPIL'S EDITION			TEACHER'S EDITION	TEACHER'S RESOURCE CENTER	
	Lesson	Extra Practice	Practice Plus	Alternative Strategies for Reteaching	Reteaching	Practice
A. Read and write whole numbers to millions	12–17	40	44	13, 15, 17	1, 2, 3	1, 2, 3
B. Write money amounts from pictures and word names, and make change for dollar amounts up to $20	22–25	41, 42		23, 25	5, 6	5, 6
C. Compare and order whole numbers, including money amounts	28–29	42		29	7	7
D. Round numbers to the nearest 10, 100, or 1,000, and money amounts to the nearest $.10, $1, or $10	30–31	42	45	31	8	8
E. Interpret and display data in a table	34–35	43		35	10	10
F. Solve problems including those that involve number sense	32–33	43			9	9

You may wish to refer to the Chapter Organizer in the Teacher's Edition to identify additional activities for meeting individual needs at basic, average, and challenge levels.

SCORING CHART
Grade 4, Chapter 2

____ Form A   ____ Form B   ____ Form C

Student _____ Date _____

Directions: For each item that is answered incorrectly, cross out the item number. Then record the number of correct responses in the appropriate Student Score column. If the student has not met the Criterion Score for an objective, circle the student's score. Recommended assignments are listed in the Prescription Table on the next page.

Objective	Item Numbers	Criterion Score	Student Score
A. Understand and use the identity, associative, and order properties of addition and subtraction	3 4 7 8 14	4/5	/5
B. Use addition and subtraction facts to 18	1 5 10 12 13 17 18 20 21 22	8/10	/10
C. Estimate and measure length using metric units	2 6 9 11 15 16 19 28	6/8	/8
D. Interpret and display data on a given bar graph from collected data	23 24 25 26 27	4/5	/5
E. Solve problems including those that involve identifying needed information and drawing a diagram	29 30 31 32 33	4/5	/5
Total Test Score		26/33	/33
Total Percent Correct			%

MACMILLAN / McGRAW-HILL

PRESCRIPTION TABLE
Grade 4, Chapter 2

Objective	PUPIL'S EDITION			TEACHER'S EDITION	TEACHER'S RESOURCE CENTER	
	Lesson	Extra Practice	Practice Plus	Alternative Strategies for Reteaching	Reteaching	Practice
A. Understand and use the identity, associative, and order properties of addition and subtraction	52–55	78		53, 55	11, 12	11, 12
B. Use addition and subtraction facts to 18	56–61	78, 79	82, 83	57, 59, 61	13, 14, 15	13, 14, 15
C. Estimate and measure length using metric units	66–69	80		67, 69	17, 18	17, 18
D. Interpret and display data on a given bar graph from collected data	72–73	81		73	20	20
E. Solve problems including those that involve identifying needed information and drawing a diagram	62–63, 70–71	79, 81			16, 19	16, 19

You may wish to refer to the Chapter Organizer in the Teacher's Edition to identify additional activities for meeting individual needs at basic, average, and challenge levels.

MACMILLAN / McGRAW-HILL

SCORING CHART
Grade 4, Chapter 3

____ Form A   ____ Form B   ____ Form C

Student _____ **Date** _____

Directions: For each item that is answered incorrectly, cross out the item number. Then record the number of correct responses in the appropriate Student Score column. If the student has not met the Criterion Score for an objective, circle the student's score. Recommended assignments are listed in the Prescription Table on the next page.

Objective	Item Numbers	Criterion Score	Student Score
A. Estimate sums and differences, including money amounts	1 4 7 11 15	4/5	/5
B. Add up to 4-digit numbers, including money amounts (including multiples of 10 and 100)	2 6 9 13 17	4/5	/5
C. Subtract up to 4-digit numbers, including money amounts (including multiples of 10 and 100)	3 8 12 16 19	4/5	/5
D. Find the perimeter of a figure in metric units	5 10 14 18 20	4/5	/5
E. Solve problems including those that involve checking that the answer is reasonable and choosing the correct operation	21 22 23 24 25	4/5	/5
Total Test Score		20/25	/25
Total Percent Correct			%

PRESCRIPTION TABLE
Grade 4, Chapter 3

Objective	PUPIL'S EDITION			TEACHER'S EDITION	TEACHER'S RESOURCE CENTER	
	Lesson	Extra Practice	Practice Plus	Alternative Strategies for Reteaching	Reteaching	Practice
A. Estimate sums and differences, including money amounts	92–95, 106–107	122, 124		93, 95, 107	22, 23, 28	22, 23, 28
B. Add up to 4-digit numbers, including money amounts (including multiples of 10 and 100)	90–91, 98–101	122, 123	126	91, 99, 101	21, 25, 26	21, 25, 26
C. Subtract up to 4-digit numbers, including money amounts (including multiples of 10 and 100)	104–105, 108–111	124, 125	127	105, 109, 111	27, 29, 30	27, 29, 30
D. Find the perimeter of a figure in metric units	116–117	125		117	32	32
E. Solve problems including those that involve checking that the answer is reasonable and choosing the correct operation	96–97, 114–115	123, 125			24, 31	24, 31

You may wish to refer to the Chapter Organizer in the Teacher's Edition to identify additional activities for meeting individual needs at basic, average, and challenge levels.

Macmillan/McGraw-Hill, MATHEMATICS IN ACTION
Grade 4

MACMILLAN / McGRAW-HILL

_____ Form A   _____ Form B   _____ Form C

Student _____ **Date** _____

Directions: For each item that is answered incorrectly, cross out the item number. Then record the number of correct responses in the appropriate Student Score column. If the student has not met the Criterion Score for an objective, circle the student's score. Recommended assignments are listed in the Prescription Table on the next page.

Objective	Item Numbers	Criterion Score	Student Score
A. Estimate, tell, and write time, and find elapsed time	1 4 8 11	3/4	/4
B. Estimate and measure capacity and mass using metric units	2 6 9 10	3/4	/4
C. Estimate and measure temperature in °C	3 5 7 12	3/4	/4
D. Locate and name ordered pairs on a coordinate grid	13 14 15 16	3/4	/4
E. Display and interpret data on a line graph	17 18 19 20	3/4	/4
F. Solve problems including those that involve extra information and two-step solutions	21 22 23 24 25	4/5	/5
Total Test Score		19/25	/25
Total Percent Correct			%

PRESCRIPTION TABLE
Grade 4, Chapter 4

Objective	PUPIL'S EDITION			TEACHER'S EDITION	TEACHER'S RESOURCE CENTER	
	Lesson	Extra Practice	Practice Plus	Alternative Strategies for Reteaching	Reteaching	Practice
A. Estimate, tell, and write time, and find elapsed time	134–139	164	168	135, 137, 139	33, 34, 35	33, 34, 35
B. Estimate and measure capacity and mass using metric units	148–151	166	169	149, 151	39, 40	39, 40
C. Estimate and measure temperature in °C	156–157	167		157	42	42
D. Locate and name ordered pairs on a coordinate grid	142–143	165		143	37	37
E. Display and interpret data on a line graph	144–145	166		145	38	38
F. Solve problems including those that involve extra information and two-step solutions	140–141, 152–153	165, 167			36, 41	36, 41

You may wish to refer to the Chapter Organizer in the Teacher's Edition to identify additional activities for meeting individual needs at basic, average, and challenge levels.

MACMILLAN / McGRAW-HILL

_____ Form A   _____ Form B   _____ Form C

Student _____ **Date** _____

Directions: For each item that is answered incorrectly, cross out the item number. Then record the number of correct responses in the appropriate Student Score column. If the student has not met the Criterion Score for an objective, circle the student's score. Recommended assignments are listed in the Prescription Table on the next page.

Objective	Item Numbers	Criterion Score	Student Score
A. Know and use the identity, order, zero, and grouping properties and fact families of multiplication and division	5 11 18 22	3/4	/4
B. Find factors and multiples of numbers, and missing factors	4 10 16 20	3/4	/4
C. Identify numbers as odd, even, prime, or composite	3 8 14 23	3/4	/4
D. Use 2 to 9 as factors or divisors	1 6 9 12 15 17 21 24	6/8	/8
E. Find the area of a figure	2 7 13 19	3/4	/4
F. Display and interpret data in a pictograph	25 26 27 28	3/4	/4
G. Solve problems including those that involve choosing the correct operation and finding a pattern	29 30 31 32 33	4/5	/5
Total Test Score		25/33	/33
Total Percent Correct			%

MACMILLAN / McGRAW-HILL

PRESCRIPTION TABLE
Grade 4, Chapter 5

Objective	PUPIL'S EDITION			TEACHER'S EDITION	TEACHER'S RESOURCE CENTER	
	Lesson	Extra Practice	Practice Plus	Alternative Strategies for Reteaching	Reteaching	Practice
A. Know and use the identity, order, zero, and grouping properties and fact families of multiplication and division	180–181	208		181	45	45
B. Find factors and multiples of numbers, and missing factors	182–183, 192–193	208, 210		183, 193	46, 50	46, 50
C. Identify numbers as odd, even, prime, or composite	196–197	210	213	197	52	52
D. Use 2 to 9 as factors or divisors	184–187	209	212	185, 187	47, 48	47, 48
E. Find the area of a figure	200–201	211		201	54	54
F. Display and interpret data in a pictograph	202–203	211		203	55	55
G. Solve problems including those that involve choosing the correct operation and finding a pattern	188–189, 198–199	209, 211			49, 53	49, 53

You may wish to refer to the Chapter Organizer in the Teacher's Edition to identify additional activities for meeting individual needs at basic, average, and challenge levels.

SCORING CHART
Grade 4, Chapter 6

____ Form A   ____ Form B   ____ Form C

Student _____ **Date** _____

Directions: For each item that is answered incorrectly, cross out the item number. Then record the number of correct responses in the appropriate Student Score column. If the student has not met the Criterion Score for an objective, circle the student's score. Recommended assignments are listed in the Prescription Table on the next page.

Objective	Item Numbers	Criterion Score	Student Score
A. Multiply multiples of 10, 100, and 1,000	1 5 9 13 17	4/5	/5
B. Estimate products, including money amounts	2 6 10 14 18	4/5	/5
C. Multiply by 1-digit factors	3 7 11 15 19	4/5	/5
D. Multiply money amounts	4 8 12 16 20	4/5	/5
E. Solve problems including those that involve guessing, testing, and revising, and finding an over- or underestimate	21 22 23 24 25	4/5	/5
Total Test Score		20/25	/25
Total Percent Correct			%

MACMILLAN / McGRAW-HILL

PRESCRIPTION TABLE
Grade 4, Chapter 6

Objective	PUPIL'S EDITION			TEACHER'S EDITION	TEACHER'S RESOURCE CENTER	
	Lesson	Extra Practice	Practice Plus	Alternative Strategies for Reteaching	Reteaching	Practice
A. Multiply multiples of 10, 100, and 1,000	220–221	246		221	56	56
B. Estimate products, including money amounts	222–223	246		223	57	57
C. Multiply by 1-digit factors	226–231, 234–235	247, 248	250	227, 229, 231, 235	59, 60, 61	59, 60, 61
D. Multiply money amounts	236–237	249	251	237	62	62
E. Solve problems including those that involve guessing, testing, and revising, and finding an over- or underestimate	224–225, 240–241	247, 249			58, 63	58, 63

You may wish to refer to the Chapter Organizer in the Teacher's Edition to identify additional activities for meeting individual needs at basic, average, and challenge levels.

SCORING CHART
Grade 4, Chapter 7

____ Form A   ____ Form B   ____ Form C

Student _____ Date _____

Directions: For each item that is answered incorrectly, cross out the item number. Then record the number of correct responses in the appropriate Student Score column. If the student has not met the Criterion Score for an objective, circle the student's score. Recommended assignments are listed in the Prescription Table on the next page.

Objective	Item Numbers	Criterion Score	Student Score
A. Divide multiples of 10, 100, and 1,000	1 3 7 13 15	4/5	/5
B. Divide by 1-digit divisors, including money amounts	5 6 8 10 12	4/5	/5
C. Estimate quotients	2 4 9 11 14	4/5	/5
D. Find average (mean), median, and range of a set of data	16 17 18 19 20	4/5	/5
E. Solve problems including those that involve making a table and interpreting quotients and remainders	21 22 23 24 25	4/5	/5
Total Test Score		20/25	/25
Total Percent Correct			%

MACMILLAN / McGRAW-HILL

Macmillan/McGraw-Hill, MATHEMATICS IN ACTION
Grade 4

TM19

PRESCRIPTION TABLE
Grade 4, Chapter 7

Objective	PUPIL'S EDITION			TEACHER'S EDITION	TEACHER'S RESOURCE CENTER	
	Lesson	Extra Practice	Practice Plus	Alternative Strategies for Reteaching	Reteaching	Practice
A. Divide multiples of 10, 100, and 1,000	260–261	292		261	65	65
B. Divide by 1-digit divisors, including money amounts	266–271, 274–279	293, 294	296, 297	267, 269, 271, 275, 277, 279	68, 69, 70, 71, 72	68, 69, 70, 71, 72
C. Estimate quotients	262–263	292		263	66	66
D. Find average (mean), median, and range of a set of data	284–287	295		285, 287	74	74
E. Solve problems including those that involve making a table and interpreting quotients and remainders	264–265, 282–283	293, 295			67, 73	67, 73

You may wish to refer to the Chapter Organizer in the Teacher's Edition to identify additional activities for meeting individual needs at basic, average, and challenge levels.

MACMILLAN / McGRAW-HILL

SCORING CHART
Grade 4, Chapter 8

_____ Form A   _____ Form B   _____ Form C

Student _____ **Date** _____

Directions: For each item that is answered incorrectly, cross out the item number. Then record the number of correct responses in the appropriate Student Score column. If the student has not met the Criterion Score for an objective, circle the student's score. Recommended assignments are listed in the Prescription Table on the next page.

Objective	Item Numbers	Criterion Score	Student Score
A. Tell if a figure is a line, line segment, or ray, and identify two lines as intersecting, parallel, or perpendicular	1 9 15 16	3/4	/4
B. Identify plane figures and their parts, and space figures and their parts	2 8 17 18 19	4/5	/5
C. Identify an angle, name the sides and vertices, and describe it relative to a right angle	10 13 14 20 21	4/5	/5
D. Transform plane figures and identify how a figure was transformed	5 11 22 23	3/4	/4
E. Identify figures as congruent, similar, and symmetrical	4 6 12 24 25	4/5	/5
F. Find the volume of a figure	3 7 26 27 28	4/5	/5
G. Solve problems including those that involve multistep solutions	29 30 31 32 33	4/5	/5
Total Test Score		26/33	/33
Total Percent Correct			%

PRESCRIPTION TABLE
Grade 4, Chapter 8

Objective	PUPIL'S EDITION			TEACHER'S EDITION	TEACHER'S RESOURCE CENTER	
	Lesson	Extra Practice	Practice Plus	Alternative Strategies for Reteaching	Reteaching	Practice
A. Tell if a figure is a line, line segment, or ray, and identify two lines as intersecting, parallel, or perpendicular	306–307	332		307	75	75
B. Identify plane figures and their parts, and space figures and their parts	310–311, 324–325	332, 335	336, 337	311, 325	77, 83	77, 83
C. Identify an angle, name the sides and vertices, and describe it relative to a right angle	308–309	332		309	76	76
D. Transform plane figures and identify how a figure was transformed	318–319	334		319	80	80
E. Identify figures as congruent, similar, and symmetrical	320–323	334		321, 323	81, 82	81, 82
F. Find the volume of a figure	326–327	335		327	84	84
G. Solve problems including those that involve multistep solutions	312–313	333			78	78

You may wish to refer to the Chapter Organizer in the Teacher's Edition to identify additional activities for meeting individual needs at basic, average, and challenge levels.

MACMILLAN / McGRAW-HILL

____ Form A   ____ Form B   ____ Form C

Student _____ **Date** _____

Directions: For each item that is answered incorrectly, cross out the item number. Then record the number of correct responses in the appropriate Student Score column. If the student has not met the Criterion Score for an objective, circle the student's score. Recommended assignments are listed in the Prescription Table on the next page.

Objective	Item Numbers	Criterion Score	Student Score
A. Read and write fractions for parts of wholes or parts of sets, and find fractional parts of a set	1 10 14 18	3/4	/4
B. Simplify and find equivalent fractions	2 6 15 19	3/4	/4
C. Read, write, and rename mixed numbers	3 7 11 20	3/4	/4
D. Compare and order fractions and mixed numbers	4 8 12 16	3/4	/4
E. Estimate and measure length in customary units	5 9 13 17	3/4	/4
F. Solve problems including those that involve working backward and using number sense	21 22 23 24 25	4/5	/5
Total Test Score		19/25	/25
Total Percent Correct			%

PRESCRIPTION TABLE
Grade 4, Chapter 9

Objective	PUPIL'S EDITION			TEACHER'S EDITION	TEACHER'S RESOURCE CENTER	
	Lesson	Extra Practice	Practice Plus	Alternative Strategies for Reteaching	Reteaching	Practice
A. Read and write fractions for parts of wholes or parts of sets, and find fractional parts of a set	344–351	374, 375		345, 347, 349, 351	85, 86, 87, 88	85, 86, 87, 88
B. Simplify and find equivalent fractions	354–355, 358–359	375, 376	378	355, 359	90, 91	90, 91
C. Read, write, and rename mixed numbers	360–361	376	379	361	92	92
D. Compare and order fractions and mixed numbers	362–363	376		363	93	93
E. Estimate and measure length in customary units	364–367	377		365, 367	94, 95	94, 95
F. Solve problems including those that involve working backward and using number sense	352–353, 368–369	375, 377			89, 96	89, 96

You may wish to refer to the Chapter Organizer in the Teacher's Edition to identify additional activities for meeting individual needs at basic, average, and challenge levels.

___ **Form A**   ___ **Form B**   ___ **Form C**

Student _____ **Date** _____

Directions: For each item that is answered incorrectly, cross out the item number. Then record the number of correct responses in the appropriate Student Score column. If the student has not met the Criterion Score for an objective, circle the student's score. Recommended assignments are listed in the Prescription Table on the next page.

Objective	Item Numbers	Criterion Score	Student Score
A. Add fractions with like denominators	1 6 11 16	3/4	/4
B. Subtract fractions with like denominators	2 7 12 17	3/4	/4
C. Find area and perimeter in customary units	3 8 13 18	3/4	/4
D. Estimate and measure capacity and weight in customary units	4 9 14 20	3/4	/4
E. Estimate and measure temperature in °F	5 10 15 19	3/4	/4
F. Solve problems including those that involve using different strategies and are simpler and similar	21 22 23 24 25	4/5	/5
Total Test Score		19/25	/25
Total Percent Correct			%

PRESCRIPTION TABLE
Grade 4, Chapter 10

Objective	PUPIL'S EDITION			TEACHER'S EDITION	TEACHER'S RESOURCE CENTER	
	Lesson	Extra Practice	Practice Plus	Alternative Strategies for Reteaching	Reteaching	Practice
A. Add fractions with like denominators	388–391	420	424	389, 391	97, 98	97, 98
B. Subtract fractions with like denominators	398–399	421	425	399	100	100
C. Find area and perimeter in customary units	404–405	422		405	102	102
D. Estimate and measure capacity and weight in customary units	406–409	423		407, 409	103, 104	103, 104
E. Estimate and measure temperature in °F	412–413	423		413	105	105
F. Solve problems including those that involve using different strategies and are simpler and similar	392–393, 402–403	421, 422			99, 101	99, 101

You may wish to refer to the Chapter Organizer in the Teacher's Edition to identify additional activities for meeting individual needs at basic, average, and challenge levels.

SCORING CHART
Grade 4, Chapter 11

____ Form A   ____ Form B   ____ Form C

Student _____ **Date** _____

Directions: For each item that is answered incorrectly, cross out the item number. Then record the number of correct responses in the appropriate Student Score column. If the student has not met the Criterion Score for an objective, circle the student's score. Recommended assignments are listed in the Prescription Table on the next page.

Objective	Item Numbers	Criterion Score	Student Score
A. Read and write decimals to tenths and hundredths	1 6 11 16	3/4	/4
B. Compare and order decimals	2 7 12 17	3/4	/4
C. Estimate the sums and differences of decimals	3 8 13 18	3/4	/4
D. Add and subtract decimals	4 9 14 19	3/4	/4
E. Find the likelihood or probability of an event and make predictions	5 10 15 20	3/4	/4
F. Solve problems including those that involve making an organized list or tree diagram and conducting an experiment	21 22 23 24 25	4/5	/5
Total Test Score		19/25	/25
Total Percent Correct			%

MACMILLAN / McGRAW-HILL

PRESCRIPTION TABLE
Grade 4, Chapter 11

Objective	PUPIL'S EDITION			TEACHER'S EDITION	TEACHER'S RESOURCE CENTER	
	Lesson	Extra Practice	Practice Plus	Alternative Strategies for Reteaching	Reteaching	Practice
A. Read and write decimals to tenths and hundredths	434–435	462		435	106	106
B. Compare and order decimals	436–437	462		437	107	107
C. Estimate the sums and differences of decimals	442–443	463		443	109	109
D. Add and subtract decimals	444–447	464	466	445, 447	110, 111	110, 111
E. Find the likelihood or probability of an event and make predictions	452–455	465	467	453, 455	113, 114	113, 114
F. Solve problems including those that involve making an organized list or tree diagram and conducting an experiment	438–439, 450–451	463, 464			108, 112	108, 112

You may wish to refer to the Chapter Organizer in the Teacher's Edition to identify additional activities for meeting individual needs at basic, average, and challenge levels.

MACMILLAN / McGRAW-HILL

SCORING CHART
Grade 4, Chapter 12

____ Form A   ____ Form B   ____ Form C

Student _____ **Date** _____

Directions: For each item that is answered incorrectly, cross out the item number. Then record the number of correct responses in the appropriate Student Score column. If the student has not met the Criterion Score for an objective, circle the student's score. Recommended assignments are listed in the Prescription Table on the next page.

Objective	Item Numbers	Criterion Score	Student Score
A. Multiply multiples of 10, 100, and 1,000 by multiples of 10	1 6 12 16	3/4	/4
B. Estimate products of 2-digit numbers, including money amounts	2 7 11 18	3/4	/4
C. Multiply by 2-digit factors, including money amounts	3 9 13 17	3/4	/4
D. Divide multiples of 10, 100, and 1,000 by multiples of 10	4 8 14 19	3/4	/4
E. Divide by multiples of 10	5 10 15 20	3/4	/4
F. Solve problems including those that involve choosing the correct operation	21 22 23 24 25	4/5	/5
Total Test Score		19/25	/25
Total Percent Correct			%

Macmillan/McGraw-Hill, MATHEMATICS IN ACTION
Grade 4

MACMILLAN / McGRAW-HILL

PRESCRIPTION TABLE
Grade 4, Chapter 12

Objective	PUPIL'S EDITION			TEACHER'S EDITION	TEACHER'S RESOURCE CENTER	
	Lesson	Extra Practice	Practice Plus	Alternative Strategies for Reteaching	Reteaching	Practice
A. Multiply multiples of 10, 100, and 1,000 by multiples of 10	474–475, 478–479	506		475, 479	115, 117	115, 117
B. Estimate products of 2-digit numbers, including money amounts	476–477	506		477	116	116
C. Multiply by 2-digit factors, including money amounts	484–487, 490–491	507, 508	510	485, 487, 491	119, 120, 121	119, 120, 121
D. Divide multiples of 10, 100, and 1,000 by multiples of 10	494–495	508		495	122	122
E. Divide by multiples of 10	496–497	509	511	497	123	123
F. Solve problems including those that involve choosing the correct operation	480–481, 498–499	507, 509			118, 124	118, 124

You may wish to refer to the Chapter Organizer in the Teacher's Edition to identify additional activities for meeting individual needs at basic, average, and challenge levels.

MACMILLAN / McGRAW-HILL

SCORING CHART
Grade 4, Cumulative 1 Test

Student _____ Date _____

Directions: Record the number of correct responses for each strand in the appropriate Student Score column. If the student has not met the Criterion Score for a strand, circle the student's score.

Strand • Objective	Item Numbers	Criterion Score	Student Score
NUMERATION AND NUMBER THEORY Read and write whole numbers to millions Write money amounts from pictures and word names, and make change for dollar amounts up to $20 Compare and order whole numbers, including money amounts Round numbers to the nearest 10, 100, or 1,000, and money amounts to the nearest $.10, $1, $10 Understand and use the identity, associative, and order properties of addition and subtraction	1–8	6/8	/8
MEASUREMENT AND GEOMETRY Find the perimeter of a figure in metric units Estimate and measure length using metric units	9–18	8/10	/10
COMPUTATION Use addition and subtraction facts to 18 Estimate sums and differences, including money amounts Add or subtract up to 4-digit numbers, including money amounts (including multiples of 10 and 100)	19–33	12/15	/15
GRAPHING, PROBABILITY, AND STATISTICS Interpret and display data in a table Interpret and display data on a given bar graph from collected data	34–40	6/7	/7

PROBLEM SOLVING
Solve problems including those that involve:
  number sense
  identifying needed information and drawing a diagram
  checking that the answer is reasonable and choosing the correct operation
	41–50	8/10	/10

Total Test Score		40/50	/50
Total Percent Correct			%

MACMILLAN / McGRAW-HILL

Macmillan/McGraw-Hill, MATHEMATICS IN ACTION
Grade 4

SCORING CHART
Grade 4, Cumulative 2 Test

Student _____ **Date** _____

Directions: Record the number of correct responses for each strand in the appropriate Student Score column. If the student has not met the Criterion Score for a strand, circle the student's score.

Strand • Objective	Item Numbers	Criterion Score	Student Score
NUMERATION AND NUMBER THEORY Read and write whole numbers to millions Write money amounts from pictures and word names, and make change for dollar amounts up to $20 Compare and order whole numbers, including money amounts Round numbers to the nearest 10, 100, or 1,000, and money amounts to the nearest $.10, $1, $10 Understand and use the identity, associative, and order properties of addition and subtraction Know and use the identity, order, zero, and grouping properties and fact families of multiplication and division Find factors and multiples of numbers, and missing factors Identify numbers as odd, even, prime, or composite	1–8	6/8	/8
MEASUREMENT AND GEOMETRY Find the area and perimeter of a figure in metric units Estimate and measure length, capacity, and mass using metric units Estimate, tell, and write time, and find elapsed time Estimate and measure temperature in °C	9–18	8/10	/10
COMPUTATION Use addition and subtraction facts to 18 Estimate sums and differences, including money amounts Add or subtract up to 4-digit numbers, including money amounts Use 2 to 9 as factors or divisors Multiply multiples of 10, 100, and 1,000 Estimate products, including money amounts Multiply by 1-digit factors Multiply money amounts	19–33	12/15	/15
GRAPHING, PROBABILITY, AND STATISTICS Interpret and display data in a table, bar graph, line graph, pictograph Locate and name ordered pairs on a coordinate grid	34–40	5/7	/7

(continued on next page)

MACMILLAN / McGRAW-HILL

Strand • Objective	Item Numbers	Criterion Score	Student Score

PROBLEM SOLVING
Solve problems including those that involve:
  number sense
  identifying needed information and drawing a diagram
  checking that the answer is reasonable and choosing the
    correct operation
  extra information and two-step solutions
  choosing the correct operation and finding a pattern
  guessing, testing, and revising, and finding an over- or underestimate
	41–50	8/10	/10

Total Test Score		39/50	/50
Total Percent Correct			%

MACMILLAN / McGRAW-HILL

SCORING CHART
Grade 4, Cumulative 3 Test

Student _____ Date _____

Directions: Record the number of correct responses for each strand in the appropriate Student Score column. If the student has not met the Criterion Score for a strand, circle the student's score.

Strand • Objective	Item Numbers	Criterion Score	Student Score
NUMERATION AND NUMBER THEORY Understand and use the identity, associative, and order properties of addition and subtraction Know and use the identity, order, zero, and grouping properties and fact families of multiplication and division Find factors and multiples of numbers, and missing factors Identify numbers as odd, even, prime, or composite Read and write fractions for parts of wholes or parts of sets, and find fractional parts of a set Simplify and find equivalent fractions Read, write, and rename mixed numbers Compare and order fractions and mixed numbers	1–8	6/8	/8
COMPUTATION Use addition and subtraction facts to 18 Estimate sums and differences, including money amounts Add or subtract up to 4-digit numbers, including money amounts Use 2 to 9 as factors or divisors Multiply by 1-digit factors and multiples of 10, 100, and 1,000 Estimate products, including money amounts Multiply money amounts Divide by 1-digit divisors, including money amounts Divide multiples of 10, 100, and 1,000 Estimate quotients	9–23	12/15	/15
MEASUREMENT AND GEOMETRY Find the area and perimeter of a figure in metric units Estimate and measure length, capacity, and mass using metric units Estimate, tell, and write time, and find elapsed time Estimate and measure temperature in °C Tell if a figure is a line, line segment, or ray, and identify two lines as intersecting, parallel, or perpendicular Identify plane figures and their parts, and space figures and their parts Identify an angle, name the sides and vertices, and describe it relative to a right angle Transform plane figures and identify how a figure was transformed Identify figures as congruent, similar, and symmetrical Find the volume of a figure Estimate and measure length in customary units	24–35	10/12	/12

(continued on next page)

MACMILLAN / McGRAW-HILL

Strand • Objective	Item Numbers	Criterion Score	Student Score
GRAPHING, PROBABILITY, AND STATISTICS Interpret and display data in a table, bar graph, line graph, pictograph Locate and name ordered pairs on a coordinate grid Find average (mean), median, and range of a set of data	36–42	6/7	/7

PROBLEM SOLVING
Solve problems including those that involve:
   choosing the correct operation and finding a pattern
   guessing, testing, and revising, and finding an over- or underestimate
   making a table and interpreting quotients and remainders
   multistep solutions
   working backward and using number sense
	43–50	6/8	/8

Total Test Score		40/50	/50
Total Percent Correct			%

MACMILLAN / McGRAW-HILL

SCORING CHART
Grade 4, End-Year Test

Student _____ **Date** _____

Directions: Record the number of correct responses for each strand in the appropriate Student Score column. If the student has not met the Criterion Score for a strand, circle the student's score.

Strand • Objective	Item Numbers	Criterion Score	Student Score
NUMERATION AND NUMBER THEORY Compare and order whole numbers, including money amounts Round numbers to the nearest 10, 100, or 1,000, and money amounts to the nearest $.10, $1, or $10 Understand and use the identity, associative, and order properties of addition and subtraction Know and use the identity, order, zero, and grouping properties and fact families of multiplication and division Find factors and multiples of numbers, and missing factors Identify numbers as odd, even, prime, or composite Read and write fractions for parts of wholes or parts of sets, and find fractional parts of a set Simplify and find equivalent fractions Read, write, and rename mixed numbers Compare and order fractions and mixed numbers Read and write decimals to tenths and hundredths Compare and order decimals	1–10	8/10	/10
COMPUTATION Use addition and subtraction facts to 18 Estimate sums and differences, including money amounts Add or subtract up to 4-digit numbers, including money amounts Use 2 to 9 as factors or divisors Multiply by 1-digit factors and multiples of 10, 100, and 1,000 Estimate products, including money amounts Multiply money amounts Divide by 1-digit divisors, including money amounts Divide multiples of 10, 100, and 1,000 Estimate quotients Add fractions with like denominators Subtract fractions with like denominators Multiply multiples of 10, 100, and 1,000 by multiples of 10 Estimate products of 2-digit numbers, including money amounts Multiply by 2-digit factors, including money amounts Divide multiples of 10, 100, and 1,000 by multiples of 10 Divide by multiples of 10 Estimate the sums and differences of decimals	11–34	19/24	/24

(continued on next page)

Strand • Objective	Item Numbers	Criterion Score	Student Score
MEASUREMENT AND GEOMETRY Find the area and perimeter of a figure in metric or customary units Estimate and measure length, capacity, and mass using metric units Estimate, tell, and write time, and find elapsed time Estimate and measure temperature in °C or °F Tell if a figure is a line, line segment, or ray, and identify two lines as intersecting, parallel, or perpendicular Identify plane figures and their parts, and space figures and their parts Identify an angle, name the sides and vertices, and describe it relative to a right angle Transform plane figures and identify how a figure was transformed Identify figures as congruent, similar, and symmetrical Find the volume of a figure Estimate and measure length, capacity, and weight in customary units	35–50	13/16	/16
GRAPHING, PROBABILITY, AND STATISTICS Interpret and display data in a table, bar graph, line graph, pictograph Locate and name ordered pairs on a coordinate grid Find average (mean), median, and range of a set of data Find the likelihood or probability of an event and make predictions	51–60	8/10	/10

PROBLEM SOLVING
Solve problems including those that involve:
  identifying needed information and drawing a diagram
  checking that the answer is reasonable
  choosing the correct operation
  extra information and two-step solutions
  finding a pattern
  guessing, testing, and revising, and finding an over- or underestimate
  making a table and interpreting quotients and remainders
  multistep solutions
  working backward and using number sense
  using different strategies and are simpler and similar
  making an organized list or tree diagram and conducting an experiment
	61–75	12/15	/15

Total Test Score		60/75	/75
Total Percent Correct			%

STUDENT PROFILE CHART
Grade 4

Name _____

Chapter	Form A Score	Form A %	Form B Score	Form B %	Form C Score	Form C %	Comments
1	/25		/25		/25		
2	/33		/33		/33		
3	/25		/25		/25		
4	/25		/25		/25		
5	/33		/33		/33		
6	/25		/25		/25		
7	/25		/25		/25		
8	/33		/33		/33		
9	/25		/25		/25		
10	/25		/25		/25		
11	/25		/25		/25		
12	/25		/25		/25		

	Score	%
Cumulative 1	/50	
Cumulative 2	/50	

	Score	%
Cumulative 3	/50	
End-Year	/75	

MACMILLAN / McGRAW-HILL

CLASS PROFILE CHART
Grade 4

Directions: Each student's name and individual test scores can be entered on a line to give an overall picture of class performance during the year.

Students	Chapter 1 Form			Chapter 2 Form			Chapter 3 Form			Cum 1	Chapter 4 Form			Chapter 5 Form			Chapter 6 Form			Cum 2
	A	B	C	A	B	C	A	B	C		A	B	C	A	B	C	A	B	C	

(continued on next page)

CLASS PROFILE CHART
Grade 4
(continued)

Students	Chapter 7 Form			Chapter 8 Form			Chapter 9 Form			Cum 3	Chapter 10 Form			Chapter 11 Form			Chapter 12 Form			End-Year
	A	B	C	A	B	C	A	B	C		A	B	C	A	B	C	A	B	C	

Card Readers: Chatsworth OMR 1000 and 2000
                    True Data Micro Mark I and Micro Mark II

actual size   reduced size

MACMILLAN / McGRAW-HILL

Card Reader: Scantron Model 1200 or 1300 Optical Mark Reader

actual size   reduced size

Answer Sheet: NCS Sentry 3000 Optical Mark Reader

actual size

NCS Trans-Optic® EP30-23192:3

COMPUTER MANAGEMENT SYSTEM
Macmillan/Scribner

STUDENT ID NO.

TEST ID NUMBER

NAME
DATE
TEACHER
GRADE

USE NO. 2 PENCIL ONLY

USE A NO. 2 PENCIL

S ⓐ ⓑ ⓒ ⓓ ⓔ

1 ⓐ ⓑ ⓒ ⓓ ⓔ
2 ⓐ ⓑ ⓒ ⓓ ⓔ
3 ⓐ ⓑ ⓒ ⓓ ⓔ
4 ⓐ ⓑ ⓒ ⓓ ⓔ
5 ⓐ ⓑ ⓒ ⓓ ⓔ
6 ⓐ ⓑ ⓒ ⓓ ⓔ
7 ⓐ ⓑ ⓒ ⓓ ⓔ
8 ⓐ ⓑ ⓒ ⓓ ⓔ

17 ⓐ ⓑ ⓒ ⓓ ⓔ
18 ⓐ ⓑ ⓒ ⓓ ⓔ
19 ⓐ ⓑ ⓒ ⓓ ⓔ
20 ⓐ ⓑ ⓒ ⓓ ⓔ
21 ⓐ ⓑ ⓒ ⓓ ⓔ
22 ⓐ ⓑ ⓒ ⓓ ⓔ
23 ⓐ ⓑ ⓒ ⓓ ⓔ
24 ⓐ ⓑ ⓒ ⓓ ⓔ

33 ⓐ ⓑ ⓒ ⓓ ⓔ
34 ⓐ ⓑ ⓒ ⓓ ⓔ
35 ⓐ ⓑ ⓒ ⓓ ⓔ
36 ⓐ ⓑ ⓒ ⓓ ⓔ
37 ⓐ ⓑ ⓒ ⓓ ⓔ
38 ⓐ ⓑ ⓒ ⓓ ⓔ
39 ⓐ ⓑ ⓒ ⓓ ⓔ
40 ⓐ ⓑ ⓒ ⓓ ⓔ

49 ⓐ ⓑ ⓒ ⓓ ⓔ
50 ⓐ ⓑ ⓒ ⓓ ⓔ
51 ⓐ ⓑ ⓒ ⓓ ⓔ
52 ⓐ ⓑ ⓒ ⓓ ⓔ
53 ⓐ ⓑ ⓒ ⓓ ⓔ
54 ⓐ ⓑ ⓒ ⓓ ⓔ
55 ⓐ ⓑ ⓒ ⓓ ⓔ
56 ⓐ ⓑ ⓒ ⓓ ⓔ

65 ⓐ ⓑ ⓒ ⓓ ⓔ
66 ⓐ ⓑ ⓒ ⓓ ⓔ
67 ⓐ ⓑ ⓒ ⓓ ⓔ
68 ⓐ ⓑ ⓒ ⓓ ⓔ
69 ⓐ ⓑ ⓒ ⓓ ⓔ
70 ⓐ ⓑ ⓒ ⓓ ⓔ
71 ⓐ ⓑ ⓒ ⓓ ⓔ
72 ⓐ ⓑ ⓒ ⓓ ⓔ

Card Reader: NCS Sentry 3000 Optical Mark Reader

reduced size

NCS Trans-Optic® EP30-23192:3

COMPUTER MANAGEMENT SYSTEM
Macmillan/Scribner

STUDENT ID NO.	TEST ID NUMBER

NAME _____

DATE _____

TEACHER _____

GRADE _____

USE A NO. 2 PENCIL

S ⓐⓑⓒⓓⓔ

USE NO. 2 PENCIL ONLY

MACMILLAN / McGRAW-HILL

TEST ANSWER SHEET

NAME _____

DATE _____

Macmillan/McGraw-Hill Mathematics

Grade 4:

Chapter _____ / Cumulative _____ / End-Year

(Choose one)

1	(a) (b) (c) (d) (e)	41	(a) (b) (c) (d) (e)
2	(a) (b) (c) (d) (e)	42	(a) (b) (c) (d) (e)
3	(a) (b) (c) (d) (e)	43	(a) (b) (c) (d) (e)
4	(a) (b) (c) (d) (e)	44	(a) (b) (c) (d) (e)
5	(a) (b) (c) (d) (e)	45	(a) (b) (c) (d) (e)
6	(a) (b) (c) (d) (e)	46	(a) (b) (c) (d) (e)
7	(a) (b) (c) (d) (e)	47	(a) (b) (c) (d) (e)
8	(a) (b) (c) (d) (e)	48	(a) (b) (c) (d) (e)
9	(a) (b) (c) (d) (e)	49	(a) (b) (c) (d) (e)
10	(a) (b) (c) (d) (e)	50	(a) (b) (c) (d) (e)
11	(a) (b) (c) (d) (e)	51	(a) (b) (c) (d) (e)
12	(a) (b) (c) (d) (e)	52	(a) (b) (c) (d) (e)
13	(a) (b) (c) (d) (e)	53	(a) (b) (c) (d) (e)
14	(a) (b) (c) (d) (e)	54	(a) (b) (c) (d) (e)
15	(a) (b) (c) (d) (e)	55	(a) (b) (c) (d) (e)
16	(a) (b) (c) (d) (e)	56	(a) (b) (c) (d) (e)
17	(a) (b) (c) (d) (e)	57	(a) (b) (c) (d) (e)
18	(a) (b) (c) (d) (e)	58	(a) (b) (c) (d) (e)
19	(a) (b) (c) (d) (e)	59	(a) (b) (c) (d) (e)
20	(a) (b) (c) (d) (e)	60	(a) (b) (c) (d) (e)
21	(a) (b) (c) (d) (e)	61	(a) (b) (c) (d) (e)
22	(a) (b) (c) (d) (e)	62	(a) (b) (c) (d) (e)
23	(a) (b) (c) (d) (e)	63	(a) (b) (c) (d) (e)
24	(a) (b) (c) (d) (e)	64	(a) (b) (c) (d) (e)
25	(a) (b) (c) (d) (e)	65	(a) (b) (c) (d) (e)
26	(a) (b) (c) (d) (e)	66	(a) (b) (c) (d) (e)
27	(a) (b) (c) (d) (e)	67	(a) (b) (c) (d) (e)
28	(a) (b) (c) (d) (e)	68	(a) (b) (c) (d) (e)
29	(a) (b) (c) (d) (e)	69	(a) (b) (c) (d) (e)
30	(a) (b) (c) (d) (e)	70	(a) (b) (c) (d) (e)
31	(a) (b) (c) (d) (e)	71	(a) (b) (c) (d) (e)
32	(a) (b) (c) (d) (e)	72	(a) (b) (c) (d) (e)
33	(a) (b) (c) (d) (e)	73	(a) (b) (c) (d) (e)
34	(a) (b) (c) (d) (e)	74	(a) (b) (c) (d) (e)
35	(a) (b) (c) (d) (e)	75	(a) (b) (c) (d) (e)
36	(a) (b) (c) (d) (e)	76	(a) (b) (c) (d) (e)
37	(a) (b) (c) (d) (e)	77	(a) (b) (c) (d) (e)
38	(a) (b) (c) (d) (e)	78	(a) (b) (c) (d) (e)
39	(a) (b) (c) (d) (e)	79	(a) (b) (c) (d) (e)
40	(a) (b) (c) (d) (e)	80	(a) (b) (c) (d) (e)

MACMILLAN / McGRAW-HILL

Name

Macmillan/McGraw-Hill
Mathematics

Chapter 1 Test

Grade 4
Form A

Page 1

Choose the letter of your answer.

1. What is the value of 6 in the number 856,202,000?

   a. 600,000   **c.** 60,000,000
   b. 6,000,000   **d.** 600,000,000

2. Round 7,839 to the nearest hundred.

   a. 8,000   **c.** 7,840
   b. 7,900   **d.** 7,800

3. Which amount is greatest?

   a. $32.70   **c.** $32.59
   b. $32.67   **d.** $32.19

4. How much is 2 five-dollar bills, 1 quarter, and 3 pennies?

   a. $2.28   **c.** $10.28
   b. $5.40   **d.** not given

5. Round 94 to the nearest ten.

   a. 90   **b.** 95   **c.** 99   **d.** 100

6. Which 3 coins make 40¢?

   a. 2 dimes, 1 nickel
   b. 1 quarter, 1 dime, 1 penny
   c. 1 quarter, 1 dime, 1 nickel
   d. not given

7. What is 100 less than 364,713?

   a. 264,713   **c.** 364,613
   b. 354,713   **d.** 364,703

8. Compare. 62,091 ● 6,289

   a. >   **b.** <   **c.** =

9. Round 3,579 to the nearest thousand.

   a. 3,000   **c.** 3,600
   b. 3,500   **d.** 4,000

10. Which number is least?

   a. 978 **b.** 789 **c.** 897 **d.** 798

11. Round $3.78 to the nearest ten cents.

   a. $3.70   **c.** $3.80
   b. $3.75   **d.** $4.00

12. What number is 1 hundred 3 tens 1 one?

   a. 131   **c.** 1,030
   b. 331   **d.** 100,301

13. Order from greatest to least.

     $86.09, $87.27, $86.35

   a. $87.27, $86.35, $86.09
   b. $86.09, $87.27, $86.35
   c. $86.35, $86.09, $87.27
   d. $86.09, $86.35, $87.27

14. Cost: $.65 Given: $1.00 Change?

   a. 5 dimes, 1 nickel
   b. 1 half dollar, 3 nickels
   c. 1 quarter, 1 dime
   d. not given

15. Which is two hundred twenty-five?

   a. 205   **c.** 20,025
   b. 225   **d.** 200,205

MACMILLAN / McGRAW-HILL

16. Find the amount.

   a. $6.00   **c.** $5.72
   b. $5.92   **d.** not given

Use the table to answer
Questions 17–20.

Store	Price		
	Roses	Tulips	Daisies
Sue's Flowers	$2.50	$1.75	$.50
Bud and Bulb	$3.00	$1.85	$.50
Town Flowers	$3.50	▓	$.50
Blooms, Inc.	$4.00	$1.85	$1.00

17. At Sue's Flowers a daisy costs ___ .

   a. $.50   **c.** $1.50
   b. $.75   **d.** $1.75

18. What is most likely the price of a
tulip at Town Flowers?

   a. $3.50   **c.** $1.85
   b. $2.50   **d.** $1.00

19. Which store sells the most
expensive roses?

   a. Sue's Flowers   **c.** Town Flowers
   b. Bud and Bulb   **d.** Blooms, Inc.

20. Which store sells the least
expensive tulip?

   a. Sue's Flowers   **c.** Town Flowers
   b. Bud and Bulb   **d.** Blooms, Inc.

STOP

21. Tomas is buying a kite that costs
$7.45. He wants to give the clerk
the exact amount using the fewest
bills and coins. Which bills and
coins should Tomas use?

   a. 1 five-dollar bill, 1 one-dollar
   bill, 4 dimes, and 1 nickel
   b. 1 five-dollar bill, 2 one-dollar
   bills, 1 quarter, and 2 dimes
   c. 1 five-dollar bill, 2 one-dollar
   bills, and 1 quarter
   d. 7 one-dollar bills, 1 quarter,
   and 5 nickels

22. The hardware store placed an
order for 1,575 nails. What is this
number to the nearest hundred?

   a. 700   **c.** 1,500
   b. 1,000   **d.** 1,600

23. Use number sense.

If every seat is taken, about how
many people are in a car?

   a. about 1   **c.** about 30
   b. about 5   **d.** about 200

24. Mr. Dougan has collected
2,693 baseball cards. What is
this number in expanded form?

   a. 200 + 60 + 9 + 3
   b. 2,000 + 900 + 60 + 3
   c. 2,000 + 600 + 90 + 3
   d. 20,000 + 6,000 + 900 + 30

25. Use number sense.

Jane buys a pad of notebook
paper. About how many sheets of
paper are in the pad?

   a. about 2   **c.** about 5,000
   b. about 100   **d.** about 12,000

Name

Macmillan/McGraw-Hill

Mathematics

Chapter 1 Test

Grade 4

Form B

Page 1

Choose the letter of your answer.

1. What is the value of 9 in the number 942,618,000?

   a. 900,000   **c.** 90,000,000
   b. 9,000,000   **d.** 900,000,000

2. Round 356 to the nearest hundred.

   a. 400   **b.** 360   **c.** 350   **d.** 300

3. Which number is greatest?

   a. 486   **b.** 648   **c.** 468   **d.** 684

4. How much is 3 one-dollar bills, 2 dimes, and 3 nickels?

   a. $3.25   **c.** $4.30
   b. $3.35   **d.** not given

5. Round $7.55 to the nearest ten cents.

   a. $8.00   **c.** $7.50
   b. $7.60   **d.** $7.00

6. Which 3 coins make 45¢?

   a. 1 quarter, 1 dime, 1 penny
   b. 1 quarter, 1 dime, 1 nickel
   c. 1 quarter, 2 dimes
   d. not given

7. Which number is 100 less than 781,319?

   a. 681,319   **c.** 780,319
   b. 771,319   **d.** 781,219

8. Compare. 51,102 ● 51,021

   a. >   **b.** <   **c.** =

9. Round 2,469 to the nearest thousand.

   a. 2,000   **c.** 2,500
   b. 2,400   **d.** 3,000

10. Which amount is least?

    a. $3.19   **c.** $2.89
    b. $3.27   **d.** $3.00

11. Round $81.43 to the nearest dollar.

    a. $82.00   **c.** $81.00
    b. $81.50   **d.** $80.00

12. What number is 2 hundreds 4 tens 3 ones?

    a. 243   **c.** 2,043
    b. 342   **d.** 200,403

13. Order from greatest to least.

    $63.87, $63.79, $64.01

    a. $63.79, $63.87, $64.01
    b. $63.79, $64.01, $63.87
    c. $64.01, $63.87, $63.79
    d. $63.87, $63.79, $64.01

14. Cost: $1.30 Given: $2.00
    Change?

    a. 3 quarters, 1 dime
    b. 1 half dollar, 3 nickels
    c. 2 quarters, 2 dimes
    d. not given

15. Which is six hundred sixty-nine?

    a. 609   **c.** 6,069
    b. 669   **d.** 600,609

MACMILLAN / McGRAW-HILL

16. Find the amount.

   a. $51.46   **c.** $5.46
   b. $5.71   **d.** not given

Use the table to answer
Questions 17–20.

Store	Number of Pens Sold		
	Fine-Point	Medium-Point	Bold-Point
The Art Shop	137	96	305
Sam's Supply	135	280	81
City Stationer	120	200	105
Write Place	132	88	212

17. How many bold-point pens did
Write Place sell?

   a. 212 **b.** 105 **c.** 96 **d.** 72

18. Which store sold the fewest
fine-point pens?

   a. The Art Shop **c.** City Stationer
   b. Sam's Supply **d.** Write Place

19. How many medium-point pens did
Sam's Supply sell?

   a. 81 **b.** 120 **c.** 200 **d.** 280

20. Which store sold more than
300 bold-point pens?

   a. The Art Shop **c.** City Stationer
   b. Sam's Supply **d.** Write Place

STOP

21. Emily has two bills and two coins,
just enough to pay the exact
amount for a pen that costs $2.60.
Which bills and coins does Emily
have?

   a. 2 one-dollar bills and 2 dimes
   b. 1 five-dollar bill, 1 one-dollar
     bill, and 2 dimes
   c. 2 one-dollar bills, 1 half dollar,
     and 1 dime
   d. 2 one-dollar bills, 2 quarters

22. The Sew Good Sewing Shop sold
21,559 spools of thread last year.
What is this number to the nearest
thousand?

   a. 20,000   **c.** 22,000
   b. 21,000   **d.** 23,000

23. Use number sense.

If every seat is taken, about how
many people are in a taxi?

   a. about 300   **c.** about 6
   b. about 50   **d.** about 1

24. Last week 4,250 people went to
the movie theater at the mall.
What is this number in expanded
form?

   a. 40,000 + 2,000 + 50
   b. 4,000 + 200 + 50
   c. 4,000 + 200 + 5
   d. 400 + 20 + 5

25. Use number sense.

Elizabeth buys a pack of pens.
About how many pens are in the
pack?

   a. about 1   **c.** about 3,000
   b. about 20   **d.** about 80,000

Name
_____

Macmillan/McGraw-Hill
Mathematics

Chapter 1 Test

Grade 4

Form C

Page 1

Mark your answer.

1. Write the value of 6 in the number 856,202,000.

   _____

2. Round 7,839 to the nearest hundred.

   _____

3. Ring the amount that is greatest.

   $32.70 $32.59

   $32.67 $32.19

4. How much is 2 five-dollar bills, 1 quarter, and 3 pennies?

   _____

5. Round 94 to the nearest ten.

   _____

6. Which 3 coins make 40¢?

   _____

7. What is 100 less than 364,713?

   _____

8. Compare. Write >, <, or =.
   62,091 ● 6,289

   _____

9. Round 3,579 to the nearest thousand.

   _____

10. Ring the number that is least.

    978   789   897   798

11. Round $3.78 to the nearest ten cents.

    _____

12. What number is 1 hundred 3 tens 1 one?

    _____

13. Order from greatest to least.
    $86.09, $87.27, $86.35

    _____

14. Cost: $.65 Given: $1.00
    What two coins make change?

    _____

15. Write two hundred twenty-five as a number.

    _____

16. Write the amount.

_____

Use the table to answer
Questions 17–20.

Store	Price		
	Roses	Tulips	Daisies
Sue's Flowers	$2.50	$1.75	$.50
Bud and Bulb	$3.00	$1.85	$.50
Town Flowers	$3.50		$.50
Blooms, Inc.	$4.00	$1.85	$1.00

17. At Sue's Flowers a daisy costs ___.

_____

18. What is most likely the price of a tulip at Town Flowers?

_____

19. Which store sells the most expensive roses?

_____

20. Which store sells the least expensive tulip?

_____

21. Tomas is buying a kite that costs $7.45. He wants to give the clerk the exact amount using the fewest bills and coins. Which bills and coins should Tomas use?

_____

22. The hardware store placed an order for 1,575 nails. Write this number to the nearest hundred.

_____

23. Use number sense.
If every seat in a car is taken, about how many people are in the car?

_____

24. Mr. Dougan has collected 2,693 baseball cards. Write this number in expanded form.

_____

25. Use number sense.
Jane buys a pad of notebook paper. Are there about 2 sheets, 100 sheets, 5,000 sheets, or 12,000 sheets of paper in the pad?

_____

Name _____

Macmillan/McGraw-Hill
Mathematics

Chapter 2 Test

Grade 4

Form A

Page 1

Choose the letter of your answer.

1. $\begin{array}{r} 9 \\ + 6 \\ \hline \end{array}$
    a. 3 **c.** 16
    b. 15 **d.** 54

2. What is the length of the goldfish?

   a. 3 cm **c.** 10 cm
   b. 4 cm **d.** 30 cm

3. $6 + 7 = \blacksquare + 6$
   a. 13 **c.** 6
   b. 7 **d.** not given

4. $\begin{array}{r} 5 \\ + 0 \\ \hline \end{array}$
    a. 0
    b. 10
    c. 50
    d. not given

5. $4 + 3 + 2 + 8$
   a. 12 **b.** 15 **c.** 17 **d.** 18

6. How wide is the stamp?

   a. 1 cm **c.** 3 cm
   b. 2 cm **d.** 4 cm

7. $\begin{array}{r} 4 \\ - 0 \\ \hline \end{array}$
    a. 0
    b. 4
    c. 8
    d. not given

8. $2 + 3 = \blacksquare + 2$
   a. 3 **c.** 9
   b. 5 **d.** not given

9. The length of a banana is about _____.
   a. 20 km **c.** 20 cm
   b. 20 m **d.** 20 dm

10. $\begin{array}{r} 10 \\ - 3 \\ \hline \end{array}$
    a. 3
    b. 6
    c. 7
    d. 13

11. How long is the bolt?

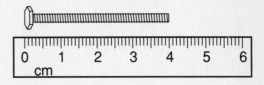

    a. 3 cm **c.** 5 cm
    b. 4 cm **d.** 6 cm

12. $3 + 9$
    a. 6 **b.** 12 **c.** 27 **d.** 39

13. $\begin{array}{r} 12 \\ - 4 \\ \hline \end{array}$
    a. 0
    b. 8
    c. 10
    d. 14

MACMILLAN / McGRAW-HILL

14. $7 + 1 = \blacksquare + 7$

  a. 1   **c.** 7

  b. 5   **d.** not given

15. Which is the best unit to measure the length of a pencil?

  a. dm   **c.** m

  b. cm   **d.** km

16. Which is the best unit to measure the length of a car?

  a. cm   **b.** dm   **c.** m   **d.** km

17. $\begin{array}{r} 18 \\ -\ 9 \\ \hline \end{array}$ **a.** 8

                 b. 9

                 c. 10

                 d. 27

18. $11 - 3$

  a. 3   **b.** 7   **c.** 8   **d.** 113

19. About how wide is the door to your classroom?

  a. about 1 meter

  b. about 1 kilometer

  c. about 1 centimeter

  d. about 1 decimeter

20. $\begin{array}{r} 5 \\ +\ 2 \\ \hline \end{array}$ **a.** 52

                 b. 10

                 c. 7

                 d. 3

21. $7 + 8$

  a. 1   **b.** 15   **c.** 16   **d.** 78

22. What is the difference between 17 and 8?

  a. 6   **b.** 9   **c.** 11   **d.** 25

Use the bar graph to answer Questions 23–27.

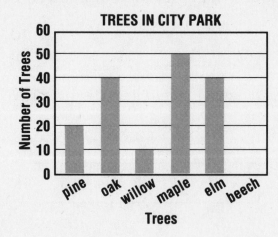

TREES IN CITY PARK

23. How many pine trees are there in City Park?

  a. 20   **b.** 30   **c.** 40   **d.** 50

24. There are more pine trees than _____.

  a. oak trees   **c.** elm trees

  b. willow trees   **d.** maple trees

25. In City Park there is an equal number of oak trees and _____.

  a. willow trees   **c.** elm trees

  b. pine trees   **d.** maple trees

26. How many beech trees are there in City Park?

  a. 160   **b.** 60   **c.** 16   **d.** 0

27. There are the greatest number of which kind of tree in City Park?

  a. pine trees   **c.** maple trees

  b. oak trees   **d.** elm trees

28. What is the length of the paper clip?

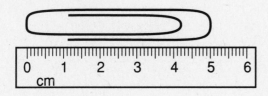

a. 1 cm   **c.** 5 cm
b. 4 cm   **d.** 6 cm

29. Mr. Garcia bought suntan lotion for $4.98, a bag of ice for $.89, and a pair of sunglasses. What else do you need to know to find out how much he spent in all?

a. the name of the store
b. the type of suntan lotion he bought
c. the temperature outside
d. the price of the sunglasses

30. Karen had 9 beads. She gave 3 beads to Susan. How many beads did Karen have left?

a. 0   **b.** 3   **c.** 6   **d.** 12

31. Use number sense.

If the waiting room at the doctor's office is full, about how many people are in the waiting room?

a. about 2   **c.** about 300
b. about 25   **d.** about 5,000

32. Cindy rode 2 km to the store. Then she rode 3 km to the bank. Then she rode 5 km back to her house. How far did she ride?

a. 20 km   **c.** 5 km
b. 10 km   **d.** 0 km

33. Mr. Chambers has a square field that measures 18 m on each side. The field has a square pasture in the middle that is 3 m from the edge of the field on all sides. What is the measurement of one side of the pasture in the middle?

a. 15 m   **c.** 6 m
b. 12 m   **d.** 3 m

Name

Macmillan/McGraw-Hill
Mathematics

Chapter 2 Test

Grade 4
Form B

Page 1

Choose the letter of your answer.

1. 9
  + 4

a. 94   **c.** 13
b. 14   **d.** 5

2. What is the length of the caterpillar?

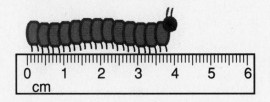

a. 1 cm   **c.** 30 cm
b. 4 cm   **d.** 40 cm

3. 5 + 6 = ■ + 5

a. 11   **c.** 6
b. 7   **d.** not given

4. 3
  + 0

a. 0
b. 3
c. 6
d. not given

5. 8 + 3 + 1 + 3

a. 16   **b.** 15   **c.** 9   **d.** 1

6. How long is the eraser?

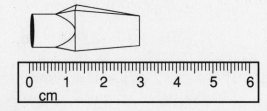

a. 2 cm   **c.** 4 cm
b. 3 cm   **d.** 5 cm

7. 2
  − 0

a. 0
b. 2
c. 4
d. not given

8. 4 + 7 = ■ + 4

a. 4   **c.** 11
b. 6   **d.** not given

9. The length of a pencil is about _____.

a. 15 cm   **c.** 15 m
b. 15 dm   **d.** 15 km

10. 10
  − 2

a. 2
b. 8
c. 9
d. 12

11. How long is the hair clip?

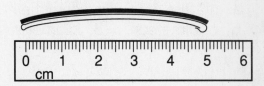

a. 2 cm   **c.** 4 cm
b. 3 cm   **d.** 5 cm

12. 2 + 9

a. 29   **b.** 18   **c.** 12   **d.** 11

13. 14
  − 5

a. 29
b. 19
c. 9
d. 8

14. $9 + 5 = \blacksquare + 9$

  a. 5   **c.** 14

  b. 9   **d.** not given

15. Which is the best unit to measure the length of your thumb?

  a. dm   **c.** m

  b. cm   **d.** km

16. Which is the best unit to measure the length of a truck?

  a. cm   **b.** dm   **c.** m   **d.** km

17.
$$\begin{array}{r} 16 \\ -\ 8 \\ \hline \end{array}$$

  a. 24

  b. 12

  c. 8

  d. 0

18. $12 - 4$

  a. 16   **b.** 8   **c.** 7   **d.** 4

19. To measure the distance between two cities, the best unit to use is _____.

  a. meters   **c.** centimeters

  b. decimeters   **d.** kilometers

20.
$$\begin{array}{r} 7 \\ +\ 5 \\ \hline \end{array}$$

  a. 2

  b. 11

  c. 12

  d. 35

21. $9 + 8$

  a. 1   **b.** 17   **c.** 72   **d.** 98

22. What is the difference between 15 and 7?

  a. 8   **b.** 9   **c.** 12   **d.** 22

Use the bar graph to answer Questions 23–27.

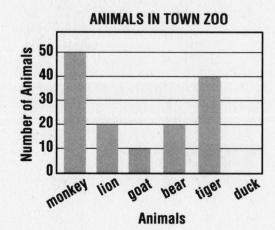

23. How many goats are there in Town Zoo?

  a. 50   **c.** 20

  b. 40   **d.** 10

24. There are more bears than _____.

  a. monkeys   **c.** goats

  b. tigers   **d.** lions

25. In Town Zoo there is an equal number of bears and _____.

  a. horses   **c.** monkeys

  b. tigers   **d.** lions

26. How many ducks are there in Town Zoo?

  a. 0   **b.** 20   **c.** 40   **d.** 140

27. There are the greatest number of which kind of animal in Town Zoo?

  a. monkeys   **c.** tigers

  b. lions   **d.** ducks

MACMILLAN / McGRAW-HILL

28. What is the length of the nail?

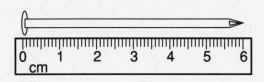

a. 6 cm   c. 50 cm

b. 10 cm   d. 60 cm

29. Marnie buys shampoo for $2.59, a hairbrush for $1.99, and toothpaste. What else do you need to know to find out how much she spends in all?

a. the price of the shampoo

b. the price of the toothpaste

c. what kind of shampoo she buys

d. what kind of toothpaste she buys

30. Lori has 7 blocks. She gives 4 blocks to Mark. How many blocks does Lori have now?

a. 3   b. 4   c. 7   d. 11

31. Use number sense.

If every seat in the train car is full, about how many people are in the train car?

a. about 5   c. about 900

b. about 100   d. about 25,000

32. Gloria drove 4 km to the zoo. Then she drove 2 km to the park. Then she drove 6 km home. How far did Gloria drive in all?

a. 0 km   c. 6 km

b. 2 km   d. 12 km

33. Mrs. Nolan has a square garden that measures 10 m on each side. The garden has a square plot in the middle that is 2 m from the edge of the garden on all sides. What is the measurement of one side of the plot in the middle?

a. 2 m   c. 6 m

b. 4 m   d. 8 m

MACMILLAN / McGRAW-HILL

Name

Macmillan/McGraw-Hill
Mathematics

Chapter 2 Test

Grade 4
Form C

Page 1

Mark your answer.

1. $\begin{array}{r} 9 \\ + 6 \\ \hline \end{array}$

_____

2. What is the length of the goldfish?

_____

3. $6 + 7 = \blacksquare + 6$

_____

4. $\begin{array}{r} 5 \\ + 0 \\ \hline \end{array}$

_____

5. $4 + 3 + 2 + 8$

_____

6. How wide is the stamp?

_____

7. $\begin{array}{r} 4 \\ - 0 \\ \hline \end{array}$

_____

8. $2 + 3 = \blacksquare + 2$

_____

9. Is the length of a banana about
    20 kilometers, 20 meters,
    20 centimeters, or 20 decimeters?

_____

10. $\begin{array}{r} 10 \\ - 3 \\ \hline \end{array}$

_____

11. How long is the bolt?

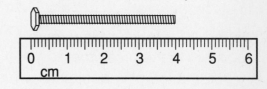

_____

12. $3 + 9$

_____

13. $\begin{array}{r} 12 \\ - 4 \\ \hline \end{array}$

_____

14. $7 + 1 = \blacksquare + 7$

_____

15. Is the best unit to measure the length of a pencil decimeters, centimeters, meters, or kilometers?

_____

16. Is the best unit to measure the length of a car centimeters, decimeters, meters, or kilometers?

_____

17.
$$\begin{array}{r} 18 \\ -9 \\ \hline \end{array}$$

_____

18. $11 - 3$

_____

19. Is the door to your classroom about 1 meter, 1 kilometer, 1 centimeter, or 1 decimeter wide?

_____

20.
$$\begin{array}{r} 5 \\ +2 \\ \hline \end{array}$$

_____

21. $7 + 8$

_____

22. What is the difference between 17 and 8?

_____

Use the bar graph to answer Questions 23–27.

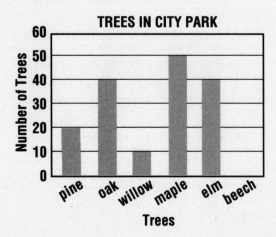

TREES IN CITY PARK

23. How many pine trees are there in City Park?

_____

24. There are more pine trees than _____.

_____

25. In City Park there is an equal number of oak trees and _____.

_____

26. How many beech trees are there in City Park?

_____

MACMILLAN / McGRAW-HILL

27. There are the greatest number of which kind of tree in City Park?

_____

28. What is the length of the paper clip?

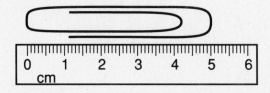

_____

29. Mr. Garcia bought suntan lotion for $4.98, a bag of ice for $.89, and a pair of sunglasses. What else do you need to know to find out how much he spent in all?

_____

30. Karen had 9 beads. She gave 3 beads to Susan. How many beads did Karen have left?

_____

31. Use number sense.

If the waiting room at the doctor's office is full, are there about 2 people, 25 people, 300 people, or 5,000 people in the waiting room?

_____

32. Cindy rode 2 kilometers to the store. Then she rode 3 kilometers to the bank. Then she rode 5 kilometers back to her house. How far did she ride?

_____

33. Mr. Chambers has a square field that measures 18 meters on each side. The field has a square pasture in the middle that is 3 meters from the edge of the field on all sides. What is the measurement of one side of the pasture in the middle?

_____

MACMILLAN / McGRAW-HILL

Choose the letter of your answer.

1. What is the best estimate of 2,072 +1,386?

   a. 10,000   **c.** 3,000

   b. 5,000   **d.** 2,000

2. $72.15 + $99.07

   a. $171.22   **c.** $19.52

   b. $161.22   **d.** not given

3.   4,978   **a.** 2,215

    – 2,763   **b.** 2,341

              c. 2,515

              d. 7,741

4. Estimate.

      $74.65 + $.24 + $25.32

   a. $150.00   **c.** $80.00

   b. $100.00   **d.** $70.00

5. Find the perimeter.

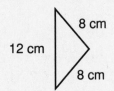

   a. 10 cm

   b. 20 cm

   c. 25 cm

   d. 28 cm

6.   342   **a.** 374

      29   **b.** 383

   + 14   **c.** 385

              d. not given

7. What is the best estimate of 4,321 – 2,215?

   a. 1,000   **c.** 3,000

   b. 2,000   **d.** 4,000

8. $76.29   **a.** $135.44

   – 59.15   **b.** $27.24

              c. $19.14

              d. $17.14

9. 2,867 + 6,731

   a. 9,598   **c.** 3,864

   b. 8,598   **d.** not given

10. Find the perimeter.

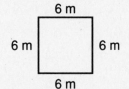

   a. 36 m

   b. 24 m

   c. 18 m

   d. 12 m

11. Estimate by rounding.

      $4.32 + $6.89 + $4.99

   a. $14.00

   b. $15.00

   c. $16.00

   d. $17.00

12. $100.00 – $10.24

   a. $79.76   **c.** $89.86

   b. $89.76   **d.** $99.06

13. 2,500   **a.** 5,200

     1,000   **b.** 4,700

       700   **c.** 3,500

   + 300   **d.** not given

14. Find the perimeter.

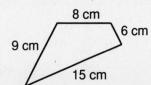

   a. 32 cm

   b. 35 cm

   c. 38 cm

   d. 46 cm

MACMILLAN / McGRAW-HILL

15. What is the best estimate of 9,243 – 4,018?

a. 200   **c.** 5,000
b. 500   **d.** 6,000

16. 526 – 19

a. 507   **b.** 514   **c.** 517   **d.** 545

17.
```
   2,946
   1,072
+    348
```
a. 3,356
b. 4,256
c. 4,366
d. not given

18. Find the perimeter.

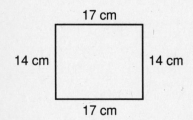

17 cm
14 cm   14 cm
17 cm

a. 31 cm   **c.** 62 cm
b. 57 cm   **d.** 68 cm

19.
```
  7,030
– 2,480
```
a. 4,550
b. 5,000
c. 5,610
d. 9,420

20. Find the perimeter.

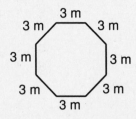

3 m
3 m   3 m
3 m   3 m
3 m   3 m
3 m

a. 30 m   **c.** 24 m
b. 27 m   **d.** 21 m

STOP

21. John's swimming pool is a rectangle. It is 6 m wide and 12 m long. What is its perimeter?

a. 72 m   **c.** 18 m
b. 36 m   **d.** 12 m

22. Ellen wants to buy a kite that costs $8.29. She gives the clerk $20.00. Which number sentence should you use to find how much change she should receive?

a. $20.00 + $8.29 =
b. $20.00 – $8.29 = ▓

23. Ms. Talbot's ranch is surrounded by fences. The lengths of the fences are 1,681 meters, 973 meters, 2,047 meters, and 1,411 meters. She wants to know the perimeter of the ranch. Which is the most reasonable answer?

a. 2,112 meters
b. 3,120 meters
c. 6,112 meters
d. 10,120 meters

24. Kim and Ted made 328 cookies to sell at the fair. They sold 276. How many cookies were left?

a. 604   **c.** 58
b. 152   **d.** 52

25. Joe has $7.00. He buys a toy car. What else do you need to know to find how much money he has left?

a. the name of the store
b. the color of the toy car
c. the size of the toy car
d. the price of the toy car

MACMILLAN / McGRAW-HILL

Name

Macmillan/McGraw-Hill
Mathematics

Chapter 3 Test

Grade 4
Form B

Page 1

Choose the letter of your answer.

1. What is the best estimate of 3,551 + 3,337?

   a. 8,000   **c.** 5,000
   b. 7,000   **d.** 1,000

2. $24.32 + $87.46

   a. $111.78   **c.** $112.76
   b. $111.88   **d.** not given

3.   7,128
     − 4,015

   a. 2,813
   b. 3,013
   c. 3,113
   d. 11,143

4. Estimate.

       $19.83 + $6.08 + $24.18

   a. $20.00   **c.** $50.00
   b. $40.00   **d.** $60.00

5. Find the perimeter.

   9 cm   16 cm
       22 cm

   a. 43 cm   **c.** 47 cm
   b. 45 cm   **d.** 50 cm

6.   4,528
        110
     +   7

   a. 4,645
   b. 4,644
   c. 4,536
   d. not given

7. What is the best estimate of 9,215 − 4,328?

   a. 500   **c.** 4,000
   b. 3,000   **d.** 5,000

8. $36.50
     − 22.98

   a. $12.52
   b. $13.42
   c. $13.52
   d. $23.12

9. 3,632 + 4,536

   a. 7,569   **c.** 9,218
   b. 8,268   **d.** not given

10. Find the perimeter.

    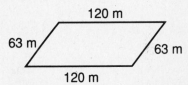

    120 m
    63 m   63 m
    120 m

    a. 183 m   **c.** 386 m
    b. 366 m   **d.** 449 m

11. Estimate by rounding.

        $21.36 + $5.79 + $9.38

    a. $34.00
    b. $35.00
    c. $36.00
    d. $41.00

12. $36.27 − $17.95

    a. $17.32   **c.** $18.32
    b. $17.52   **d.** $18.35

13.   9,000
       2,060
        840
      +   300

    a. 12,200
    b. 12,010
    c. 11,300
    d. not given

MACMILLAN / McGRAW-HILL

14. Find the perimeter.

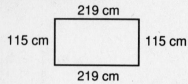

219 cm

115 cm · 115 cm

219 cm

a. 700 cm c. 558 cm
b. 668 cm d. 334 cm

15. What is the best estimate of 7,812 – 5,704?

a. 6,000 c. 3,000
b. 5,000 d. 2,000

16. 738 – 615

a. 113 b. 123 c. 153 d. 223

17. 4,123
  2,235
+ 894
  ———

a. 7,252
b. 7,262
c. 8,252
d. not given

18. Find the perimeter.

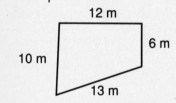

12 m

6 m

10 m

13 m

a. 36 m c. 41 m
b. 38 m d. 45 m

19. 5,200
– 3,670
———

a. 8,870
b. 2,970
c. 2,600
d. 1,530

20. Find the perimeter.

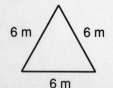

6 m 6 m

6 m

a. 12 m
b. 18 m
c. 24 m
d. 36 m

21. The playground is a rectangle. It is 60 m long and 50 m wide. What is its perimeter?

a. 110 m c. 220 m
b. 200 m d. 250 m

22. Peter has $5.78. His aunt gives him $10.50 for his birthday. Which number sentence should you use to find how much money he has in all?

a. $5.78 + $10.50 = ▣
b. $10.50 – $5.78 = ▣

23. Stony Island has sides that measure 2,240 meters, 3,398 meters, 1,427 meters, and 2,412 meters. Bob wants to find the perimeter of the island. Which is the most reasonable answer?

a. 4,461 meters c. 8,477 meters
b. 7,578 meters d. 9,477 meters

24. Joan has 1,200 stamps in her collection. She sells 864 stamps. How many stamps does she have left?

a. 2,064 c. 446
b. 1,446 d. 336

25. Lita has $8.00. She buys a ring at the store. What else do you need to know to find how much money she has left?

a. the price of the ring
b. the name of the store
c. the name of Lita's town
d. the color of the ring

STOP

MACMILLAN / McGRAW-HILL

Name

Macmillan/McGraw-Hill
Mathematics

Chapter 3 Test

Grade 4
Form C

Page 1

Mark your answer.

1. Estimate.   2,072 + 1,386

_____

2. $72.15 + $99.07

_____

3. 4,978 − 2,763

_____

4. Estimate.
    $74.65 + $.24 + $25.32

_____

5. Find the perimeter.

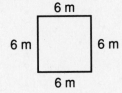

_____

6.   342
          29
      + 14
      _____

_____

7. Estimate.   4,321 − 2,215

_____

8. $76.29 − $59.15

_____

9. 2,867 + 6,731

_____

10. Find the perimeter.

          6 m
      ┌────────┐
  6 m │   │ 6 m
      └────────┘
          6 m

_____

11. Estimate by rounding.
    $4.32 + $6.89 + $4.99

_____

12. $100.00 − $10.24

_____

13.   2,500
          1,000
            700
      +   300
      _____

_____

14. Find the perimeter.

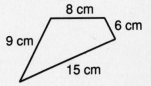

_____

MACMILLAN / McGRAW-HILL

15. Estimate. 9,243 − 4,018

_____

16. 526 − 19

_____

17.   2,946
    1,072
 +   348
_____

_____

18. Find the perimeter.

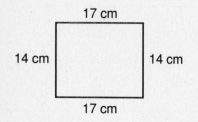

17 cm

14 cm   14 cm

17 cm

_____

19.   7,030
 − 2,480
_____

_____

20. Find the perimeter.

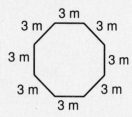

3 m

3 m   3 m

3 m   3 m

3 m   3 m

3 m

_____

21. John's swimming pool is a rectangle. It is 6 m wide and 12 m long. What is its perimeter?

_____

22. Ellen wants to buy a kite that costs $8.29. She gives the clerk $20.00. Write the number sentence you should use to find how much change she should receive.

_____

23. Ms. Talbot's ranch is surrounded by fences. The lengths of the fences are 1,681 meters, 973 meters, 2,047 meters, and 1,411 meters. She wants to know the perimeter of the ranch. Is the most reasonable answer 2,112 meters, 3,120 meters, 6,112 meters, or 10,120 meters?

_____

24. Kim and Ted made 328 cookies to sell at the fair. They sold 276. How many cookies were left?

_____

25. Joe has $7.00. He buys a toy car. What else do you need to know to find how much money he has left?

_____

MACMILLAN / McGRAW-HILL

Name _____

Macmillan/McGraw-Hill
Mathematics

Chapter 4 Test

Grade 4
Form A

Page 1

Choose the letter of your answer.

1. About how long is a movie?
   a. about 2 hours
   b. about 2 minutes
   c. about 200 seconds
   d. about 20 minutes

2. Which is the best estimate for the mass of a bicycle?
   a. 15 mL   c. 15 kg
   b. 5 g   d. 5 L

3. On a good day for ice-skating, the temperature would be _____.
   a. 212°C
   b. 100°C
   c. 32°C
   d. ⁻5°C

4. The time shown is _____.

   a. 7:25
   b. 6:25
   c. 6:05
   d. 5:30

5. Which is the best estimate for the temperature on a warm, sunny day?
   a. ⁻10°C
   b. 0°C
   c. 5°C
   d. 25°C

6. The capacity of a kitchen sink is about _____.
   a. 10 mL   c. 100 L
   b. 10 L   d. 1 mL

7. What is the temperature shown?
   a. 10°C
   b. 25°C
   c. 30°C
   d. 40°C

   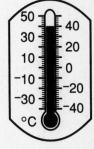

8. What time is 40 min after 7:10?
   a. 6:30
   b. 7:40
   c. 7:50
   d. 11:10

9. Which is the best estimate for the mass of a fourth-grade student?
   a. 31 g   c. 31 kg
   b. 310 g   d. 310 kg

10. The capacity of a cereal bowl is about _____.
    a. 250 mL   c. 250 L
    b. 1 L   d. 1 mL

11. How much time passes between 3:10 P.M. and 3:52 P.M.?
    a. 62 minutes
    b. 42 minutes
    c. 40 minutes
    d. 12 minutes

12. You usually need a jacket when the temperature outside is _____.
    a. 5°C
    b. 25°C
    c. 30°C
    d. 40°C

Macmillan/McGraw-Hill, MATHEMATICS IN ACTION
Grade 4, Chapter 4, Form A   CMS Test ID 124041

MACMILLAN / McGRAW-HILL

Use the grid to answer
Questions 13–16.

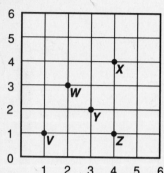

13. Which letter is at the point (4, 4)?

  a. *V*   **c.** *X*

  b. *W*   **d.** not given

14. The ordered pair for point *Z*
is _____ .

  a. (1, 4)

  b. (4, 1)

  c. (5, 5)

  d. not given

15. Which letter is at the point (3, 2)?

  a. *W*

  b. *X*

  c. *Y*

  d. not given

16. The ordered pair for point *W*
is _____ .

  a. (1, 1)

  b. (2, 2)

  c. (3, 2)

  d. not given

Use the graph to answer
Questions 17–20.

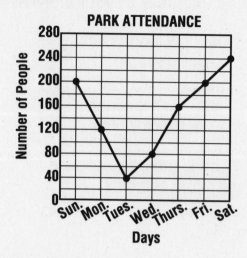

17. On which day were the most
people at the park?

  a. Tuesday

  b. Saturday

  c. Sunday

  d. Friday

18. How many people were at the
park on Wednesday?

  a. 80   **c.** 160

  b. 120   **d.** 200

19. On which day were the fewest
people at the park?

  a. Saturday

  b. Friday

  c. Thursday

  d. Tuesday

20. How many people were at the
park on Thursday?

  a. 40   **c.** 160

  b. 120   **d.** 240

MACMILLAN / McGRAW-HILL

21. At 12 noon the temperature was 28°C. By 5:00 P.M. the temperature was 3° lower. At 9:00 P.M. it was 21°C. How much did the temperature change between 5:00 P.M. and 9:00 P.M.?

    a. 7°C   **c.** 3°C
    b. 4°C   **d.** 1°C

22. Al and Nick got to the park at 3:30 P.M. Their parents picked them up at 4:45 P.M. How long were the boys at the park?

    a. 15 min   **c.** 1 h 15 min
    b. 45 min   **d.** 1 h 45 min

23. Jan is cleaning her yard. She spends 1 hour raking leaves. She then takes about 45 minutes to pick up sticks and sweep the sidewalk. About how long does she take to clean the yard?

    a. about 2 hours
    b. about 1 hour
    c. about 45 minutes
    d. about 30 minutes

24. Otis has 459 old coins. He sells 128 coins and buys 205 stamps. How many coins does he have left?

    a. 536   **c.** 254
    b. 331   **d.** 128

25. Mrs. Howe buys a book for $13.73. She gives the clerk $20.00. Which number sentence should you use to find how much change she should receive?

    a. $20.00 − $13.73 = ▓
    b. $20.00 + $13.73 = ▓

Name

Macmillan/McGraw-Hill
Mathematics

Chapter 4 Test

Grade 4

Form B

Page 1

Choose the letter of your answer.

1. About how long does it take to sing a song?

   a. about 3 seconds
   b. about 3 minutes
   c. about 3 hours
   d. about 30 hours

2. Which is the best estimate for the mass of a large television?

   a. 20 kg   **c.** 20 mL
   b. 2 g   **d.** 2 L

3. At what temperature would ice cream probably start melting?

   a. ⁻20°C
   b. ⁻10°C
   c. 0°C
   d. 10°C

4. What time does the clock show?

   a. 4:20
   b. 4:25
   c. 5:20
   d. 5:40

5. Which is the best estimate for the temperature on a cold, snowy day?

   a. ⁻5°C
   b. 5°C
   c. 20°C
   d. 50°C

6. The capacity of a water glass is about _____ .

   a. 250 L   **c.** 25 mL
   b. 25 L   **d.** 250 mL

7. What is the temperature shown?

   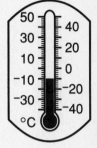

   a. 15°C
   b. 0°C
   c. ⁻10°C
   d. ⁻20°C

8. What time is 30 min before 5:15?

   a. 6:15
   b. 5:45
   c. 4:45
   d. 4:30

9. Which is the best estimate for the mass of a nine-year-old child?

   a. 10 kg   **c.** 25 g
   b. 25 kg   **d.** 90 g

10. The capacity of a cooking pot is about _____ .

    a. 1 L   **c.** 2 mL
    b. 25 mL   **d.** 50 L

11. How much time passes between 2:25 P.M. and 2:57 P.M.?

    a. 25 minutes
    b. 28 minutes
    c. 32 minutes
    d. 82 minutes

12. You can usually wear shorts when the temperature outside is _____ .

    a. 0°C
    b. 5°C
    c. 10°C
    d. 30°C

MACMILLAN / McGRAW-HILL

Use the grid to answer
Questions 13–16.

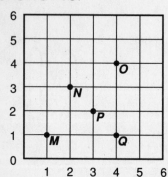

13. Which letter is at the point (4, 1)?

  a. *M*   **c.** *P*

  b. *N*   **d.** not given

14. The ordered pair for point *P*
is _____ .

  a. (3, 2)

  b. (3, 3)

  c. (2, 3)

  d. not given

15. Which letter is at the point (2, 3)?

  a. *M*   **c.** *O*

  b. *N*   **d.** not given

16. The ordered pair for point *M*
is _____ .

  a. (1, 1)

  b. (3, 2)

  c. (4, 4)

  d. not given

Use the graph to answer
Questions 17–20.

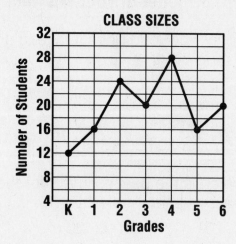

17. Which grade has the most
students?

  a. K   **c.** 4th

  b. 2nd   **d.** 6th

18. How many students are in the
6th grade?

  a. 16   **c.** 24

  b. 20   **d.** 28

19. Which grade has the fewest
students?

  a. 4th   **c.** 1st

  b. 2nd   **d.** K

20. How many students are in the
2nd grade?

  a. 12   **c.** 24

  b. 20   **d.** 32

21. At 7:00 A.M. the temperature was 24°C. By 12 noon it was 2° higher. At 3:00 P.M. it was 29°C. How much did the temperature change between 12 noon and 3:00 P.M.?

   a. 2°C   **c.** 4°C
   b. 3°C   **d.** 6°C

22. The movie started at 6:30 P.M. It ended at 8:15 P.M. How long was the movie?

   a. 2 h 15 min   **c.** 1 h 15 min
   b. 1 h 45 min   **d.** 45 min

23. Rhonda is painting the living room. She takes 2 hours to paint the walls and about 40 minutes to paint the ceiling. About how long does she take to paint the living room?

   a. about 20 minutes
   b. about 40 minutes
   c. about 2 hours
   d. about 3 hours

24. The baker makes 212 loaves of bread and 434 muffins. He sells 186 muffins. How many muffins are left?

   a. 26   **c.** 248
   b. 146   **d.** 398

25. Ernie buys a hammer and nails for $23.27. He gives the clerk $25.00. Which number sentence should you use to find how much change he should receive?

   a. $25.00 − $23.27 = ▮
   b. $25.00 + $23.27 = ▮

Name _____

Macmillan/McGraw-Hill
Mathematics

Chapter 4 Test

Grade 4
Form C

Page 1

Mark your answer.

1. Is the length of a movie about 2 hours, 2 minutes, 200 seconds, or 20 minutes?

_____

2. Is the best estimate for the mass of a bicycle 15 milliliters, 5 grams, 15 kilograms, or 5 liters?

_____

3. On a good day for ice-skating, would the temperature be 212°C, 100°C, 32°C, or ⁻5°C?

_____

4. The time shown is _____.

_____

5. Is the best estimate for the temperature on a warm, sunny day ⁻10°C, 0°C, 5°C, or 25°C?

_____

6. Is the capacity of a kitchen sink about 10 milliliters, 10 liters, 100 liters, or 1 milliliter?

_____

7. What is the temperature shown?

_____

8. What time is 40 minutes after 7:10?

_____

9. Is the best estimate for the mass of a fourth-grade student 31 grams, 310 grams, 31 kilograms, or 310 kilograms?

_____

10. Is the capacity of a cereal bowl about 250 liters, 1 liter, 250 milliliters, or 1 milliliter?

_____

11. How much time passes between 3:10 P.M. and 3:52 P.M.?

_____

12. Do you usually need a jacket when the temperature outside is 5°C, 25°C, 30°C, or 40°C?

_____

MACMILLAN / McGRAW-HILL

Use the grid to answer
Questions 13–16.

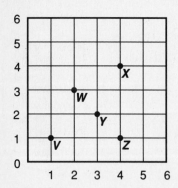

13. Which letter is at the point (4, 4)?

_____

14. The ordered pair for point *Z*
is _____ .

_____

15. Which letter is at the point (3, 2)?

_____

16. The ordered pair for point *W*
is _____ .

_____

Use the graph to answer
Questions 17–20.

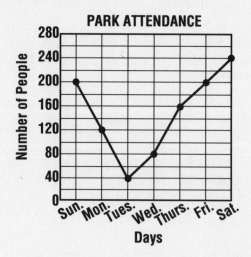

17. On which day were the most
people at the park?

_____

18. How many people were at the
park on Wednesday?

_____

19. On which day were the fewest
people at the park?

_____

20. How many people were at the
park on Thursday?

_____

_____

MACMILLAN / McGRAW-HILL

21. At 12 noon the temperature was 28°C. By 5:00 P.M. the temperature was 3° lower. At 9:00 P.M. it was 21°C. How much did the temperature change between 5:00 P.M. and 9:00 P.M.?

_____

22. Al and Nick got to the park at 3:30 P.M. Their parents picked them up at 4:45 P.M. How long were the boys at the park?

_____

23. Jan is cleaning her yard. She spends 1 hour raking leaves. She then takes about 45 minutes to pick up sticks and sweep the sidewalk. In hours, about how long does she take to clean the yard?

_____

24. Otis has 459 old coins. He sells 128 coins and buys 205 stamps. How many coins does he have left?

_____

25. Mrs. Howe buys a book for $13.73. She gives the clerk $20.00. Write the number sentence you should use to find how much change she should receive.

_____

Name

Macmillan/McGraw-Hill
Mathematics

Chapter 5 Test

Grade 4
Form A

Page 1

Choose the letter of your answer.

1. $2\overline{)16}$

   a. 2   **c.** 8

   b. 6   **d.** not given

2. Find the area.

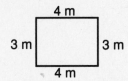

   a. 7 square m   **c.** 14 square m

   b. 12 square m   **d.** 24 square m

3. Which of the following has only even numbers?

   a. 3, 12, 24, 27

   b. 7, 9, 18, 24

   c. 3, 11, 13, 24

   d. 12, 24, 36, 48

4. $4 \times \blacksquare = 36$

   a. 3   **b.** 9   **c.** 15   **d.** 18

5. $0 \div 5$

   a. 0   **b.** 1   **c.** 5   **d.** 10

6. 2×7

   a. 21   **c.** 10

   b. 14   **d.** not given

7. What is the area of a square with 7-cm sides?

   a. 52 square cm

   b. 49 square cm

   c. 28 square cm

   d. 14 square cm

8. Which number is prime?

   a. 49   **b.** 36   **c.** 15   **d.** 3

9. $9\overline{)81}$

   a. 9   **c.** 18

   b. 12   **d.** not given

10. Which numbers are all factors of 36?

   a. 1, 8, 9, 36

   b. 4, 6, 9, 36

   c. 5, 6, 8, 9

   d. 1, 4, 6, 7

11. $(3 \times 3) \times \blacksquare = 3 \times (3 \times 7)$

   a. 2   **c.** 7

   b. 3   **d.** 21

12. $6 \div 3$

   a. 4   **c.** 1

   b. 3   **d.** not given

13. What is the area of a rectangle 8 cm long and 2 cm wide?

   a. 16 square cm

   b. 15 square cm

   c. 12 square cm

   d. 10 square cm

14. Which number is composite?

   a. 1   **b.** 2   **c.** 19   **d.** 21

15. 5×8

   a. 13   **c.** 48

   b. 40   **d.** not given

MACMILLAN / McGRAW-HILL

16. $18 \div \blacksquare = 9$

   a. 2   **b.** 5   **c.** 7   **d.** 10

17. $5\overline{)25}$

   a. 15   **c.** 5
   b. 7   **d.** not given

18. 7×0

   a. 0   **b.** 1   **c.** 3   **d.** 7

19. Find the area in square centimeters.

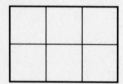

   a. 6 square cm   **c.** 9 square cm
   b. 8 square cm   **d.** 12 square cm

20. Which numbers are all multiples of 5?

   a. 5, 7, 13, 18
   b. 5, 15, 25, 40
   c. 3, 10, 15, 18
   d. 10, 12, 20, 36

21. 3×7

   a. 21   **c.** 7
   b. 18   **d.** not given

22. $48 \div 8$

   a. 12   **b.** 9   **c.** 8   **d.** 6

23. Which of the following has only odd numbers?

   a. 8, 13, 21, 24
   b. 15, 19, 23, 27
   c. 3, 11, 14, 21
   d. 13, 15, 18, 24

24. 7×9

   a. 63   **b.** 54   **c.** 36   **d.** 16

Use the pictograph to answer Questions 25 – 28.

TAXIS IN LONGVIEW CITY

City Taxis	🚕 🚕 🚕 🚕
ABC Taxis	🚕 🚕 🚕
Acme Taxi Co.	🚕 🚕
Harry's Taxis	🚕

🚕 = 50 taxis

25. How many taxis does ABC Taxis own?

   a. 50   **b.** 60   **c.** 150 **d.** 225

26. What is each 🚕 worth?

   a. 200 taxis   **c.** 100 taxis
   b. 150 taxis   **d.** 50 taxis

27. How many taxis does City Taxis own?

   a. 150   **c.** 350
   b. 200   **d.** 450

28. How many more taxis does Acme Taxi Co. own than Harry's Taxis?

   a. 50   **b.** 75   **c.** 100 **d.** 200

STOP

29. James has 45 model planes. He puts them on shelves that hold 9 planes each. Which number sentence should you use to find how many shelves he will fill with the planes?

  a. $45 \times 9 =$ ■

  b. $45 + 9 =$ ■

  c. $45 \div 9 =$ ■

  d. $45 - 9 =$ ■

30. What is the area of a rectangular strip of paper 9 cm long and 2 cm wide?

  a. 11 square cm

  b. 18 square cm

  c. 20 square cm

  d. 29 square cm

31. A new movie is playing at the Palace Theater. The first show is at 1:30. The second show is at 3:45. The third show is at 6:00. If the pattern continues, at what time is the fifth show?

  a. 9:30   **c.** 10:15

  b. 9:45   **d.** 10:30

32. Mr. Gomez wants to divide the class into 3 equal lines. There are 27 children in the class. How many children should be in each line?

  a. 24   **c.** 7

  b. 9   **d.** 5

33. Tanya mailed 5 cards yesterday. She mailed 8 cards today. She received 4 cards. How many cards did she mail in all?

  a. 4   **b.** 9   **c.** 13   **d.** 17

Name

Macmillan/McGraw-Hill
Mathematics

Chapter 5 Test

Grade 4
Form B

Page 1

Choose the letter of your answer.

1. $3\overline{)15}$

   a. 3   **c.** 45
   b. 5   **d.** not given

2. Find the area.

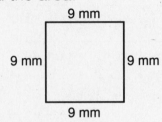

   a. 81 square mm
   b. 40.5 square mm
   c. 36 square mm
   d. 9 square mm

3. Which of the following has only odd numbers?

   a. 1, 3, 7, 8   **c.** 3, 7, 9, 13
   b. 3, 7, 13, 32 **d.** 2, 5, 7, 9

4. $5 \times \blacksquare = 45$

   a. 10 **b.** 9 **c.** 5 **d.** 4

5. $0 \div 14$

   a. 14 **b.** 7 **c.** 1 **d.** 0

6. 3×6

   a. 18   **c.** 9
   b. 12   **d.** not given

7. What is the area of a rectangle 5 cm long and 2 cm wide?

   a. 3 square cm
   b. 7 square cm
   c. 10 square cm
   d. 14 square cm

8. Which number is prime?

   a. 5 **b.** 9 **c.** 10 **d.** 14

9. $7\overline{)42}$

   a. 7   **c.** 3
   b. 6   **d.** not given

10. Which numbers are all factors of 24?

   a. 1, 3, 8, 24
   b. 1, 4, 6, 7
   c. 2, 6, 8, 9
   d. 3, 6, 7, 24

11. $(8 \times 3) \times 3 = 8 \times (3 \times \blacksquare)$

   a. 72   **c.** 6
   b. 24   **d.** 3

12. $8 \div 2$

   a. 2   **c.** 16
   b. 4   **d.** not given

13. What is the area of a square with 3-cm sides?

   a. 3 square cm
   b. 9 square cm
   c. 18 square cm
   d. 81 square cm

14. Which number is composite?

   a. 36 **b.** 13 **c.** 7 **d.** 3

15. 7×8

   a. 15   **c.** 64
   b. 49   **d.** not given

MACMILLAN / McGRAW-HILL

16. ■ ÷ 4 = 4

   a. 3   **b.** 8   **c.** 16   **d.** 36

17. 6)‾30‾

   a. 10   **c.** 4

   b. 6   **d.** not given

18. 5 × 0

   a. 10   **b.** 5   **c.** 1   **d.** 0

19. Find the area in square centimeters.

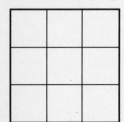

   a. 9 square cm
   b. 12 square cm
   c. 15 square cm
   d. 25 square cm

20. Which numbers are all multiples of 7?

   a. 1, 7, 14, 21
   b. 7, 14, 20, 28
   c. 7, 21, 28, 56
   d. 21, 28, 36, 42

21. 6 × 9

   a. 48   **c.** 72

   b. 54   **d.** not given

22. 36 ÷ 9

   a. 9   **b.** 5   **c.** 4   **d.** 3

23. Which of the following has only even numbers?

   a. 2, 4, 6, 9
   b. 4, 10, 12, 15
   c. 6, 10, 13, 18
   d. 4, 8, 12, 22

24. 4 × 7

   a. 11   **b.** 16   **c.** 21   **d.** 28

Use the pictograph to answer Questions 25–28.

DAILY MILK PRODUCTION IN THE U.S.

Wisconsin	🐄 🐄 🐄 🐄
Minnesota	🐄 🐄 🐄
California	🐄 🐄 🐄
New York	🐄 🐄

🐄 = 1,000 gallons

25. Which two states produce about the same amount of milk?

   a. Wisconsin and New York
   b. California and Minnesota
   c. California and New York
   d. New York and Minnesota

26. What is each 🐄 worth?

   a. 50 gal   **c.** 1,000 gal
   b. 100 gal   **d.** 2,500 gal

27. How much milk is produced daily in New York?

   a. 1,000 gal   **c.** 3,500 gal
   b. 2,000 gal   **d.** 4,000 gal

28. How much more milk is produced in Wisconsin than in California?

   a. 2,000 gal   **c.** 1,000 gal
   b. 1,500 gal   **d.** 500 gal

MACMILLAN / McGRAW-HILL

29. Theresa has 21 toy cars. She puts them in baskets that hold 7 toy cars each. Which number sentence should you use to find how many baskets she will fill with the toy cars?

   a. $21 \div 7 = $ ▨

   b. $21 \times 7 = $ ▨

   c. $21 + 7 = $ ▨

   d. $21 - 7 = $ ▨

30. What is the area of a rectangular bookmark 4 cm wide and 9 cm long?

   a. 5 square cm
   b. 13 square cm
   c. 26 square cm
   d. 36 square cm

31. Nancy stacks 7 rows of cans in a pattern for a store display. She puts 31 cans on the bottom row, 27 cans in the row above that, and 23 cans in the next row. How many cans will be in the top row?

   a. 3   **c.** 7
   b. 4   **d.** 9

32. There are 54 students riding in 6 vans. If there is an equal number of students in each van, how many students are in each van?

   a. 10   **c.** 8
   b. 9   **d.** 6

33. Nat read 9 books last month. He read 6 books this month. He saw 3 movies this month. How many books did he read in all?

   a. 15   **b.** 18   **c.** 27   **d.** 54

Name

Macmillan/McGraw-Hill
Mathematics

Chapter 5 Test

Grade 4
Form C

Page 1

Mark your answer.

1. $2\overline{)16}$

2. Find the area.

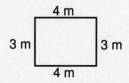

3 m   3 m

4 m (top)

4 m (bottom)

3. Ring the even numbers.

   3,   11,   12,   24,   27,   36

4. $4 \times \blacksquare = 36$

5. $0 \div 5$

6. 2×7

7. What is the area of a square with 7-cm sides?

8. Is 49, 36, 15, or 3 a prime number?

9. $9\overline{)81}$

10. Ring the factors of 36.

    4,   5,   6,   8,   9,   36

11. $(3 \times 3) \times \blacksquare = 3 \times (3 \times 7)$

12. $6 \div 3$

13. What is the area of a rectangle 8 cm long and 2 cm wide?

14. Is 1, 2, 19, or 21 a composite number?

15. 5×8

16. $18 \div \blacksquare = 9$

MACMILLAN / McGRAW-HILL

17. 5$\overline{)25}$

_____

18. 7×0

_____

19. Find the area in square centimeters.

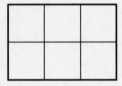

_____

20. Ring the multiples of 5.

3,   5,   12,   15,   18,   25

21. 3×7

_____

22. $48 \div 8$

_____

23. Ring the odd numbers.

3,   8,   11,   12,   14,   15

24. 7×9

_____

Use the pictograph to answer Questions 25 – 28.

TAXIS IN LONGVIEW CITY

City Taxis	🚕 🚕 🚕 🚕
ABC Taxis	🚕 🚕 🚕
Acme Taxi Co.	🚕 🚕
Harry's Taxis	🚕
🚕 = 50 taxis	

25. How many taxis does ABC Taxis own?

_____

26. What is each 🚕 worth?

_____

27. How many taxis does City Taxis own?

_____

28. How many more taxis does Acme Taxi Co. own than Harry's Taxis?

_____

STOP

29. James has 45 model planes. He puts them on shelves that hold 9 planes each. Write the number sentence that you should use to find how many shelves he will fill with the planes.

_____

30. What is the area of a rectangular strip of paper 9 cm long and 2 cm wide?

_____

31. A new movie is playing at the Palace Theater. The first show is at 1:30. The second show is at 3:45. The third show is at 6:00. If the pattern continues, at what time is the fifth show?

_____

32. Mr. Gomez wants to divide the class into 3 equal lines. There are 27 children in the class. How many children should be in each line?

_____

33. Tanya mailed 5 cards yesterday. She mailed 8 cards today. She received 4 cards. How many cards did she mail in all?

_____

Name _____

Macmillan/McGraw-Hill
Mathematics

Chapter 6 Test

Grade 4
Form A

Page 1

Choose the letter of your answer.

1. 4×100

  a. 400   **c.** 40
  b. 104   **d.** not given

2. Estimate by rounding.
        5×62

  a. 20   **c.** 200
  b. 30   **d.** 300

3. 3×927

  a. 2,781   **c.** 2,761
  b. 2,771   **d.** 2,751

4. $\$5.33$
  $\times \quad 2$

  a. $\$10.06$
  b. $\$10.55$
  c. $\$10.66$
  d. $\$10.99$

5. 60
  $\times \quad 6$

  a. 30
  b. 36
  c. 300
  d. not given

6. About how much is $3 \times \$42$?

  a. about $70   **c.** about $700
  b. about $120   **d.** about $1,200

7. 6×89

  a. 534   **c.** 474
  b. 484   **d.** 194

8. $4 \times \$4.95$

  a. $16.60   **c.** $19.80
  b. $17.39   **d.** $22.00

9. 7×80

  a. 56   **c.** 5,600
  b. 560   **d.** not given

10. Estimate by using the front digits.
        2×285

  a. 300   **c.** 500
  b. 400   **d.** 600

11. 708
  $\times \quad 4$

  a. 2,332
  b. 2,802
  c. 2,812
  d. 2,832

12. $\$.80$
  $\times \quad 2$

  a. $.16
  b. $1.60
  c. $16.00
  d. $160.00

13. $8 \times 9,000$

  a. 720   **c.** 72,000
  b. 7,200   **d.** not given

14. Estimate by rounding.
        $9 \times 2,023$

  a. 700   **c.** 7,000
  b. 1,800   **d.** 18,000

15. 5×698

  a. 3,620   **c.** 3,090
  b. 3,490   **d.** 3,050

16. $8 \times \$4.70$

  a. $32.60   **c.** $36.58
  b. $33.58   **d.** $37.60

17. 300
  × 5

  a. 1,500
  b. 150
  c. 15
  d. not given

18. About how much is 5 × $3.95?

  a. about $20.00
  b. about $15.00
  c. about $2.00
  d. about $1.50

19. 821
  × 7

  a. 6,547
  b. 5,747
  c. 5,647
  d. 4,947

20. $7.89
  × 6

  a. $47.34
  b. $46.95
  c. $42.84
  d. $42.04

STOP

21. In a baseball game, Ernie and Tanya made 12 hits. Tanya got twice as many hits as Ernie did. How many hits did Ernie make?

  a. 12   **c.** 5
  b. 8   **d.** 4

22. Jim has some shells he wants to glue onto a board. He puts 14 shells in each of 4 rows. How many shells does he have?

  a. 56   **c.** 18
  b. 46   **d.** 14

23. The fourth-grade students wanted to raise $75.00 for the library. They held a car wash to raise the money. They made $48.50 on Saturday and $31.89 on Sunday. Did the students reach their goal?

  a. Yes.   **b.** No.

24. Jeanne has 19 pieces of string. She puts 8 beads on each string. About how many beads does she have in all? Use rounding.

  a. about 250
  b. about 160
  c. about 100
  d. about 50

25. Each row in the auditorium has 9 seats. There are 36 students in Mr. Marquez's class. Which number sentence should you use to find how many rows they will fill in the auditorium?

  a. 36 × 9 =
  b. 36 ÷ 9 = ▮
  c. 36 + 9 = ▮
  d. 36 − 9 = ▮

MACMILLAN / McGRAW-HILL

Name

Macmillan/McGraw-Hill
Mathematics

Chapter 6 Test

Grade 4

Form B

Page 1

Choose the letter of your answer.

1. 3×600
   - **a.** 18
   - **b.** 180
   - **c.** 1,800
   - **d.** not given

2. Estimate by rounding.
   5×38
   - **a.** 500
   - **b.** 200
   - **c.** 50
   - **d.** 20

3. 2×755
   - **a.** 1,400
   - **b.** 1,410
   - **c.** 1,500
   - **d.** 1,510

4. $\begin{array}{r} \$8.49 \\ \times \quad 7 \\ \hline \end{array}$
   - **a.** $59.43
   - **b.** $58.96
   - **c.** $56.83
   - **d.** $56.23

5. $\begin{array}{r} 30 \\ \times \quad 9 \\ \hline \end{array}$
   - **a.** 270
   - **b.** 210
   - **c.** 21
   - **d.** not given

6. About how much is $4 \times \$21$?
   - **a.** about $1,500
   - **b.** about $800
   - **c.** about $150
   - **d.** about $80

7. 3×59
   - **a.** 222
   - **b.** 217
   - **c.** 177
   - **d.** 157

8. $9 \times \$5.08$
   - **a.** $45.02
   - **b.** $45.17
   - **c.** $45.72
   - **d.** $54.72

9. 6×70
   - **a.** 42,000
   - **b.** 4,200
   - **c.** 420
   - **d.** not given

10. Estimate by using the front digits.
    4×312
    - **a.** 120
    - **b.** 900
    - **c.** 1,100
    - **d.** 1,200

11. $\begin{array}{r} 634 \\ \times \quad 7 \\ \hline \end{array}$
    - **a.** 4,438
    - **b.** 4,238
    - **c.** 4,231
    - **d.** 4,218

12. $\begin{array}{r} \$.50 \\ \times \quad 3 \\ \hline \end{array}$
    - **a.** $150.00
    - **b.** $15.00
    - **c.** $1.50
    - **d.** $.15

13. $2 \times 5,000$
    - **a.** 1,000
    - **b.** 100
    - **c.** 10
    - **d.** not given

14. Estimate by rounding.
    $8 \times 3,011$
    - **a.** 24,000
    - **b.** 16,000
    - **c.** 2,400
    - **d.** 1,600

15. 6×452
    - **a.** 2,402
    - **b.** 2,412
    - **c.** 2,712
    - **d.** 2,718

16. $8 \times \$6.30$
    - **a.** $48.40
    - **b.** $49.10
    - **c.** $50.10
    - **d.** $50.40

MACMILLAN / McGRAW-HILL

17.   100
　　× 5

a. 5,000
b. 500
c. 50
d. not given

18. About how much is 4 × $9.89?

a. about $3.60
b. about $4.00
c. about $20.00
d. about $40.00

19.   990
　　× 6

a. 5,940
b. 5,720
c. 5,440
d. 4,850

20. $5.68
　　× 9

a. $45.42
b. $50.42
c. $51.12
d. $51.21

STOP

21. Sondra and Clarence read 24 books. Clarence read 3 times as many books as Sondra read. How many books did Clarence read?

a. 6　　　c. 21
b. 18　　 d. 72

22. Mike is planting vegetables. He puts 25 plants in each of 6 rows. How many plants does he have?

a. 200　　c. 31
b. 150　　d. 4

23. The fourth-grade students held a bake sale to raise $50.00 for their class trip. The students made $39.15 on Saturday and $21.60 on Sunday. Did they make enough money?

a. Yes.　　　　b. No.

24. Seth makes 17 stacks of baseball cards. There are 9 cards in each stack. About how many cards does Seth have in all? Use rounding.

a. about 250
b. about 170
c. about 30
d. about 2

25. There are 25 children at soccer practice. The coach wants to make 5 teams. Which number sentence should you use to find how many children will be on each team?

a. 25 ÷ 5 =
b. 25 + 5 = ▥
c. 25 × 5 = ▥
d. 25 − 5 = ▥

Name

Macmillan/McGraw-Hill
Mathematics

Chapter 6 Test

Grade 4
Form C

Page 1

Mark your answer.

1. 4×100

_____

2. Estimate by rounding.
5×62

_____

3. 3×927

_____

4. $\begin{array}{r} \$5.33 \\ \times\quad 2 \\ \hline \end{array}$

_____

5. $\begin{array}{r} 60 \\ \times\ 6 \\ \hline \end{array}$

_____

6. About how much is $3 \times \$42$?

_____

7. 6×89

_____

8. $4 \times \$4.95$

_____

9. 7×80

_____

10. Estimate by using the front digits.
2×285

_____

11. $\begin{array}{r} 708 \\ \times\quad 4 \\ \hline \end{array}$

_____

12. $\begin{array}{r} \$.80 \\ \times\quad 2 \\ \hline \end{array}$

_____

13. $8 \times 9,000$

_____

14. Estimate by rounding.
$9 \times 2,023$

_____

15. 5×698

_____

16. $8 \times \$4.70$

_____

MACMILLAN / McGRAW-HILL

17. 300
     × 5

_____

18. About how much is 5 × $3.95?

_____

19. 821
     × 7

_____

20. $7.89
     ×   6

_____

_____

21. In a baseball game, Ernie and Tanya made 12 hits. Tanya got twice as many hits as Ernie did. How many hits did Ernie make?

_____

22. Jim has some shells he wants to glue onto a board. He puts 14 shells in each of 4 rows. How many shells does he have?

_____

23. The fourth-grade students wanted to raise $75.00 for the library. They held a car wash to raise the money. They made $48.50 on Saturday and $31.89 on Sunday. Did the students reach their goal?

_____

24. Jeanne has 19 pieces of string. She puts 8 beads on each string. About how many beads does she have in all? Use rounding.

_____

25. Each row in the auditorium has 9 seats. There are 36 students in Mr. Marquez's class. Write a number sentence to find how many rows the students will fill in the auditorium.

_____

MACMILLAN / McGRAW-HILL

Name

Macmillan/McGraw-Hill
Mathematics

Chapter 7 Test

Grade 4
Form A

Page 1

Choose the letter of your answer.

1. 60 ÷ 2

a. 3   **c.** 120
b. 30   **d.** 1,200

2. Which is the best estimate of 3,892 ÷ 9?

a. greater than 1,000
b. greater than 400
c. less than 300
d. less than 200

3. 800 ÷ 4

a. 2   **c.** 200
b. 40   **d.** 400

4. Which is the best estimate of 2,513 ÷ 6?

a. less than 300
b. between 300 and 400
c. between 400 and 500
d. greater than 500

5. 65 ÷ 9

a. 6 R3   **c.** 70
b. 17   **d.** not given

6. 5)$\overline{509}$

a. 11 R4   **c.** 110
b. 101 R4   **d.** not given

7. 560 ÷ 7

a. 8   **c.** 800
b. 80   **d.** 8,000

8. 47 ÷ 3

a. 15   **c.** 16 R1
b. 15 R2   **d.** not given

9. Estimate by using compatible numbers. $50.00 ÷ 6

a. $.80   **c.** $8.00
b. $1.00   **d.** $10.00

10. 8)$\overline{\$7.44}$

a. $.93   **c.** $93.00
b. $9.30   **d.** not given

11. About how much is 271 ÷ 4?

a. about 100   **c.** about 70
b. about 90   **d.** about 7

12. 4)$\overline{362}$

a. 9 R2   **c.** 92
b. 90 R2   **d.** not given

13. 4,500 ÷ 9

a. 5,000   **c.** 50
b. 500   **d.** 5

14. Estimate by rounding. 4,213 ÷ 5

a. 80   **c.** 800
b. 90   **d.** 9,000

15. 9,000 ÷ 3

a. 3,000   **c.** 300
b. 360   **d.** 36

MACMILLAN / McGRAW-HILL

Use the set of numbers to answer Questions 16 and 17.

103; 92; 95; 100; 115

16. What is the average?

a. 92   **b.** 95   **c.** 100   **d.** 101

17. What is the median?

a. 100   **b.** 95   **c.** 92   **d.** 16

Use the set of numbers to answer Questions 18–20.

32; 26; 38; 40; 34

18. What is the average?

a. 136   **b.** 40   **c.** 34   **d.** 32

19. What is the median?

a. 35   **b.** 34   **c.** 32   **d.** 26

20. What is the range?

a. 8   **b.** 14   **c.** 26   **d.** 34

21. Seth is selling candles for his softball team. He sells 12 on Monday, 20 on Tuesday, 14 on Friday, and 30 on Saturday. What is the average number of candles he sells each day?

a. 18   **b.** 19   **c.** 22   **d.** 30

22. A can of 3 tennis balls costs $4.59. What is the cost of each tennis ball?

a. $.15
b. $1.50
c. $1.53
d. $13.77

23. Laura made 84 posters for the fair in two days. She made twice as many on Saturday as she did on Sunday. How many posters did Laura make on Sunday?

a. 64   **b.** 56   **c.** 28   **d.** 14

24. There are 23 children in line for the roller coaster. If 5 children can sit in each car, how many cars will be needed?

a. 3   **b.** 4   **c.** 5   **d.** 6

25. Complete and use the table to answer the question.

One apple, one pear, and one orange are on the table. Mark, Kim, and Todd each pick one of the fruits. Mark does not pick the apple or the pear. Kim does not pick the pear. Who picks the apple?

	Orange	Apple	Pear
Mark		no	no
Kim			no
Todd			

a. Kim   **b.** Todd   **c.** Mark

Name

Macmillan/McGraw-Hill
Mathematics

Chapter 7 Test

Grade 4
Form B

Page 1

Choose the letter of your answer.

1. 80 ÷ 2

   a. 4   **c.** 160
   b. 40   **d.** 1,600

2. Which is the best estimate of 449 ÷ 7?

   a. less than 30
   b. less than 60
   c. greater than 60
   d. greater than 80

3. 900 ÷ 3

   a. 300   **c.** 30
   b. 90   **d.** 9

4. Which is the best estimate of 2,641 ÷ 9?

   a. less than 200
   b. between 200 and 300
   c. between 300 and 400
   d. greater than 400

5. 49 ÷ 8

   a. 5 R3   **c.** 16
   b. 6 R1   **d.** 60

6. 3)$\overline{605}$

   a. 202   **c.** 21 R2
   b. 201 R2   **d.** not given

7. 350 ÷ 7

   a. 5,000   **c.** 50
   b. 500   **d.** 5

8. 74 ÷ 5

   a. 10 R3   **c.** 14 R4
   b. 13 R4   **d.** not given

9. Estimate by using compatible numbers. $27.00 ÷ 4

   a. $.05   **c.** $5.00
   b. $.70   **d.** $7.00

10. 9)$\overline{\$5.22}$

   a. $.58   **c.** $58.00
   b. $5.80   **d.** not given

11. About how much is 365 ÷ 5?

   a. about 70   **c.** about 700
   b. about 90   **d.** about 800

12. 6)$\overline{543}$

   a. 9 R3   **c.** 93
   b. 92   **d.** not given

13. 6,000 ÷ 3

   a. 2   **c.** 200
   b. 20   **d.** 2,000

14. Estimate by rounding. 5,641 ÷ 3

   a. 6,000   **c.** 2,000
   b. 4,000   **d.** 200

15. 2,400 ÷ 6

   a. 4,000   **c.** 40
   b. 400   **d.** 4

MACMILLAN / McGRAW-HILL

Use the set of numbers to answer Questions 16 and 17.

115; 84; 92; 101; 123

16. What is the average?

a. 84   **b.** 103   **c.** 123   **d.** 515

17. What is the median?

a. 123   **b.** 103   **c.** 101   **d.** 39

Use the set of numbers to answer Questions 18–20.

32; 41; 52; 35; 40

18. What is the average?

a. 160   **b.** 52   **c.** 41   **d.** 40

19. What is the median?

a. 38   **b.** 40   **c.** 41   **d.** 52

20. What is the range?

a. 3   **b.** 17   **c.** 20   **d.** 32

21. During the first quarter of the game, the basketball team scores 23 points. The team scores 31 points in the second quarter, 18 points in the third quarter, and 40 points in the fourth quarter. What is the average number of points the team scores in a quarter?

a. 22   **b.** 27   **c.** 28   **d.** 40

22. A bag of 7 apples costs $2.59. What is the cost of each apple?

a. $.37   **c.** $18.13
b. $3.70   **d.** $18.79

23. The twins made $27.30 selling lemonade last weekend. They made twice as much on Sunday as they did on Saturday. How much did they make on Sunday?

a. $4.55   **c.** $27.30
b. $18.20   **d.** $50.00

24. There are 25 children waiting for the bus. If 3 children can sit in each seat, how many seats will be needed?

a. 10   **b.** 9   **c.** 8   **d.** 6

25. Complete and use the table to answer the question.

The children leave one blue, one green, and one red bike in the driveway. Jen's bike is not red or blue. Nick's bike is not blue. Who has the red bike?

	Red	Blue	Green
Nick		no	
Jen	no	no	
Julie			

a. Nick   **b.** Julie   **c.** Jen

Macmillan/McGraw-Hill, MATHEMATICS IN ACTION
Grade 4, Chapter 7, Form B

MACMILLAN / McGRAW-HILL

Name

Macmillan/McGraw-Hill
Mathematics

Chapter 7 Test

Grade 4
Form C

Page 1

Mark your answer.

1. $60 \div 2$

_____

2. Which is the best estimate of $3{,}892 \div 9$? Ring your answer.

   greater than 1,000

   greater than 400

   less than 300

   less than 200

3. $800 \div 4$

_____

4. Which is the best estimate of $2{,}513 \div 6$? Ring your answer.

   less than 300

   between 300 and 400

   between 400 and 500

   greater than 500

5. $65 \div 9$

_____

6. $5\overline{)509}$

_____

7. $560 \div 7$

_____

8. $47 \div 3$

_____

9. Estimate by using compatible numbers.

   $$\$50.00 \div 6$$

_____

10. $8\overline{)\$7.44}$

_____

11. About how much is $271 \div 4$?

_____

12. $4\overline{)362}$

_____

13. $4{,}500 \div 9$

_____

14. Estimate by rounding.

   $$4{,}213 \div 5$$

_____

15. $9{,}000 \div 3$

_____

MACMILLAN / McGRAW-HILL

Use the set of numbers to answer
Questions 16 and 17.

    103; 92; 95; 100; 115

16. What is the average?

_____

17. What is the median?

_____

Use the set of numbers to answer
Questions 18–20.

    32; 26; 38; 40; 34

18. What is the average?

_____

19. What is the median?

_____

20. What is the range?

_____

21. Seth is selling candles for his
softball team. He sells 12 on
Monday, 20 on Tuesday, 14 on
Friday, and 30 on Saturday. What
is the average number of candles
he sells each day?

_____

22. A can of 3 tennis balls costs
$4.59. What is the cost of each
tennis ball?

_____

23. Laura made 84 posters for the fair
in two days. She made twice as
many on Saturday as she did on
Sunday. How many posters did
Laura make on Sunday?

_____

24. There are 23 children in line for the
roller coaster. If 5 children can sit
in each car, how many cars will be
needed?

_____

25. Complete and use the table to
answer the question.

One apple, one pear, and one
orange are on the table. Mark,
Kim, and Todd each pick one of
the fruits. Mark does not pick the
apple or the pear. Kim does not
pick the pear. Who picks the
apple?

	Orange	Apple	Pear
Mark		no	no
Kim			no
Todd			

_____

Name
Macmillan/McGraw-Hill
Mathematics

Chapter 8 Test

Grade 4
Form A

Page 1

Choose the letter of your answer.

1. Which describes the figure?

a. angle *RS* **c.** ray *SR*
b. line *RS* **d.** plane *RS*

2. Which word describes this figure?

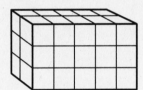

a. square
b. pentagon
c. hexagon
d. octagon

3. What is the volume of the figure?

a. 5 cubic units
b. 10 cubic units
c. 25 cubic units
d. not given

4. Which figure is symmetrical?

a.   **c.**

b.   **d.**

5. Is the figure the result of a flip, slide, or turn?

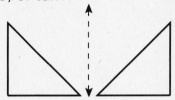

a. flip **b.** slide **c.** turn

6. Which two figures are congruent?

7. What is the volume of this figure?

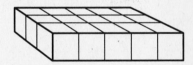

a. 30 cubic units
b. 15 cubic units
c. 12 cubic units
d. not given

8. How many sides does a hexagon have?

a. 3 **b.** 4 **c.** 5 **d.** 6

MACMILLAN / McGRAW-HILL

9. Which figure shows ray $\overrightarrow{PQ}$?

a.

c.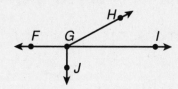

b.

d.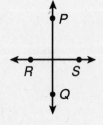

10. Which describes the figure?

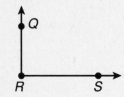

a. plane *QRS*
b. $\overline{EG}$
c. ∠*QRS*
d. $\overrightarrow{QR}$ ∥ $\overrightarrow{RS}$

11. Which pair of figures shows a slide?

a.

c.

b.

d.

12. Which is a line of symmetry in this figure?

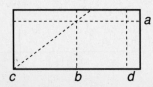

a. *a*　**b.** *b*　**c.** *c*　**d.** *d*

Use the figure below to answer Questions 13 and 14.

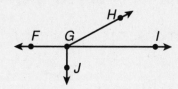

13. Which angle is a right angle?

a. ∠*HGI*　**c.** ∠*JGI*
b. ∠*FGI*　**d.** ∠*FGH*

14. Find the angle that is greater than a right angle.

a. ∠*FGJ*　**c.** ∠*HGI*
b. ∠*FGH*　**d.** ∠*JGI*

Use the figures below to answer Questions 15 and 16.

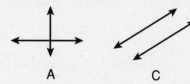

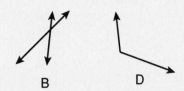

15. Which figure shows two parallel lines?

a. A　**b.** B　**c.** C　**d.** D

16. Which figure shows two perpendicular lines?

a. A　**b.** B　**c.** C　**d.** D

Use the figures below to answer
Questions 17–19.

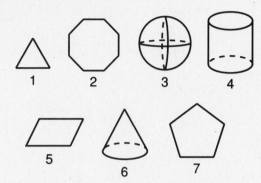

17. Which figure is a quadrilateral?

 a. 4 b. 5 c. 6 d. 7

18. Which figure is a sphere?

 a. 1 b. 2 c. 3 d. 4

19. Which figure has one curved face?

 a. 1 b. 4 c. 5 d. 7

Use the figures below to answer
Questions 20 and 21.

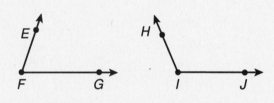

20. Point _F_ is the vertex of _____.

 a. ∠FEG c. ∠HIJ
 b. ∠JIH d. ∠EFG

21. Which is a side of ∠HIJ?

 a. $\overrightarrow{IJ}$ c. $\overrightarrow{FG}$
 b. $\overrightarrow{FE}$ d. $\overrightarrow{HJ}$

Use the figures below to answer
Questions 22 and 23.

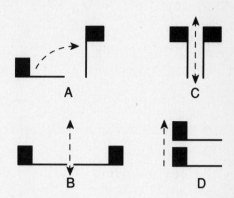

22. Which pair of figures shows a
 turn?

 a. A b. B c. C d. D

23. Which pair of figures shows a
 slide?

 a. A b. B c. C d. D

Use the figures below to answer
Questions 24 and 25.

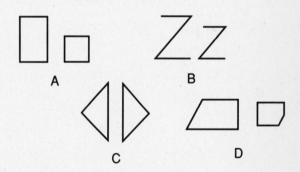

24. Which two figures are congruent?

 a. A b. B c. C d. D

25. Which two figures are similar, but
 not congruent?

 a. A b. B c. C d. D

26. Find the volume of a rectangular prism 6 units long, 3 units wide, and 2 units high.

   a. 11 cubic units
   b. 20 cubic units
   c. 36 cubic units
   d. not given

27. Find the volume of a cube with sides 4 units long.

   a. 64 cubic units
   b. 16 cubic units
   c. 12 cubic units
   d. not given

28. Find the volume.

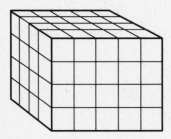

   a. 13 cubic units
   b. 36 cubic units
   c. 80 cubic units
   d. not given

29. There are 29 people waiting to rent canoes. Each canoe holds 3 people. How many canoes will be needed to hold all the people?

   a. 9   **b.** 10   **c.** 11   **d.** 12

30. Tickets to the science museum cost $3.50 for an adult and $2.00 for a child. Mr. and Mrs. Moy and their 5 children go to the museum. How much will the tickets cost in all?

   a. $13.50   **c.** $20.00
   b. $17.00   **d.** $21.50

31. Ron measures a wooden box. It is 2 units long, 3 units wide, and 2 units high. What is the volume of the box?

   a. 7 cubic units
   b. 10 cubic units
   c. 12 cubic units
   d. 15 cubic units

32. Martín hands out 10 posters on each of 3 streets. Kim hands out 14 posters on each of 2 streets. Andrea hands out 71 posters in all. How many more posters does Andrea hand out than Martín and Kim together?

   a. 43   **b.** 41   **c.** 30   **d.** 13

33. Grace wraps a gift box that is 8 cm long, 8 cm wide, and 8 cm tall. What space figure does the box suggest?

   a. cylinder   **c.** cube
   b. sphere   **d.** cone

Name

Macmillan/McGraw-Hill
Mathematics

Chapter 8 Test

Grade 4
Form B

Page 1

Choose the letter of your answer.

1. Which describes the figure?

   a. angle *YZ*   **c.** ray *YZ*

   b. line *ZY*   **d.** plane *XY*

2. Which word describes this figure?

   a. pentagon
   b. octagon
   c. quadrilateral
   d. decagon

3. What is the volume of the figure?

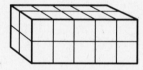

   a. 24 cubic units
   b. 20 cubic units
   c. 12 cubic units
   d. not given

4. Which figure is symmetrical?

  a.    **c.**

  b.   **d.**

5. Is the figure the result of a slide, flip, or turn?

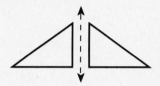

   a. slide   **b.** flip   **c.** turn

6. Which two figures are congruent?

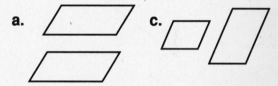

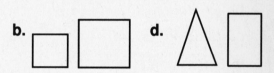

7. What is the volume of this figure?

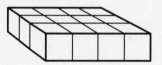

   a. 19 cubic units
   b. 15 cubic units
   c. 12 cubic units
   d. not given

8. How many sides does a pentagon have?

   a. 10   **b.** 8   **c.** 6   **d.** 5

MACMILLAN / McGRAW-HILL

9. Which figure shows line $\overleftrightarrow{LM}$?

a.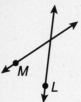

c.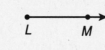

b.

d.

10. Which describes the figure?

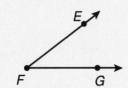

a. $\overline{EG}$
b. $\overrightarrow{EF} \parallel \overrightarrow{FG}$
c. plane *EFG*
d. $\angle EFG$

11. Which pair of figures shows a slide?

a.

c.

b.

d.

12. Which is the line of symmetry in this figure?

a. *a*
b. *b*
c. *c*
d. *d*

Use the figure below to answer Questions 13 and 14.

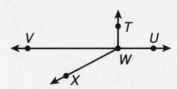

13. Which angle is a right angle?

a. $\angle XWU$ c. $\angle TWU$
b. $\angle VWX$ d. $\angle TWX$

14. Find the angle that is less than a right angle.

a. $\angle VWX$ c. $\angle VWU$
b. $\angle XWU$ d. $\angle VWT$

Use the figures below to answer Questions 15 and 16.

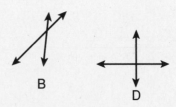

15. Which figure shows two perpendicular lines?

a. A   b. B   c. C   d. D

16. Which figure shows two parallel lines?

a. A   b. B   c. C   d. D

Use the figures below to answer Questions 17–19.

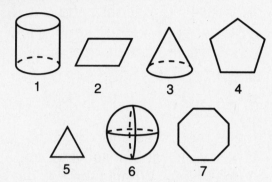

17. Which figure is a triangle?

a. 1   **b.** 2   **c.** 5   **d.** 6

18. Which figure is a cone?

a. 1   **b.** 2   **c.** 3   **d.** 4

19. Which figure has two flat faces?

a. 1   **b.** 3   **c.** 5   **d.** 7

Use the figures below to answer Questions 20 and 21.

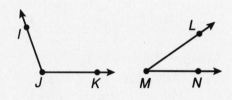

20. Which is a side of $\angle IJK$?

a. $\overrightarrow{ML}$ **c.** $\overrightarrow{IK}$

b. $\overrightarrow{JK}$ **d.** $\overrightarrow{MN}$

21. Which point is the vertex of $\angle LMN$?

a. N **c.** L

b. J **d.** M

Use the figures below to answer Questions 22 and 23.

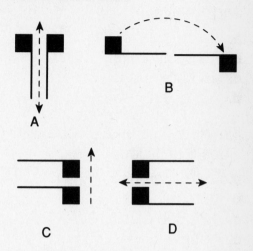

22. Which pair of figures shows a slide?

a. A   **b.** B   **c.** C   **d.** D

23. Which pair of figures shows a turn?

a. A   **b.** B   **c.** C   **d.** D

Use the figures below to answer Questions 24 and 25.

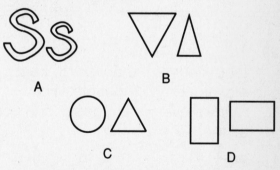

24. Which two figures are similar, but not congruent?

a. A   **b.** B   **c.** C   **d.** D

25. Which two figures are congruent?

a. A   **b.** B   **c.** C   **d.** D

26. Find the volume of a rectangular prism 5 units long, 3 units wide, and 1 unit high.

  a. 9 cubic units
  b. 15 cubic units
  c. 16 cubic units
  d. not given

27. Find the volume of a cube with sides 5 units long.

  a. 15 cubic units
  b. 25 cubic units
  c. 125 cubic units
  d. not given

28. Find the volume.

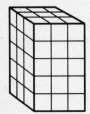

  a. 11 cubic units
  b. 18 cubic units
  c. 30 cubic units
  d. not given

29. There are 43 people going to the tenth floor of the building. Each elevator holds 9 people. How many elevators are needed to hold all the people?

  a. 4   **b.** 5   **c.** 6   **d.** 9

30. Tickets to the circus cost $3.00 for a child and $5.00 for an adult. A group of 3 teachers and 9 students go to the circus. How much will the tickets cost in all?

  a. $15.00   **c.** $42.00
  b. $27.00   **d.** $54.00

31. Marie measures a jewelry box. It is 4 units long, 3 units wide, and 3 units high. What is the volume of the box?

  a. 10 cubic units
  b. 12 cubic units
  c. 18 cubic units
  d. 36 cubic units

32. Terence baked 3 batches of 12 cookies each. Nina baked 4 batches of 11 cookies each. Kent baked 91 cookies in all. How many more cookies did Kent bake than Terence and Nina together?

  a. 8   **b.** 11   **c.** 44   **d.** 47

33. Lon has a flashlight that has one curved face and two circular bases. What space figure does the flashlight suggest?

  a. cylinder   **c.** cube
  b. sphere   **d.** cone

Name

Macmillan/McGraw-Hill
Mathematics

Chapter 8 Test

Grade 4
Form C

Page 1

Mark your answer.

1. Write the name of the figure.

_____

2. Name the figure.

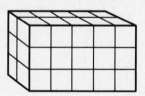

_____

3. What is the volume of the figure?

_____

4. Ring the figure that is symmetrical.

5. Is the figure the result of a flip, slide, or turn?

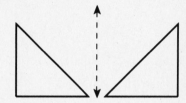

_____

6. Ring the pair of congruent figures.

7. What is the volume of this figure?

_____

8. How many sides does a hexagon have?

_____

9. Ring the figure that shows ray $\overrightarrow{PQ}$.

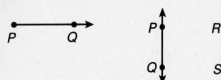

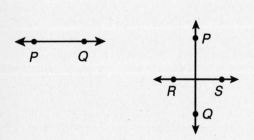

10. Write the name of the figure.

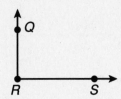

_____

11. Ring the pair of figures that shows a slide.

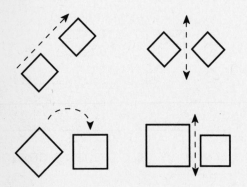

12. Which is a line of symmetry in this figure?

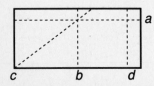

_____

Use the figure below to answer Questions 13 and 14.

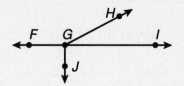

13. Which angle is a right angle?

_____

14. Find the angle that is greater than a right angle.

_____

Use the figures below to answer Questions 15 and 16.

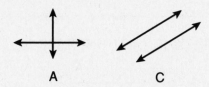

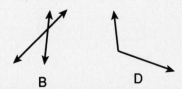

15. Which figure shows two parallel lines?

_____

16. Which figure shows two perpendicular lines?

_____

MACMILLAN / McGRAW-HILL

Use the figures below to answer Questions 17–19.

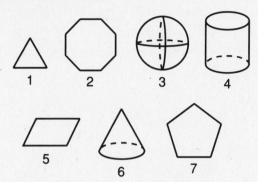

17. Which figure is a quadrilateral?

_____

18. Which figure is a sphere?

_____

19. Which figure has one curved face?

_____

Use the figures below to answer Questions 20 and 21.

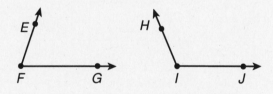

20. Point _F_ is the vertex of _____.

_____

21. Name a side of ∠_HIJ_.

_____

Use the figures below to answer Questions 22 and 23.

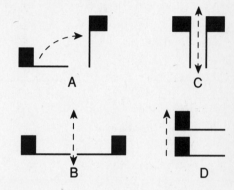

22. Which pair of figures shows a turn?

_____

23. Which pair of figures shows a slide?

_____

Use the figures below to answer Questions 24 and 25.

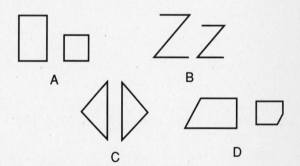

24. Which figures are congruent?

_____

25. Which figures are similar, but not congruent?

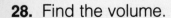

26. Find the volume of a rectangular prism 6 units long, 3 units wide, and 2 units high.

27. Find the volume of a cube with sides 4 units long.

28. Find the volume.

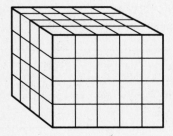

STOP

29. There are 29 people waiting to rent canoes. Each canoe holds 3 people. How many canoes will be needed to hold all the people?

30. Tickets to the science museum cost $3.50 for an adult and $2.00 for a child. Mr. and Mrs. Moy and their 5 children go to the museum. How much will the tickets cost in all?

31. Ron measures a wooden box. It is 2 units long, 3 units wide, and 2 units high. What is the volume of the box?

32. Martín hands out 10 posters on each of 3 streets. Kim hands out 14 posters on each of 2 streets. Andrea hands out 71 posters in all. How many more posters does Andrea hand out than Martín and Kim together?

33. Grace wraps a gift box that is 8 cm long, 8 cm wide, and 8 cm tall. What space figure does the box suggest?

Name

Macmillan/McGraw-Hill
Mathematics

Chapter 9 Test

Grade 4

Form A

Page 1

Choose the letter of your answer.

1. What fraction is shaded?

  a. $\frac{2}{9}$ **b.** $\frac{2}{7}$ **c.** $\frac{7}{2}$ **d.** $\frac{9}{2}$

2. Which fraction is equivalent to $\frac{3}{6}$?

  a. $\frac{3}{12}$ **b.** $\frac{1}{3}$ **c.** $\frac{6}{12}$ **d.** $\frac{6}{3}$

3. What is $\frac{17}{5}$ in simplest form?

  a. $2\frac{3}{5}$ **c.** $5\frac{2}{3}$

  b. $3\frac{2}{5}$ **d.** not given

4. Which number is greatest?

  a. 1   **c.** $1\frac{7}{12}$

  b. $1\frac{2}{12}$ **d.** $\frac{4}{9}$

5. About how tall is a horse?

  a. about 6 miles
  b. about 6 yards
  c. about 6 feet
  d. about 6 inches

6. Complete. $\frac{2}{7} = \frac{\blacksquare}{21}$

  a. 3   **b.** 6   **c.** 8   **d.** 10

7. Which is two and one-half?

  a. $1\frac{2}{2}$ **c.** $2\frac{2}{1}$

  b. $2\frac{1}{3}$ **d.** not given

8. Compare. $3\frac{1}{5}$ ● $3\frac{3}{5}$

  a. >   **b.** <   **c.** =

9. Measure this small pencil to the nearest inch.

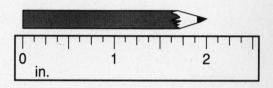

  a. 1 inch   **c.** 3 inches
  b. 2 inches   **d.** 4 inches

10. What part of the set is shaded?

  a. $\frac{5}{12}$ **b.** $\frac{7}{12}$ **c.** $\frac{5}{7}$ **d.** $\frac{7}{5}$

11. What is $\frac{15}{5}$ in simplest form?

  a. 3   **c.** 10
  b. 5   **d.** not given

12. Which number is least?

  a. $2\frac{1}{2}$ **c.** $2\frac{5}{8}$

  b. $3\frac{1}{4}$ **d.** $3\frac{1}{5}$

13. Which is the best estimate for the length of a fork?

  a. 8 feet   **c.** 8 miles
  b. 8 inches   **d.** 8 yards

14. What is $\frac{3}{8}$ of the set?

  a. 3   **b.** 4   **c.** 5   **d.** 6

MACMILLAN / McGRAW-HILL

15. What is $\frac{4}{12}$ in simplest form?

   a. $\frac{1}{8}$ **b.** $\frac{1}{4}$ **c.** $\frac{1}{3}$ **d.** $\frac{12}{4}$

16. Compare. $5\frac{2}{9}$ ● $5\frac{2}{18}$

   a. >   **b.** <   **c.** =

17. Measure this line segment to the nearest $\frac{1}{2}$ inch.

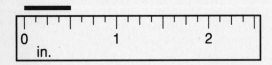

   a. $\frac{1}{2}$ inch   **c.** 2 inches

   b. $1\frac{1}{2}$ inches   **d.** $2\frac{1}{2}$ inches

18. What is $\frac{4}{5}$ of 15?

   a. 4   **b.** 8   **c.** 12   **d.** 16

19. What is $\frac{12}{16}$ in simplest form?

   a. $\frac{1}{4}$ **b.** $\frac{1}{2}$ **c.** $\frac{2}{3}$ **d.** $\frac{3}{4}$

20. What is $\frac{14}{3}$ in simplest form?

   a. $2\frac{3}{4}$ **c.** $4\frac{2}{3}$

   b. $3\frac{2}{4}$ **d.** not given

STOP

21. Miguel asked 8 of his friends to choose their favorite sport. Football was chosen by 2 friends, soccer by 3 friends, tennis by 2 friends, and lacrosse by 1 friend. What fraction of Miguel's friends chose soccer?

   a. $\frac{2}{8}$ **b.** $\frac{3}{8}$ **c.** $\frac{4}{8}$ **d.** $\frac{5}{8}$

22. Carol read 3 times as many books as Tom. Pete read 3 more books than Tom. Sally read 2 fewer books than Pete. Sally read 7 books. How many books did Carol read?

   a. 18   **b.** 15   **c.** 9   **d.** 6

23. Henry collected 437 baseball cards. His grandfather gave him 148 more cards. Henry gave 74 cards to his friend Joyce. How many baseball cards did Henry have left?

   a. 289   **b.** 366   **c.** 511   **d.** 733

24. Annette made 24 sandwiches. She wants to take $\frac{2}{3}$ of them to her class. How many should she take?

   a. 2   **b.** 8   **c.** 12   **d.** 16

25. Use number sense.

Helena wants to make 2 skirts in sewing class. She will need $2\frac{3}{4}$ yards of fabric for each skirt. She has 5 yards of fabric. Does she have enough fabric?

   a. Yes.   **b.** No.

Name

Macmillan/McGraw-Hill
Mathematics

Chapter 9 Test

Grade 4

Form B

Page 1

Choose the letter of your answer.

1. What fraction is shaded?

  a. $\frac{3}{5}$ **b.** $\frac{3}{8}$ **c.** $\frac{5}{8}$ **d.** $\frac{5}{3}$

2. Which fraction is equivalent to $\frac{4}{7}$?

  a. $\frac{7}{14}$ **b.** $\frac{8}{14}$ **c.** $\frac{8}{7}$ **d.** $\frac{7}{4}$

3. What is $\frac{19}{7}$ in simplest form?

  a. $2\frac{5}{7}$ **c.** $7\frac{2}{5}$

  b. $5\frac{2}{7}$ **d.** not given

4. Which number is greatest?

  a. $3\frac{2}{9}$ **c.** $4\frac{1}{2}$

  b. $\frac{8}{12}$ **d.** $\frac{10}{16}$

5. About how tall is a sheep?

  a. about 3 inches
  b. about 3 feet
  c. about 3 yards
  d. about 3 miles

6. Complete. $\frac{7}{8} = \frac{14}{\blacksquare}$

  a. 2   **b.** 16   **c.** 21   **d.** 24

7. Which is three and four-fifths?

  a. $4\frac{3}{5}$ **c.** $3\frac{4}{5}$

  b. $3\frac{5}{4}$ **d.** not given

8. Compare. $3\frac{2}{7}$ ⬤ $3\frac{3}{14}$

  a. >   **b.** <   **c.** =

9. Measure this toothpick to the nearest inch.

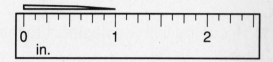

  a. 4 inches   **c.** 2 inches
  b. 3 inches   **d.** 1 inch

10. What part of the set is shaded?

  a. $\frac{1}{6}$ **b.** $\frac{1}{5}$ **c.** $\frac{5}{6}$ **d.** $\frac{5}{1}$

11. What is $\frac{20}{4}$ in simplest form?

  a. 3   **c.** 16
  b. 10   **d.** not given

12. Which number is least?

  a. $1\frac{8}{9}$ **b.** $2\frac{6}{10}$ **c.** $1\frac{7}{9}$ **d.** $1\frac{4}{9}$

13. Which is the best estimate for the length of a spoon?

  a. 6 feet   **c.** 6 miles
  b. 6 inches   **d.** 6 yards

14. What is $\frac{5}{12}$ of the set?

  a. 5   **b.** 6   **c.** 9   **d.** 10

MACMILLAN / McGRAW-HILL

15. What is $\frac{12}{16}$ in simplest form?

   a. $\frac{1}{3}$ **b.** $\frac{5}{8}$ **c.** $\frac{3}{4}$ **d.** $\frac{16}{12}$

16. Compare. $5\frac{1}{4}$ ● $4\frac{7}{8}$

   a. >   **b.** <   **c.** =

17. Measure this line segment to the nearest $\frac{1}{2}$ inch.

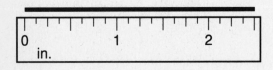

   a. $1\frac{1}{2}$ inches   **c.** $2\frac{1}{2}$ inches

   b. 2 inches   **d.** 3 inches

18. What is $\frac{5}{9}$ of 18?

   a. 10   **b.** 9   **c.** 6   **d.** 5

19. What is $\frac{10}{15}$ in simplest form?

   a. $\frac{1}{5}$ **b.** $\frac{2}{3}$ **c.** $\frac{2}{5}$ **d.** $\frac{1}{2}$

20. What is $\frac{8}{3}$ in simplest form?

   a. $2\frac{2}{3}$ **c.** $1\frac{2}{3}$

   b. $3\frac{2}{3}$ **d.** not given

21. Juan asked 10 of his friends to choose their favorite fruit. Apples were chosen by 3 friends, oranges by 1 friend, plums by 4 friends, and pears by 2 friends. What fraction of Juan's friends chose plums?

   a. $\frac{1}{10}$ **b.** $\frac{2}{10}$ **c.** $\frac{3}{10}$ **d.** $\frac{4}{10}$

22. The fourth-grade class holds a car wash. Tamara washes 2 fewer cars than Jim. Jesse washes 3 times as many cars as Jim. Sue washes 7 fewer cars than Jesse. Sue washes 2 cars. How many cars does Jim wash?

   a. 14   **b.** 9   **c.** 5   **d.** 3

23. Mr. Scott bought 8 boxes of paper clips. Each box contained 150 paper clips. Mr. Scott gave 3 boxes to Ms. Winthrop. How many paper clips did Mr. Scott have left?

   a. 400   **c.** 1,200

   b. 750   **d.** 1,650

24. Sandy baked 20 cookies. She wants to take $\frac{3}{4}$ of them to her class. How many should she take?

   a. 5   **b.** 10   **c.** 15   **d.** 18

25. Use number sense.

Rosa needs at least 6 pounds of cold cuts for her party. She buys $2\frac{3}{4}$ pounds of ham and $3\frac{1}{2}$ pounds of turkey. Does she buy enough cold cuts?

   a. Yes.   **b.** No.

MACMILLAN / McGRAW-HILL

Macmillan/McGraw-Hill, MATHEMATICS IN ACTION
Grade 4, Chapter 9, Form B

Name _____

Macmillan/McGraw-Hill
Mathematics

Chapter 9 Test

Grade 4
Form C

Page 1

Mark your answer.

1. Write a fraction for the part that is shaded.

    _____

2. Ring the fraction that is equivalent to $\frac{3}{6}$.

    $\frac{3}{12}$ $\frac{1}{3}$ $\frac{6}{12}$ $\frac{6}{3}$

3. What is $\frac{17}{5}$ in simplest form?

    _____

4. Order $1\frac{2}{12}$, $\frac{4}{9}$, and $1\frac{7}{12}$ from greatest to least.

    _____

5. Is the best estimate for the height of a horse 6 miles, 6 yards, 6 feet, or 6 inches?

    _____

6. Complete. $\frac{2}{7} = \frac{\blacksquare}{21}$

    _____

7. Write the number for two and one-half.

    _____

8. Compare. Write >, <, or =.

    $3\frac{1}{5}$  $3\frac{3}{5}$

    _____

9. Measure this small pencil to the nearest inch.

    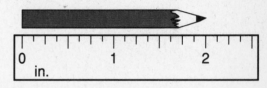

    _____

10. Write a fraction for the part of the set that is shaded.

    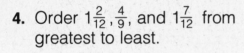

    _____

11. What is $\frac{15}{5}$ in simplest form?

    _____

12. Order $3\frac{1}{4}$, $3\frac{1}{5}$, and $2\frac{5}{8}$ from least to greatest.

    _____

13. Estimate the length of a fork.

    _____

MACMILLAN / McGRAW-HILL

14. What is $\frac{3}{8}$ of the set?

_____

15. What is $\frac{4}{12}$ in simplest form?

_____

16. Compare. Write >, <, or =.

$$5\frac{2}{9} \quad \bullet \quad 5\frac{2}{18}$$

_____

17. Measure this line segment to the nearest $\frac{1}{2}$ inch.

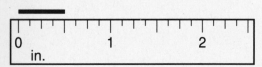

_____

18. What is $\frac{4}{5}$ of 15?

_____

19. What is $\frac{12}{16}$ in simplest form?

_____

20. What is $\frac{14}{3}$ in simplest form?

_____

 STOP

21. Miguel asked 8 of his friends to choose their favorite sport. Football was chosen by 2 friends, soccer by 3 friends, tennis by 2 friends, and lacrosse by 1 friend. What fraction of Miguel's friends chose soccer?

_____

22. Carol read 3 times as many books as Tom. Pete read 3 more books than Tom. Sally read 2 fewer books than Pete. Sally read 7 books. How many books did Carol read?

_____

23. Henry collected 437 baseball cards. His grandfather gave him 148 more cards. Henry gave 74 cards to his friend Joyce. How many baseball cards did Henry have left?

_____

24. Annette made 24 sandwiches. She wants to take $\frac{2}{3}$ of them to her class. How many should she take?

_____

25. Use number sense.

Helena wants to make 2 skirts in sewing class. She will need $2\frac{3}{4}$ yards of fabric for each skirt. She has 5 yards of fabric. Does she have enough fabric?

_____

MACMILLAN / McGRAW-HILL

Macmillan/McGraw-Hill, **MATHEMATICS IN ACTION**
Grade 4, Chapter 9, Form C

Name _____

Macmillan/McGraw-Hill
Mathematics

Chapter 10 Test

Grade 4
Form A

Page 1

Choose the letter of your answer.

1. $\frac{3}{5} + \frac{1}{5}$

   a. $\frac{2}{5}$ **c.** $\frac{4}{5}$

   b. $\frac{3}{10}$ **d.** not given

2. What is $\frac{5}{6} - \frac{1}{6}$ in simplest form?

   a. $\frac{2}{3}$ **c.** 1

   b. $\frac{4}{5}$ **d.** 4

3. What is the area of the figure?

6 ft

3 ft

   a. 3 square ft   **c.** 18 square ft

   b. 9 square ft   **d.** 32 square ft

4. Which is the best unit to measure the capacity of a jelly jar?

   a. cup   **c.** quart

   b. pint   **d.** gallon

5. Which is the most reasonable estimate for the temperature of a glass of cold juice?

   a. 40°F   **c.** 60°F

   b. 55°F   **d.** 75°F

6.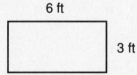

   a. $\frac{1}{3}$

   b. $\frac{2}{3}$

   c. $\frac{7}{9}$

   d. not given

7. What is $\frac{6}{7} - \frac{2}{7}$ in simplest form?

   a. $\frac{4}{14}$ **c.** $\frac{4}{7}$

   b. $\frac{3}{7}$ **d.** $1\frac{1}{7}$

8. What is the perimeter of the figure?

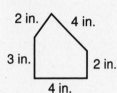
2 in.   4 in.
3 in.   2 in.
4 in.

   a. 13 in.

   b. 15 in.

   c. 19 in.

   d. 30 in.

9. About how much does a car weigh?

   a. about 35 oz

   b. about 35 lb

   c. about 350 oz

   d. about 3,500 lb

10. What is the temperature?

   a. ⁻12°F

   b. 22°F

   c. 35°F

   d. 47°F

11. What is $\frac{2}{10} + \frac{3}{10}$ in simplest form?

   a. $\frac{1}{10}$ **c.** $\frac{2}{3}$

   b. $\frac{1}{2}$ **d.** not given

12. What is $\frac{11}{12} - \frac{7}{12}$ in simplest form?

   a. 4   **c.** $\frac{5}{12}$

   b. $1\frac{1}{2}$ **d.** $\frac{1}{3}$

13. What is the area of the figure?

4 yd

4 yd

   a. 64 square yd

   b. 16 square yd

   c. 8 square yd

   d. 4 square yd

MACMILLAN / McGRAW-HILL

14. Which is the most reasonable estimate for the capacity of a large fish tank?

   a. 3 pt   **c.** 3 qt

   b. 30 c   **d.** 30 gal

15. Which is the most reasonable estimate for the temperature of bath water?

   a. 40°F   **c.** 95°F

   b. 60°F   **d.** 125°F

16. What is $\frac{3}{8} + \frac{3}{8}$ in simplest form?

   a. $\frac{2}{3}$ **c.** $\frac{1}{3}$

   b. $\frac{1}{2}$ **d.** not given

17. $\begin{array}{r} \frac{8}{11} \\ -\frac{1}{11} \\ \hline \end{array}$

   a. $\frac{1}{7}$

   b. $\frac{7}{22}$

   c. $\frac{7}{11}$

   d. $\frac{9}{11}$

18. What is the perimeter of the figure?

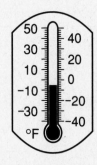

   a. 11 in.

   b. 20 in.

   c. 32 in.

   d. 40 in.

19. What is the temperature?

   a. 35°F

   b. 20°F

   c. 5°F

   d. −5°F

20. Which is the best estimate for the weight of an orange?

   a. 14 oz   **c.** 4 oz

   b. 14 lb   **d.** 4 lb

21. Melinda has a vegetable garden. She planted twice as many beans as cucumbers. She planted 7 more cucumbers than carrots. She planted 40 beans. How many carrots did she plant?

   a. 54   **b.** 27   **c.** 13   **d.** 8

22. Samuel has 327 pennies, 211 nickels, and 159 dimes. How many coins does he have in all?

   a. 116 **b.** 370 **c.** 588 **d.** 697

23. Mrs. Rico buys $\frac{7}{8}$ yd of lace. She sews $\frac{5}{8}$ yd onto a dress. How much lace does she have left?

   a. $\frac{1}{8}$ yd **b.** $\frac{1}{4}$ yd **c.** $\frac{3}{8}$ yd **d.** $\frac{1}{2}$ yd

24. Use number sense.

Mr. Connell wants to wash the second floor windows of his house. His $11\frac{1}{2}$-ft ladder is too short to reach the windows. Should he get an $11\frac{1}{4}$-ft ladder or an $11\frac{5}{8}$-ft ladder?

   a. $11\frac{1}{4}$-ft ladder   **b.** $11\frac{5}{8}$-ft ladder

25. Lea has a square garden that measures 7 yards on each side. What is the area of the garden?

   a. 14 square yd   **c.** 49 square yd

   b. 21 square yd   **d.** 98 square yd

Name

Macmillan/McGraw-Hill
Mathematics

Chapter 10 Test

Grade 4

Form B

Page 1

Choose the letter of your answer.

1. $\frac{4}{9} + \frac{1}{9}$
   - **a.** $\frac{5}{9}$
   - **c.** $\frac{5}{18}$
   - **b.** $\frac{1}{3}$
   - **d.** not given

2. What is $\frac{7}{8} - \frac{3}{8}$ in simplest form?
   - **a.** $\frac{1}{4}$
   - **c.** $\frac{5}{8}$
   - **b.** $\frac{1}{2}$
   - **d.** $1\frac{1}{4}$

3. What is the area of the figure?

3 in.

3 in.

   - **a.** 81 square in.
   - **c.** 9 square in.
   - **b.** 12 square in.
   - **d.** 6 square in.

4. Which is the best unit to measure the capacity of a washing machine?
   - **a.** gallon
   - **c.** pint
   - **b.** quart
   - **d.** cup

5. Which is the most reasonable estimate for the temperature of a cup of hot coffee?
   - **a.** ⁻10°F
   - **c.** 75°F
   - **b.** 40°F
   - **d.** 120°F

6. $\begin{array}{r} \frac{2}{5} \\ + \frac{1}{5} \\ \hline \end{array}$
   - **a.** $\frac{2}{25}$
   - **b.** $\frac{1}{5}$
   - **c.** $\frac{3}{5}$
   - **d.** not given

7. What is $\frac{5}{8} - \frac{3}{8}$ in simplest form?
   - **a.** $\frac{1}{4}$
   - **c.** $\frac{3}{4}$
   - **b.** $\frac{3}{8}$
   - **d.** $1\frac{1}{8}$

8. What is the perimeter of the figure?

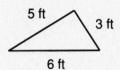

5 ft   3 ft

6 ft

   - **a.** 11 ft
   - **b.** 14 ft
   - **c.** 28 ft
   - **d.** 90 ft

9. About how much does a pencil weigh?
   - **a.** about 1 oz
   - **c.** about 10 lb
   - **b.** about 1 lb
   - **d.** about 100 oz

10. What is the temperature?

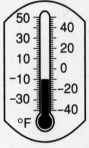

   - **a.** ⁻10°F
   - **b.** 10°F
   - **c.** 25°F
   - **d.** 50°F

11. What is $\frac{7}{12} + \frac{1}{12}$ in simplest form?
   - **a.** $\frac{1}{8}$
   - **c.** $\frac{1}{2}$
   - **b.** $\frac{1}{4}$
   - **d.** not given

12. What is $\frac{5}{11} - \frac{2}{11}$ in simplest form?
   - **a.** $\frac{3}{11}$
   - **c.** $\frac{7}{11}$
   - **b.** $\frac{7}{22}$
   - **d.** 3

13. What is the area of the figure?

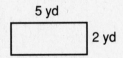

5 yd

2 yd

   - **a.** 20 square yd
   - **c.** 10 square yd
   - **b.** 14 square yd
   - **d.** 7 square yd

MACMILLAN / McGRAW-HILL

14. Which is the most reasonable estimate for the capacity of a Thermos bottle?

   a. 8 c   **c.** 80 qt
   b. 8 pt   **d.** 8 gal

15. Which is the best estimate for the temperature of snow?

   a. 25°F   **c.** 55°F
   b. 40°F   **d.** 70°F

16. What is $\frac{1}{8} + \frac{1}{8}$ in simplest form?

   a. 1   **c.** $\frac{1}{4}$
   b. $\frac{1}{2}$ **d.** not given

17. $\frac{7}{10}$
        $-\frac{4}{10}$ **a.** $1\frac{1}{10}$
                  b. $\frac{11}{20}$
                          c. $\frac{1}{2}$
                          d. $\frac{3}{10}$

18. What is the perimeter of the figure?

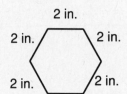

   a. 10 in.
   b. 12 in.
   c. 24 in.
   d. 64 in.

2 in. on each side

19. What is the temperature?

   a. ⁻5°F
   b. 12°F
   c. 25°F
   d. 40°F

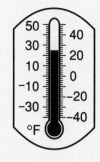

20. Which is the best estimate for the weight of a school bus?

   a. 200 oz   **c.** 20,000 oz
   b. 200 lb   **d.** 20,000 lb

 STOP

21. Jay is buying art supplies. A paint tube costs $2.79. A paintbrush costs $6.00. A pad of special paper costs $9.59. Jay needs 5 paint tubes, 2 brushes, and 1 pad of paper. Will $25.00 be enough to pay for these items?

   a. Yes.   **b.** No.

22. Calvin has 446 red tiles, 318 blue tiles, and 120 green tiles. How many tiles does he have in all?

   a. 884   **b.** 750   **c.** 568   **d.** 87

23. Mr. Girard buys $\frac{3}{4}$ yd of canvas. He uses $\frac{1}{4}$ yd to repair a tent. How much canvas does he have left?

   a. $\frac{1}{8}$ yd   **b.** $\frac{1}{4}$ yd   **c.** $\frac{1}{2}$ yd   **d.** 1 yd

24. Use number sense.

Sarah needs to tie up a large box. A $9\frac{1}{4}$-ft piece of twine is not long enough. Should she use a $9\frac{1}{2}$-ft or a $9\frac{1}{8}$-ft piece of twine?

   a. $9\frac{1}{2}$-ft piece of twine

   b. $9\frac{1}{8}$-ft piece of twine

25. A rectangular swimming pool measures 8 yards by 10 yards. What is the area of the pool?

   a. 160 square yd   **c.** 36 square yd
   b. 80 square yd   **d.** 18 square yd

Name

Macmillan/McGraw-Hill
Mathematics

Chapter 10 Test

Grade 4

Form C

Page 1

Mark your answer.

1. $\frac{3}{5} + \frac{1}{5}$

_____

2. What is $\frac{5}{6} - \frac{1}{6}$ in simplest form?

_____

3. What is the area of the figure?

6 ft

3 ft

_____

4. Is a cup, a pint, a quart, or a gallon the best unit to measure the capacity of a jelly jar?

_____

5. Ring the most reasonable estimate for the temperature of a glass of cold juice.

40°F	60°F
55°F	75°F

6.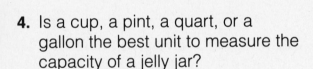
$$\begin{array}{r}\frac{5}{9}\\[-2pt]+\ \frac{2}{9}\\\hline\end{array}$$

_____

7. What is $\frac{6}{7} - \frac{2}{7}$ in simplest form?

8. What is the perimeter of the figure?

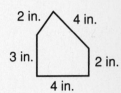
2 in.   4 in.
3 in.   2 in.
4 in.

_____

9. Is the best estimate of a car's weight 35 oz, 35 lb, 350 oz, or 3,500 lb?

_____

10. What is the temperature?

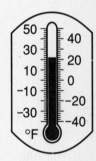

_____

11. What is $\frac{2}{10} + \frac{3}{10}$ in simplest form?

_____

12. What is $\frac{11}{12} - \frac{7}{12}$ in simplest form?

_____

13. What is the area of the figure?

4 yd

4 yd

_____

MACMILLAN / McGRAW-HILL

14. Is the most reasonable estimate for the capacity of a large fish tank 3 pints, 30 cups, 3 quarts, or 30 gallons?

_____

15. Ring the most reasonable estimate for the temperature of bath water.

40°F   95°F

60°F   125°F

16. What is $\frac{3}{8} + \frac{3}{8}$ in simplest form?

_____

17. $\frac{8}{11}$
         $-\frac{1}{11}$
         _____

_____

18. What is the perimeter of the figure?

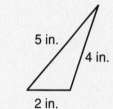

5 in.

4 in.

2 in.

_____

19. What is the temperature?

_____

20. Is the best estimate for the weight of an orange 14 oz, 14 lb, 4 oz, or 4 lb?

_____

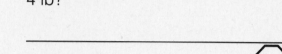
STOP

21. Melinda has a vegetable garden. She planted twice as many beans as cucumbers. She planted 7 more cucumbers than carrots. She planted 40 beans. How many carrots did she plant?

_____

22. Samuel has 327 pennies, 211 nickels, and 159 dimes. How many coins does he have in all?

_____

23. Mrs. Rico buys $\frac{7}{8}$ yd of lace. She sews $\frac{5}{8}$ yd onto a dress. How much lace does she have left?

_____

24. Use number sense.

Mr. Connell wants to wash the second floor windows of his house. His $11\frac{1}{2}$-ft ladder is too short to reach the windows. Should he get an $11\frac{1}{4}$-ft ladder or an $11\frac{5}{8}$-ft ladder?

_____

25. Lea has a square garden that measures 7 yards on each side. What is the area of the garden?

_____

MACMILLAN / McGRAW-HILL

Name

Macmillan/McGraw-Hill
Mathematics

Chapter 11 Test

Grade 4
Form A

Page 1

Choose the letter of your answer.

1. What is the decimal for $\frac{6}{10}$?
- **a.** 6.0
- **b.** 0.6
- **c.** 0.06
- **d.** not given

2. Compare.

$$0.45 \; \bullet \; \frac{45}{100}$$
- **a.** >
- **b.** <
- **c.** =

3. Estimate by rounding.

$$5.12 + 7.79$$
- **a.** 5
- **b.** 8
- **c.** 12
- **d.** 13

4. 4.5 + 2.3
- **a.** 6.8
- **b.** 2.2
- **c.** 0.68
- **d.** 0.22

5. A quarter is tossed 150 times. Predict how many times it will land heads up.
- **a.** 150
- **b.** 125
- **c.** 100
- **d.** 75

6. Seven hundredths is the word name for _____.
- **a.** 7
- **b.** 1.7
- **c.** 0.07
- **d.** not given

7. Compare.

$$3.8 \; \bullet \; 8.3$$
- **a.** >
- **b.** <
- **c.** =

8. Estimate. Use the front digits and adjust.

$$18.23 - 9.37$$
- **a.** < 8
- **b.** < 9
- **c.** > 9
- **d.** > 18

9. 0.9 – 0.5
- **a.** 4.0
- **b.** 1.4
- **c.** 0.4
- **d.** 0.04

10. Predict how many times the spinner will land on ▲ in 8 spins.

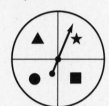
- **a.** 2
- **b.** 4
- **c.** 6
- **d.** 8

11. What is the decimal for $2\frac{3}{10}$?
- **a.** 2.3
- **b.** 1.3
- **c.** 0.3
- **d.** not given

12. Compare.

$$5.90 \; \bullet \; 5.09$$
- **a.** >
- **b.** <
- **c.** =

13. Which is the best estimate of 6.8 – 5.4?
- **a.** < 0
- **b.** > 0
- **c.** > 1
- **d.** >10

14.
$$\begin{array}{r} 0.75 \\ + 0.81 \\ \hline \end{array}$$
- **a.** 0.06
- **b.** 0.16
- **c.** 1.56
- **d.** 15.6

15. There are 3 blue cubes, 2 red cubes, and 1 green cube in a bag. What is the probability of picking a red cube?
- **a.** $\frac{1}{3}$
- **b.** $\frac{1}{2}$
- **c.** $\frac{1}{5}$
- **d.** $\frac{1}{6}$

MACMILLAN / McGRAW-HILL

16. Which is nine-tenths?

  a. 9.1   **c.** 1.9

  b. 9.01   **d.** not given

17. Which set of numbers is ordered from least to greatest?

  a. 0.13, 0.3, 3.1   **c.** 1.3, 0.3, 0.13

  b. 5.6, 6.5, 0.65   **d.** 0.65, 6.5, 5.6

18. Estimate by rounding. 3.7 + 8.9

  a. 11   **b.** 12   **c.** 13   **d.** 15

19.   12.1
   – 8.25

  a. 3.25

  b. 3.85

  c. 16.15

  d. 20.35

20. Predict how many times the spinner will land on R in 12 spins.

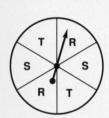

  a. 12

  b. 6

  c. 4

  d. 2

STOP

21. Roger has $1.79 in his pocket. He has $3.33 in his coin jar. About how much money does he have in all?

  a. about $1.00   **c.** about $5.00

  b. about $3.00   **d.** about $7.00

22. Each student in the school play plans to wear a white, black, or red hat with a red or blue scarf. How many different combinations can each student make?

  a. 3   **b.** 4   **c.** 5   **d.** 6

23. Janna collected 57 seashells. Peter and Steve collected 49 seashells each. Sophie collected 31 seashells. How many seashells did the children collect in all?

  a. 96   **b.** 137   **c.** 186   **d.** 217

24. Marcia and her mother drive $13\frac{6}{10}$ miles to the store. Which decimal shows how many miles Marcia and her mother drive?

  a. 0.13 mi   **c.** 6.13 mi

  b. 1.36 mi   **d.** 13.6 mi

Use the tree diagram to answer Question 25.

Tree Diagram		List
3-speed bike	basket rack	_____ 3-speed—basket _____ 3-speed—rack
5-speed bike	basket rack	_____ ▨ _____ ▨
10-speed bike	▨ ▨	_____ ▨ _____ ▨

25. Jeb wants to get a new bicycle. He has a choice of a 3-speed, a 5-speed, or a 10-speed bike. All three types come with either a handlebar basket or a rear-wheel rack. How many choices does Jeb have?

  a. 6   **b.** 9   **c.** 12   **d.** 18

MACMILLAN / McGRAW-HILL

Name

Macmillan/McGraw-Hill
Mathematics

Chapter 11 Test

Grade 4
Form B

Page 1

Choose the letter of your answer.

1. What is the decimal for $\frac{3}{10}$?
a. 0.03   **c.** 3.0
b. 1.3   **d.** not given

2. Compare.

     2.5 ● 5.2

a. >   **b.** <   **c.** =

3. Estimate by rounding.

     4.22 + 6.85

a. 63   **b.** 11   **c.** 10   **d.** 3

4. 7.6 + 1.3
a. 0.89   **c.** 6.3
b. 0.63   **d.** 8.9

5. A quarter is tossed 100 times. Predict how many times it will land tails up.
a. 10   **b.** 20   **c.** 50   **d.** 100

6. Eight tenths is the word name for _____.
a. 0.08   **c.** 1.8
b. 0.8   **d.** not given

7. Compare.

     0.72 ● $\frac{72}{100}$

a. >   **b.** <   **c.** =

8. Estimate. Use the front digits and adjust.

     14.13 − 6.33

a. < 8   **b.** > 8   **c.** < 20   **d.** >20

9. 0.8 − 0.2
a. 0.06   **c.** 1.0
b. 0.6   **d.** 6.0

10. Predict how many times the spinner will land on J in 10 spins.

a. 1
b. 2
c. 3
d. 4

11. What is the decimal for $8\frac{5}{10}$?
a. 0.58   **c.** 8.5
b. 0.85   **d.** not given

12. Compare.

     1.40 ● 1.04

a. >   **b.** <   **c.** =

13. Which is the best estimate of 5.7 − 4.2?
a. < 0   **c.** > 1
b. < 1   **d.** > 10

14.   0.97
   + 0.62
   ‾‾‾‾‾
     a. 0.95
     b. 1.59
     c. 9.5
     d. 15.9

15. There are 4 apples, 2 pears, and 1 orange in a bag. What is the probability of picking a pear?
a. $\frac{1}{7}$ **b.** $\frac{2}{7}$ **c.** $\frac{2}{5}$ **d.** $\frac{4}{7}$

MACMILLAN / McGRAW-HILL

16. Which is three hundredths?

   a. 0.03   **c.** 3.00

   b. 0.3   **d.** not given

17. Which set of numbers is ordered from least to greatest?

   a. 2.7, 0.27, 0.7   **c.** 0.27, 0.7, 2.7

   b. 0.5, 1.5, 0.15   **d.** 0.15, 1.5, 0.5

18. Estimate by rounding.

          6.3 + 4.8

   a. 12   **b.** 11   **c.** 10   **d.** 9

19.   17.5   **a.** 25.87

    – 8.37   **b.** 11.27

                 c. 9.27

                 d. 9.13

20. Predict how many times the spinner will land on ♥ in 4 spins.

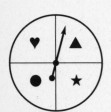

   a. 4

   b. 3

   c. 2

   d. 1

STOP

21. Monica earns $4.85 selling newspapers on Saturday. She earns $7.32 selling newspapers on Sunday. About how much money does she earn in all?

   a. about $10.00   **c.** about $14.00

   b. about $12.00   **d.** about $15.00

22. Each clown in the parade plans to wear an orange, green, or purple wig with a black, white, or red hat. How many different combinations can each clown make?

   a. 9   **b.** 6   **c.** 5   **d.** 4

23. Carol saved 205 pennies. Mitch saved 39 nickels. Henry saved 54 dimes and 146 pennies. How many coins did they save in all?

   a. 351   **b.** 444   **c.** 550   **d.** 1,086

24. The Lord family drives $23\frac{7}{10}$ miles to the beach. Which decimal shows how many miles the Lord family drives?

   a. 0.7 mi   **c.** 23.7 mi

   b. 2.37 mi   **d.** 70.23 mi

Use the tree diagram to answer Question 25.

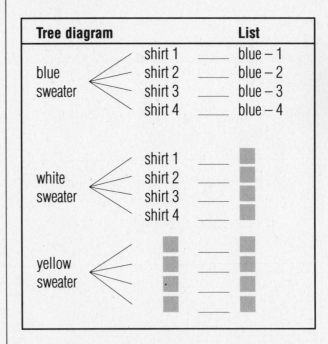

Tree diagram		List
blue sweater	shirt 1	_____ blue – 1
	shirt 2	_____ blue – 2
	shirt 3	_____ blue – 3
	shirt 4	_____ blue – 4
white sweater	shirt 1	_____
	shirt 2	_____
	shirt 3	_____
	shirt 4	_____
yellow sweater		_____
		_____
		_____
		_____

25. Kathy wants to wear a shirt and sweater combination. She has a blue sweater, a white sweater, and a yellow sweater. She has 4 shirts. How many different combinations can she put together?

   a. 7   **b.** 12   **c.** 24   **d.** 32

MACMILLAN / McGRAW-HILL

Name

Macmillan/McGraw-Hill
Mathematics

Chapter 11 Test

Grade 4

Form C

Page 1

Mark your answer.

1. What is the decimal for $\frac{6}{10}$?

   _____

2. Compare. Write >, <, or =.

   0.45 ⬤ $\frac{45}{100}$

   _____

3. Estimate by rounding.

   5.12 + 7.79

   _____

4. 4.5 + 2.3

   _____

5. A quarter is tossed 150 times. Predict how many times it will land heads up.

   _____

6. Seven hundredths is the word name for what decimal?

   _____

7. Compare. Write >, <, or =.

   3.8 ⬤ 8.3

   _____

8. Estimate. Use the front digits and adjust.

   18.23 − 9.37

   _____

9. 0.9 − 0.5

   _____

10. Predict how many times the spinner will land on ▲ in 8 spins.

   _____

11. What is the decimal for $2\frac{3}{10}$?

   _____

12. Compare. Write >, <, or =.

   5.90 ⬤ 5.09

   _____

13. Ring the best estimate of 6.8 − 5.4.

< 0	> 1
> 0	> 10

14.   0.75
    + 0.81

   _____

15. There are 3 blue cubes, 2 red cubes, and 1 green cube in a bag. What is the probability of picking a red cube?

   _____

MACMILLAN / McGRAW-HILL

16. Write the decimal for nine-tenths.

_____

17. Write in order from least to greatest.

0.3, 0.13, 3.1

_____

18. Estimate by rounding. 3.7 + 8.9

_____

19.   12.1
        – 8.25
        _____

_____

20. Predict how many times the spinner will land on R in 12 spins.

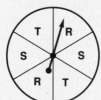

_____

21. Roger has $1.79 in his pocket. He has $3.33 in his coin jar. About how much money does he have in all?

_____

22. Each student in the school play plans to wear a white, black, or red hat with a red or blue scarf. How many different combinations can each student make?

_____

23. Janna collected 57 seashells. Peter and Steve collected 49 seashells each. Sophie collected 31 seashells. How many seashells did the children collect in all?

_____

24. Marcia and her mother drive $13\frac{6}{10}$ miles to the store. Write the decimal that shows how many miles Marcia and her mother drive.

_____

Use the tree diagram to answer Question 25.

Tree Diagram			List
3-speed bike	<	basket	_____ 3-speed—basket
		rack	_____ 3-speed—rack
5-speed bike	<	basket	_____ ▨
		rack	_____ ▨
10-speed bike	<	▨	_____ ▨
		▨	_____ ▨

25. Jeb wants to get a new bicycle. He has a choice of a 3-speed, a 5-speed, or a 10-speed bike. All three types come with either a handlebar basket or a rear-wheel rack. How many choices does Jeb have?

_____

Macmillan/McGraw-Hill
Mathematics

Chapter 12 Test

Grade 4
Form A

Page 1

Choose the letter of your answer.

1. 20×40

   a. 8   **c.** 800
   b. 80   **d.** not given

2. Estimate by using the front digits.

          23×56

   a. 100   **c.** 1,000
   b. 120   **d.** 1,200

3. 18×97

   a. 1,755   **c.** 1,696
   b. 1,746   **d.** 873

4. $10\overline{)500}$

   a. 5   **c.** 500
   b. 50   **d.** 5,000

5. $25 \div 10$

   a. 2 R5   **c.** 10 R5
   b. 2 R15   **d.** 20 R10

6.   500
  $\times$ 40

   a. 200
   b. 2,000
   c. 200,000
   d. not given

7. Estimate by rounding.

         $97 \times \$68$

   a. $700   **c.** $70,000
   b. $7,000   **d.** $700,000

8. $20 \div 20$

   a. 20   **b.** 10   **c.** 1   **d.** 0

9. $24
  $\times$ 23

   a. $110
   b. $120
   c. $552
   d. $561

10. $90\overline{)360}$

   a. 4   **b.** 40   **c.** 270   **d.** 400

11. Which is the best estimate of
     $26 \times \$84$?

   a. $240   **c.** $24,000
   b. $2,400   **d.** $240,000

12. $80 \times 9,000$

   a. 720,000   **c.** 7,200
   b. 72,000   **d.** not given

13. $42 \times \$32$

   a. $210   **c.** $1,234
   b. $814   **d.** $1,344

14. $800 \div 40$

   a. 32,000   **c.** 200
   b. 3,200   **d.** 20

15. $30\overline{)525}$

   a. 2 R25   **c.** 20 R25
   b. 17 R15   **d.** 170 R15

16.   300
  $\times$ 60

   a. 18,000
   b. 1,800
   c. 180
   d. not given

MACMILLAN / McGRAW-HILL

17. 69
× 41

  a. 28
  b. 345
  c. 2,589
  d. 2,829

18. Estimate by using the front digits.

44 × 72

  a. 2,800   **c.** 28,000
  b. 3,500   **d.** 35,000

19. 50)3,000

  a. 6   **c.** 600
  b. 60   **d.** 6,000

20. 120 ÷ 10

  a. 1,200   **c.** 30
  b. 110   **d.** 12

STOP

21. Carla wants to collect
600 baseball cards. The cards
come in packages of 20. How
many packages will she need?

  a. 3   **b.** 20   **c.** 30   **d.** 200

22. The Blue Kites baseball team
bought 30 new T-shirts. Each
T-shirt cost $12. How much did
the team spend in all?

  a. $2   **c.** $42
  b. $18   **d.** $360

23. Each student in the rally plans to
make a poster with a red or white
background and blue or black
letters. How many color
combinations of background and
letters can each student make?

  a. 2   **b.** 4   **c.** 6   **d.** 8

24. The school band must sell
500 boxes of fruit. If each
member sells 10 boxes, all the fruit
will be gone. How many band
members are there?

  a. 5   **c.** 500
  b. 50   **d.** 5,000

25. There are 25 classrooms in Brian's
school. Each classroom holds
20 desks. Which number
sentence should you use to find
how many desks there are
in all?

  a. 25 + 20 =
  b. 25 – 20 = ▓
  c. 25 × 20 = ▓
  d. 25 ÷ 20 = ▓

MACMILLAN / McGRAW-HILL

Name

Macmillan/McGraw-Hill
Mathematics

Chapter 12 Test

Grade 4
Form B

Page 1

Choose the letter of your answer.

1. 30×60
- **a.** 18
- **b.** 180
- **c.** 1,800
- **d.** not given

2. Estimate by using the front digits.

35×47
- **a.** 20,000
- **b.** 2,000
- **c.** 1,600
- **d.** 1,200

3. 15×79
- **a.** 474
- **b.** 1,185
- **c.** 1,190
- **d.** 1,194

4. $70\overline{)700}$
- **a.** 1
- **b.** 10
- **c.** 100
- **d.** 1,000

5. $83 \div 10$
- **a.** 8 R3
- **b.** 8 R13
- **c.** 10 R3
- **d.** 10 R13

6. $\begin{array}{r} 200 \\ \times\ 50 \\ \hline \end{array}$
- **a.** 10,000
- **b.** 1,000
- **c.** 100
- **d.** not given

7. Estimate by using the front digits.

$43 \times \$95$
- **a.** $36,000
- **b.** $4,000
- **c.** $3,600
- **d.** $320

8. $40 \div 10$
- **a.** 400
- **b.** 40
- **c.** 30
- **d.** 4

9. $\begin{array}{r} \$53 \\ \times\ 38 \\ \hline \end{array}$
- **a.** $304
- **b.** $1,594
- **c.** $1,672
- **d.** $2,014

10. $80\overline{)480}$
- **a.** 6
- **b.** 7
- **c.** 60
- **d.** 600

11. Which is the best estimate of $61 \times \$73$?
- **a.** $420
- **b.** $480
- **c.** $4,200
- **d.** $48,000

12. $70 \times 5,000$
- **a.** 35,000
- **b.** 3,500
- **c.** 350
- **d.** not given

13. $54 \times \$86$
- **a.** $4,644
- **b.** $4,392
- **c.** $4,324
- **d.** $744

14. $600 \div 30$
- **a.** 30
- **b.** 20
- **c.** 3
- **d.** 2

15. $20\overline{)166}$
- **a.** 8 R6
- **b.** 71 R3
- **c.** 80 R6
- **d.** 710 R3

16. $\begin{array}{r} 700 \\ \times\ 90 \\ \hline \end{array}$
- **a.** 63,000
- **b.** 6,300
- **c.** 630
- **d.** not given

MACMILLAN / McGRAW-HILL

17. 71
   × 65

   a. 45,565
   b. 4,615
   c. 781
   d. 620

18. Estimate by rounding.

   16 × 88

   a. 80   c. 1,800
   b. 180   d. 8,000

19. 50)‾4,000‾

   a. 8   c. 800
   b. 80   d. 8,000

20. 190 ÷ 10

   a. 9   c. 180
   b. 19   d. 1,900

STOP

21. Sally has 300 stamps. She plans to put them in books that hold 30 stamps each. How many books will she need?

   a. 100   b. 30   c. 20   d. 10

22. The Jets baseball team bought 20 new uniforms this year. Each uniform cost $38. How much did the team spend in all?

   a. $760   c. $18
   b. $58   d. $2

23. Each student in the Halloween parade plans to wear orange or black socks with black, white, or gray sneakers. How many color combinations of sneakers and socks can each student make?

   a. 2   b. 4   c. 6   d. 8

24. There are 20 cabins at Connie's summer camp for girls. Each cabin houses 10 girls. How many girls can stay at the camp at one time?

   a. 20   c. 200
   b. 100   d. 1,000

25. There are 36 teachers in Claudia's school. Each teacher has 20 students. Which number sentence should you use to find how many students there are in all?

   a. 36 + 20 =
   b. 36 − 20 = ▧
   c. 36 ÷ 20 = ▧
   d. 36 × 20 = ▧

MACMILLAN / McGRAW-HILL

Name _____

Macmillan/McGraw-Hill
Mathematics

Chapter 12 Test

Grade 4
Form C

Page 1

Mark your answer.

1. 20×40

_____

2. Estimate by using the front digits.

23×56

_____

3. 18×97

_____

4. $10\overline{)500}$

_____

5. $25 \div 10$

_____

6. $\begin{array}{r} 500 \\ \times\ 40 \\ \hline \end{array}$

_____

7. Estimate by rounding.

$97 \times \$68$

_____

8. $20 \div 20$

_____

9. $\begin{array}{r} \$24 \\ \times\ 23 \\ \hline \end{array}$

_____

10. $90\overline{)360}$

_____

11. Estimate. $26 \times \$84$

_____

12. $80 \times 9{,}000$

_____

13. $42 \times \$32$

_____

14. $800 \div 40$

_____

15. $30\overline{)525}$

_____

16. $\begin{array}{r} 300 \\ \times\ 60 \\ \hline \end{array}$

_____

17. 69
    × 41
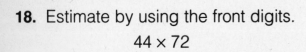

_____

18. Estimate by using the front digits.

44 × 72

_____

19. 50)‾3,000‾

_____

20. 120 ÷ 10

_____

STOP

═══════════════════════════════

21. Carla wants to collect
600 baseball cards. The cards
come in packages of 20. How
many packages will she need?

_____

22. The Blue Kites baseball team
bought 30 new T-shirts. Each
T-shirt cost $12. How much did
the team spend in all?

_____

23. Each student in the rally plans to
make a poster with a red or white
background and blue or black
letters. How many color
combinations of background and
letters can each student make?

_____

24. The school band must sell
500 boxes of fruit. If each
member sells 10 boxes, all the fruit
will be gone. How many band
members are there?

_____

25. There are 25 classrooms in Brian's
school. Each classroom holds
20 desks. Write a number
sentence to find how many desks
there are in all.

_____

MACMILLAN / McGRAW-HILL

Name

Macmillan/McGraw-Hill
Mathematics
Cumulative 1 Test
Grade 4

Page 1

Choose the letter of your answer.

1. What is the value of 7 in the number 247,102,000?

  a. 7,000   **c.** 7,000,000
  b. 70,000   **d.** 700,000,000

2. How much is 1 five-dollar bill, 3 one-dollar bills, 2 quarters, and 1 dime?

  a. $5.60   **c.** $8.99
  b. $8.60   **d.** not given

3. Compare. 34,798 ⬤ 35,100

  a. >   **b.** <   **c.** =

4. Round 892 to the nearest hundred.

  a. 800   **c.** 900
  b. 850   **d.** 1,000

5. 9 − 0

  a. 0   **b.** 9   **c.** 10   **d.** 90

6. Cost: $4.70 Given: $5.00 Change?

  a. 3 dimes, 1 nickel
  b. 2 dimes, 3 nickels
  c. 1 quarter, 1 dime
  d. 1 quarter, 1 nickel

7. Which amount is greatest?

  a. $2.99   **c.** $2.20
  b. $3.00   **d.** $3.02

8. Round $11.47 to the nearest ten cents.

  a. $11.00   **c.** $11.50
  b. $11.45   **d.** $11.60

9. Find the perimeter.

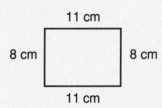

  a. 88 cm   **c.** 29 cm
  b. 38 cm   **d.** not given

10. What is the length of the flower?

  a. 1 cm   **c.** 5 cm
  b. 2 cm   **d.** 10 cm

11. Find the perimeter.

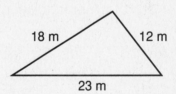

  a. 35 m   **c.** 53 m
  b. 48 m   **d.** 63 m

12. Which is the best unit to measure the length of a river?

  a. cm **b.** dm **c.** m **d.** km

13. Which is the best unit to measure the length of a house?

  a. km **b.** m **c.** dm **d.** cm

MACMILLAN / McGRAW-HILL

14. Find the perimeter.

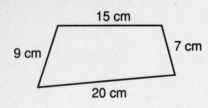

15 cm
9 cm
7 cm
20 cm

a. 28 cm   c. 51 cm
b. 44 cm   d. 56 cm

15. What is the length of the bolt?

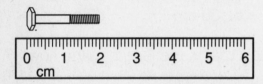

a. 1 cm   c. 28 cm
b. 2 cm   d. 200 cm

16. Find the perimeter.

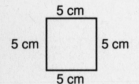

5 cm
5 cm   5 cm
5 cm

a. 25 cm
b. 20 cm
c. 18 cm
d. 10 cm

17. The length of an envelope is about _____.

a. 22 km   c. 22 dm
b. 22 m   d. 22 cm

18. Find the perimeter.

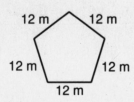

12 m   12 m
12 m   12 m
12 m

a. 60 m   c. 108 m
b. 72 m   d. 144 m

19. 5 + 9

a. 4   b. 14   c. 15   d. 45

20. $45.98 − $23.50

a. $23.50   c. $21.18
b. $22.48   d. not given

21.
    369
    112
+ 67

a. 458
b. 498
c. 525
d. not given

22. 7 + 3 + 2 + 4

a. 12   b. 13   c. 16   d. 18

23. What is the best estimate of 4,342 − 253?

a. 5,000   c. 4,300
b. 4,500   d. 4,000

24. 700 + 2,200

a. 1,500   c. 3,000
b. 2,900   d. not given

25. 11 − 2

a. 9   b. 13   c. 22   d. 112

26.
    $28.32
    16.01
+ 9.17

a. $53.50
b. $51.10
c. $35.05
d. not given

27. 2,497 − 1,846

a. 4,343   c. 651
b. 1,651   d. not given

28. Estimate. 4,569 + 1,301

a. 10,000   c. 6,000
b. 9,000   d. 3,000

MACMILLAN / McGRAW-HILL

29.   17
   – 9

a. 7   **c.** 9
b. 8   **d.** 10

30. $54.62 + $19.90

a. $74.52   **c.** $75.62
b. $74.65   **d.** not given

31. Estimate by rounding.

$8.99 + $1.03 + $4.24

a. $12.00   **c.** $14.00
b. $13.00   **d.** $15.00

32. $97.28 – $82.36

a. $14.92   **c.** $16.89
b. $15.02   **d.** not given

33.   7,800
   + 700

a. 1,480
b. 7,700
c. 14,800
d. not given

Use the table to answer
Questions 34–36.

Store	Price		
	Wrench	Bolt	Nail
Discount Wares	$5.95	$.28	$.08
T & B Hardware	$7.95	$.33	$.03
Nails and Things	$7.50		$.08
Home Works	$9.99	$.33	$.15

34. What is the price of a nail at
T & B Hardware?

a. $.01   **b.** $.03   **c.** $.15   **d.** $.28

35. What is the most likely price of a
bolt at Nails and Things?

a. $.53   **c.** $.08
b. $.28   **d.** $.01

36. Which store sells the most
expensive wrench?

a. Discount Wares
b. T & B Hardware
c. Nails and Things
d. Home Works

Use the bar graph to answer
Questions 37–40.

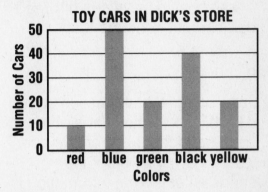

TOY CARS IN DICK'S STORE

37. Dick's store has the most of which
color toy car?

a. black   **c.** blue
b. red   **d.** yellow

38. How many black toy cars are there
in Dick's store?

a. 40   **b.** 30   **c.** 20   **d.** 10

39. How many red toy cars are there
in Dick's store?

a. 50   **b.** 30   **c.** 10   **d.** 0

40. The store has an equal number of
green toy cars and _____
toy cars.

a. red   **c.** yellow
b. blue   **d.** black

41. Use number sense.

If Wenona buys 3 notebooks, about how much money will she spend?

a. about $.50   **c.** about $50.00
b. about $5.00   **d.** about $100.00

42. Use number sense.

Anita buys one loaf of bread. About how many slices of bread can she cut from one loaf?

a. about 5   **c.** about 200
b. about 20   **d.** about 500

43. Jane builds 8 sandcastles at the beach. She puts 2 flags on top of each sandcastle. Then the ocean washes away some of the sandcastles. What information is needed to find how many sandcastles are left?

a. the amount of time Jane takes to build each sandcastle
b. the colors of the flags
c. the number of sandcastles the ocean washes away

44. Use number sense.

If Roy gives a flower to each student in his fourth-grade classroom, about how many flowers will he give out?

a. about 30   **c.** about 3,000
b. about 300   **d.** about 30,000

45. Alex spends $2.98 at the store. He gives the clerk $5.00. Which number sentence tells how much change Alex should receive?

a. $5.00 − $2.98 = ▨
b. $5.00 + $2.98 = ▨

46. At the park Karl spent $6.50 on rides, $3.35 on games, and $4.80 on food. Which is the most reasonable answer for how much Karl spent in all?

a. $14.65   **c.** $146.50
b. $24.65   **d.** $1,465.00

47. May has $10.00 to buy 25 cookies at the store. What else do you need to know to find if May has enough money for the cookies?

a. the name of the store
b. how large the cookies are
c. how much each cookie costs
d. what the cookies are made of

48. Stan's Juice Stand sold 948 glasses of lemonade and 432 glasses of orange juice. Which number sentence should you use to find how many more glasses of lemonade than orange juice were sold?

a. 948 − 432 = ▨
b. 948 + 432 = ▨

49. Mr. Okiko is building a fence that is 10 meters long. He puts a post at each end and at every 2 meters along the inside of the fence. How many posts are there in all?

a. 4   **b.** 5   **c.** 6   **d.** 7

50. On their vacation the Nash family drove 74 km on Sunday, 117 km on Monday, and 153 km on Tuesday. They want to know how many km they drove in all. Which is the most reasonable answer?

a. 191 km   **c.** 344 km
b. 270 km   **d.** 497 km

MACMILLAN / McGRAW-HILL

Cumulative 2 Test

Choose the letter of your answer.

1. Which number is greatest?
- **a.** 3,894
- **b.** 3,498
- **c.** 3,984
- **d.** 3,489

2. Round $15.43 to the nearest ten cents.
- **a.** $15.50
- **b.** $15.40
- **c.** $15.00
- **d.** not given

3. $0 \div 8$
- **a.** 16
- **b.** 8
- **c.** 1
- **d.** 0

4. Which numbers are all factors of 32?
- **a.** 2, 4, 6, 8
- **b.** 2, 4, 8, 16
- **c.** 2, 4, 8, 18
- **d.** 2, 8, 16, 18

5. Which of the following has only even numbers?
- **a.** 2, 4, 6, 9
- **b.** 12, 16, 21, 32
- **c.** 1, 10, 14, 28
- **d.** 20, 24, 28, 46

6. 5×4
- **a.** 15
- **b.** 20
- **c.** 25
- **d.** not given

7. Which numbers are all multiples of 9?
- **a.** 3, 9, 18, 27
- **b.** 9, 18, 27, 32
- **c.** 9, 18, 27, 36
- **d.** 18, 27, 45, 56

8. Which number is prime?
- **a.** 35
- **b.** 21
- **c.** 18
- **d.** 11

9. Find the perimeter.

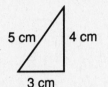

- **a.** 7 cm
- **b.** 8 cm
- **c.** 9 cm
- **d.** 12 cm

10. How long is the doll necklace?

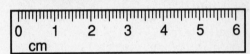

- **a.** 6 cm
- **b.** 5 cm
- **c.** 4 cm
- **d.** 3 cm

11. What time does the clock show?

- **a.** 11:10
- **b.** 11:50
- **c.** 1:10
- **d.** 1:50

12. You can usually go ice-skating outside when the temperature is _____.
- **a.** ⁻10°C
- **b.** 20°C
- **c.** 30°C
- **d.** 100°C

13. What is the area?

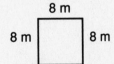

- **a.** 16 square m
- **b.** 32 square m
- **c.** 40 square m
- **d.** 64 square m

14. What is the best estimate for the mass of a large dog?
- **a.** 20 kg
- **b.** 20 mg
- **c.** 2 g
- **d.** 2 mg

15. How much time passes between 9:05 A.M. and 9:50 A.M.?

   a. 55 minutes   **c.** 45 minutes

   b. 50 minutes   **d.** not given

16. What is the temperature shown?

   a. ⁻40°C

   b. ⁻10°C

   c. 10°C

   d. 40°C

17. What is the area of a rectangle 7 cm long and 5 cm wide?

   a. 12 square cm

   b. 24 square cm

   c. 35 square cm

   d. not given

18. About how long is a school day?

   a. about 6 seconds

   b. about 60 minutes

   c. about 6 hours

   d. about 60 hours

19. 9 + 3

   a. 11   **b.** 12   **c.** 13   **d.** 93

20. What is the best estimate of 5,703 − 2,981?

   a. 1,000   **c.** 3,000

   b. 2,000   **d.** 4,000

21. 4,538 + 9,876

   a. 14,414   **c.** 14,304

   b. 14,314   **d.** 13,304

22. 5 × 6,000

   a. 30,000   **c.** 3,000,000

   b. 300,000   **d.** not given

23. About how much is 7 × $9.89?

   a. about $50.00

   b. about $60.00

   c. about $70.00

   d. about $100.00

24. 3 × 534

   a. 1,502   **c.** 1,597

   b. 1,592   **d.** 1,602

25. 2 × $8.55

   a. $17.10   **c.** $16.77

   b. $17.00   **d.** not given

26. Estimate by rounding.

$$\$7.16 + \$4.87 + \$5.31$$

   a. $16.00   **c.** $18.00

   b. $17.00   **d.** $19.00

27. $87.14 − 39.85

   a. $58.39

   b. $58.29

   c. $47.39

   d. $47.29

28. 70 × 8

   a. 56

   b. 5,600

   c. 56,000

   d. not given

29. Estimate. 5 × 78

   a. 350   **c.** 3,500

   b. 400   **d.** 4,000

30. 112 × 8

   a. 886

   b. 890

   c. 896

   d. 904

31. $5 \times \$7.01$

   a. $12.06   **c.** $35.55
   b. $35.05   **d.** not given

32.
$$\begin{array}{r} 29 \\ \times\ 9 \\ \hline \end{array}$$
   a. 181 **c.** 261
   b. 252 **d.** 299

33. $4 \times \$.62$

   a. $3.10   **c.** $2.48
   b. $2.58   **d.** not given

Use the bar graph to answer
Questions 34–36.

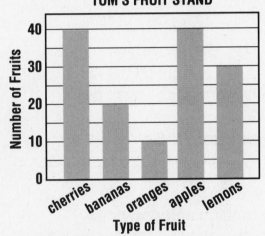

TOM'S FRUIT STAND

34. Tom's Fruit Stand has the least
amount of which fruit?

   a. cherries   **c.** apples
   b. oranges   **d.** lemons

35. Tom's Fruit Stand has the same
amount of _____.

   a. lemons and oranges
   b. oranges and bananas
   c. apples and lemons
   d. cherries and apples

36. How many bananas does Tom's
Fruit Stand have?

   a. 10 **b.** 20 **c.** 30 **d.** 40

Use the grid to answer
Questions 37 and 38.

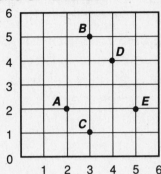

37. The ordered pair for point *E*
is _____.

   a. (1, 2)   **c.** (3, 3)
   b. (2, 4)   **d.** not given

38. Which letter is at the point (2, 2)?

   a. *A* **b.** *B* **c.** *C* **d.** *E*

Use the line graph to answer
Questions 39 and 40.

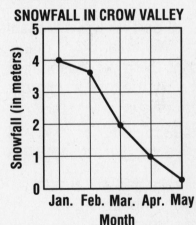

SNOWFALL IN CROW VALLEY

39. Which month had the greatest
amount of snowfall?

   a. January   **c.** April
   b. March   **d.** May

40. How much snow fell in March?

   a. 4 meters   **c.** 2 meters
   b. 3 meters   **d.** 1 meters

41. Find the pattern to solve.

The night watchman first checks Building A at 12:30. The second time he checks the building is at 1:45. The third time he checks the building is at 3:00. At what time does he check the building for the fifth time?

a. 5:15   **c.** 5:45
b. 5:30   **d.** 6:00

42. Lou had 23 toy trains. He received 2 more as gifts. He bought some more. What else do you need to know to find how many toy trains he has now?

a. what city the store is in
b. how many toy trains he bought
c. what color the toy trains are
d. how many cars are in each train

43. Three airport runways measure 613 m, 789 m, and 574 m long. Which is the most reasonable answer for the total length of all three runways?

a. 7,493 m   **c.** 1,402 m
b. 1,976 m   **d.** 1,187 m

44. The library had 4,368 books. The library then bought 546 more books. How many books does the library have now?

a. 1,092   **c.** 4,914
b. 3,822   **d.** 9,828

45. Draper's Ranch has 435 horses and 552 cows. The ranch sells 143 cows. How many cows does the ranch have now?

a. 292   **b.** 409   **c.** 844   **d.** 987

46. Ed takes $15.63 to the baseball game. He spends $2.27. His mother gives him $5.75 more. How much money does he have now?

a. $3.48   **c.** $19.11
b. $8.36   **d.** $23.65

47. Mr. Polk has 736 pieces of wood. He has 8 crates and wants to put an equal amount of wood into each crate. How many pieces of wood should he put in each crate?

a. 92   **c.** 744
b. 728   **d.** 5,888

48. Use number sense.

Anna bought 2 cookies. About how much did she spend?

a. about $1
b. about $15
c. about $100
d. about $500

49. Susana and Andy drew 28 pictures. Andy drew 3 times as many pictures as Susana drew. How many pictures did Andy draw?

a. 3   **b.** 7   **c.** 14   **d.** 21

50. Wyatt and Cindy wanted to save $50.00 to buy a radio. Wyatt saved $27.25 and Cindy saved $18.50. Did they save enough money to buy the radio?

a. Yes.   **b.** No.

Name _____

Macmillan/McGraw-Hill
Mathematics

Cumulative 3 Test

Grade 4

Page 1

Choose the letter of your answer.

1. 7 ÷ 1

a. 6   **c.** 8
b. 7   **d.** not given

2. Which numbers are all factors of 60?

a. 0, 2, 3, 9
b. 1, 3, 12, 15
c. 2, 4, 8, 10
d. 3, 10, 12, 24

3. Which number is composite?

a. 61   **b.** 71   **c.** 87   **d.** 97

4. What fraction is shaded?

a. $\frac{3}{7}$ **b.** $\frac{4}{7}$ **c.** $\frac{3}{4}$ **d.** $\frac{4}{3}$

5. Complete. $\frac{7}{10} = \frac{\blacksquare}{50}$

a. 14   **b.** 35   **c.** 47   **d.** 70

6. What is $\frac{28}{3}$ in simplest form?

a. $1\frac{3}{9}$ **c.** $9\frac{1}{3}$
b. $3\frac{1}{9}$ **d.** not given

7. Which number is greatest?

a. $6\frac{4}{5}$ **b.** 6   **c.** $5\frac{6}{7}$ **d.** $6\frac{3}{4}$

8. What is $\frac{5}{6}$ of 30?

a. 5   **b.** 15   **c.** 20   **d.** 25

9. 6 × 396

a. 1,846   **c.** 2,346
b. 1,926   **d.** 2,376

10. 6)$6.42

a. $1.07   **c.** $17.00
b. $1.70   **d.** $107.00

11. $34.69 + $9.05

a. $34.64   **c.** $43.64
b. $34.74   **d.** not given

12. 8,000 ÷ 4

a. 2,000   **c.** 32
b. 320   **d.** 20

13. Which is the best estimate of 205 ÷ 5?

a. 4   **c.** 400
b. 40   **d.** 4,000

14. Estimate by rounding.

$9.84 − $3.46

a. $6.00   **c.** $8.00
b. $7.00   **d.** $13.00

15.   5,302
     − 2,709

a. 2,593
b. 2,693
c. 3,603
d. not given

16.   75
     × 5

a. 130
b. 145
c. 355
d. 375

17. About how much is 3 × $9.89?

a. about $30.00
b. about $36.00
c. about $300.00
d. about $360.00

MACMILLAN / McGRAW-HILL

18. 3 × $6.44

   a. $9.77   **c.** $18.32

   b. $18.22   **d.** $19.32

19. 369 ÷ 8

   a. 40 R9   **c.** 46 R1

   b. 41 R1   **d.** 46 R6

20. 630 ÷ 9

   a. 7   **c.** 700

   b. 70   **d.** 7,000

21. Estimate by rounding. 5,149 ÷ 5

   a. 100   **c.** 800

   b. 200   **d.** 1,000

22. 40 × 70

   a. 21,000   **c.** 280

   b. 2,800   **d.** 210

23. 5)‾83‾

   a. 10 R3   **c.** 16 R3

   b. 13 R3   **d.** not given

24. Find the perimeter.

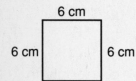

   a. 36 cm

   b. 24 cm

   c. 18 cm

   d. not given

25. Which is the best estimate for the capacity of a water pitcher?

   a. 2 mL   **c.** 2 L

   b. 20 mL   **d.** 20 L

26. How much time passes between 11:50 A.M. and 1:30 P.M.?

   a. 40 min   **c.** 2 h 40 min

   b. 1 h 40 min **d.** 25 h 40 min

27. Which pair of figures shows a flip?

a.   **c.**

b.   **d.**

28. Which word describes this figure?

   a. pentagon

   b. hexagon

   c. octagon

   d. not given

29. Which figure is symmetrical?

a.   **c.**

b.   **d.**

30. Which word describes this figure?

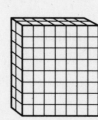

   a. pyramid

   b. prism

   c. sphere

   d. cylinder

31. What is the volume of the figure?

   a. 17 cubic units

   b. 30 cubic units

   c. 56 cubic units

   d. not given

MACMILLAN / McGRAW-HILL

32. Which is the best estimate for the length of a fourth-grade student's arm?

   a. 18 inches   **c.** 18 yards

   b. 18 feet   **d.** 18 miles

Use the diagram to answer Questions 33–35.

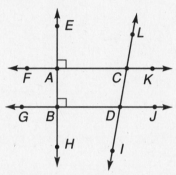

33. Point C is the vertex of _____.

   a. ∠ABD   **c.** ∠CDB

   b. ∠EAB   **d.** ∠LCK

34. Which two lines are parallel?

   a. $\overleftrightarrow{EH}$ and $\overleftrightarrow{LI}$ **c.** $\overleftrightarrow{FK}$ and $\overleftrightarrow{EH}$

   b. $\overleftrightarrow{GJ}$ and $\overleftrightarrow{FK}$ **d.** not given

35. Which names a line segment in the diagram?

   a. $\overline{BD}$ **c.** ∠LCK

   b. $\overleftrightarrow{EH}$ **d.** $\overrightarrow{AF}$

Use the grid to answer Question 36.

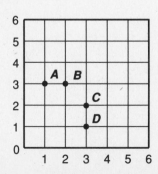

36. What is the ordered pair for point B?

   a. (1, 3)   **c.** (3, 2)

   b. (2, 3)   **d.** not given

Use the pictograph to answer Questions 37–39.

FLOWERS IN LANDVIEW GARDEN

Kind of Flower	Number
Rose	✿ ✿ ✿ ✿
Tulip	✿ ✿ ✿
Poppy	✿ ✿
Daisy	✿ ✿ ✿ ✿
Lily	✿
✿ = 20 flowers	

37. Which type of flower is least common at Landview Garden?

   a. rose   **c.** daisy

   b. lily   **d.** tulip

38. Landview Garden has the same number of which two flowers?

   a. tulip, daisy   **c.** daisy, rose

   b. rose, tulip   **d.** lily, poppy

39. How many more daisies than poppies are there at Landview Garden?

   a. 2   **b.** 10   **c.** 20   **d.** 40

Use the set of numbers to answer Questions 40–42.

     25, 39, 43, 53

40. What is the median?

   a. 25   **b.** 39   **c.** 41   **d.** 48

41. What is the range?

   a. 53   **b.** 41   **c.** 40   **d.** 28

42. What is the average?

    a. 160   **b.** 53   **c.** 40   **d.** 32

43. The manager of the Tire Hut has 48 tires and 6 racks for the tires. If the manager puts an equal number of tires on each rack, how many tires will be on each rack?

    a. 8   **b.** 42   **c.** 44   **d.** 54

44. Inés and Wally raked 36 yards. Inés raked twice as many yards as Wally raked. How many yards did Inés rake?

    a. 12   **b.** 18   **c.** 24   **d.** 72

45. Mrs. Cleary is putting 134 reports into files. Each file can hold 9 reports. How many files will Mrs. Cleary need?

    a. 9   **b.** 14   **c.** 15   **d.** 21

46. Lindy has 45 stamps. She divides the stamps into 5 equal piles. Then she takes the stamps from the first pile and gives 5 of those stamps to Joan. How many stamps are left in the first pile?

    a. 4   **b.** 5   **c.** 9   **d.** 25

47. Trevor bakes 12 cupcakes. Angela bakes 3 times as many cupcakes as Trevor. Then they sell 16 cupcakes. How many cupcakes are left?

    a. 3   **b.** 20   **c.** 32   **d.** 64

48. Complete and use the table to answer the question.

A ring, a necklace, and a bracelet are in a box. Gina, Mary, and Dawn each pick one of the items. Gina does not pick the ring or the bracelet. Dawn does not pick the ring. Who picks the bracelet?

	ring	bracelet	necklace
Gina	no	no	
Mary			
Dawn	no		

    a. Gina   **b.** Mary   **c.** Dawn

49. Laverne has twice as many marbles as Don. Terry has 6 more marbles than Don. Elise has 4 fewer marbles than Terry. Elise has 12 marbles. How many marbles does Laverne have?

    a. 4   **b.** 11   **c.** 20   **d.** 24

50. Use number sense.

Addie needs 2 pieces of rope to make a swing. She will need $8\frac{1}{3}$ feet of rope for each piece. She has a piece of rope 17 feet long. Does she have enough rope to make the swing?

    a. Yes.   **b.** No.

Macmillan/McGraw-Hill, MATHEMATICS IN ACTION
Grade 4, Cumulative 3 Test

MACMILLAN / McGRAW-HILL

Name

Macmillan/McGraw-Hill
Mathematics

End-Year Test

Grade 4

Page 1

Choose the letter of your answer.

1. Which amount is greatest?
- **a.** $24.52
- **c.** $24.39
- **b.** $24.48
- **d.** $24.61

2.
$$\begin{array}{r} 13 \\ -\ 0 \\ \hline \end{array}$$
- **a.** 0
- **b.** 13
- **c.** 130
- **d.** not given

3. Which numbers are all factors of 48?
- **a.** 3, 6, 9, 12
- **c.** 3, 4, 12, 15
- **b.** 4, 8, 12, 24
- **d.** 1, 2, 3, 5

4. What is $\frac{2}{5}$ of the set?

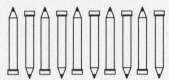

- **a.** 2
- **b.** 4
- **c.** 5
- **d.** 25

5. Which fraction is equivalent to $\frac{9}{18}$?
- **a.** $\frac{9}{36}$
- **b.** $\frac{1}{3}$
- **c.** $\frac{1}{2}$
- **d.** $\frac{18}{9}$

6. Compare. $1.6 \bullet 1\frac{6}{10}$
- **a.** >
- **b.** <
- **c.** =

7. Which number is least?
- **a.** $1\frac{4}{10}$
- **b.** $2\frac{1}{5}$
- **c.** $1\frac{7}{10}$
- **d.** $1\frac{3}{10}$

8. What is the decimal for $\frac{43}{100}$?
- **a.** 0.04
- **c.** 4.3
- **b.** 0.43
- **d.** not given

9. Compare. $5.2 \bullet 4.9$
- **a.** >
- **b.** <
- **c.** =

10. What fraction is shaded?

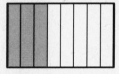

- **a.** $\frac{1}{3}$
- **b.** $\frac{3}{8}$
- **c.** $\frac{1}{2}$
- **d.** $\frac{5}{8}$

11. Estimate by rounding.
$$\$7.71 + \$3.28 + \$4.10$$
- **a.** $14.00
- **c.** $16.00
- **b.** $15.00
- **d.** $17.00

12. $2,312 + 4,896$
- **a.** 2,584
- **c.** 7,108
- **b.** 6,228
- **d.** not given

13. $25 \div 5$
- **a.** 29
- **b.** 24
- **c.** 10
- **d.** 5

14. 60×90
- **a.** 480
- **c.** 4,800
- **b.** 540
- **d.** not given

15. Which is the best estimate of 5×803?
- **a.** 400
- **c.** 4,000
- **b.** 1,300
- **d.** 13,000

16. $3 \times \$7.00$
- **a.** $21.00
- **c.** $2.10
- **b.** $18.00
- **d.** not given

17. What is $\frac{4}{9} + \frac{2}{9}$ in simplest form?
- **a.** $\frac{2}{9}$
- **b.** $\frac{6}{18}$
- **c.** $\frac{2}{3}$
- **d.** 6

MACMILLAN / McGRAW-HILL

18. 8)480

  a. 6   **c.** 600
  b. 60   **d.** 6,000

19. $9.95 ÷ 5

  a. $1.99   **c.** $49.75
  b. $19.90   **d.** not given

20. What is $\frac{7}{8} - \frac{3}{8}$ in simplest form?

  a. $\frac{1}{2}$ **c.** $1\frac{1}{4}$
  b. $\frac{5}{8}$ **d.** not given

21. 30 × 300

  a. 900,000   **c.** 9,000
  b. 90,000   **d.** 900

22. Estimate by using the front digits.

         13 × $65

  a. $70   **c.** $700
  b. $600   **d.** $6,000

23. 63 × 71

  a. 42,813   **c.** 639
  b. 4,473   **d.** not given

24. 50)8,000

  a. 16   **c.** 160
  b. 106   **d.** 1,060

25. 40)360

  a. 8   **b.** 9   **c.** 90   **d.** 120

26. Estimate by rounding.

      2.81 + 1.31

  a. 1   **b.** 2   **c.** 3   **d.** 4

27. 9 × 305

  a. 2,705   **c.** 2,745
  b. 2,714   **d.** 2,835

28. $\frac{5}{7} - \frac{2}{7}$

  a. $\frac{3}{7}$ **b.** $\frac{1}{2}$ **c.** $\frac{4}{7}$ **d.** 3

29. 40 × 5,000

  a. 2,000   **c.** 200,000
  b. 20,000   **d.** not given

30. Estimate by rounding.

        49 × 66

  a. 2,800   **c.** 3,500
  b. 3,200   **d.** 4,000

31. $64   **a.** $768
  × 12   **b.** $192
  ―――   **c.** $120
             d. $52

32. 2,100 ÷ 30

  a. 700   **b.** 70   **c.** 30   **d.** 7

33. 71 ÷ 30

  a. 2 R11   **c.** 20 R1
  b. 3 R1   **d.** not given

34. Which is the best estimate
of 9.8 − 7.4?

  a. less than 0.2
  b. less than 2
  c. greater than 2
  d. greater than 16

35. How much time passes between
6:15 P.M. and 11:59 P.M.?

  a. 5 h 16 min   **c.** 6 h 16 min
  b. 5 h 44 min   **d.** not given

36. You can usually go roller-skating outside when the temperature is _____.

   a. 80°C   **c.** 30°C
   b. 60°C   **d.** ⁻10°C

37. Which is the best estimate of the length of a candle?

   a. 10 cm   **c.** 10 m
   b. 100 cm   **d.** 100 m

38. Which figure shows perpendicular lines?

a.   **c.**

b.   **d.**

39. Find the perimeter.

   a. 10 ft
   b. 11 ft
   c. 13 ft
   d. not given

40. Which figure is a rectangle?

a.   **c.**

b.   **d.**

41. Which angle has point *E* as a vertex?

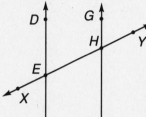

   a. ∠*DEX*
   b. ∠*GHY*
   c. ∠*EHI*
   d. not given

42. Which pair of figures shows a slide?

a.   **c.**

b.   **d.**

43. Which figure is symmetrical?

a.    **c.**

b.    **d.**

44. What is the volume of the figure?

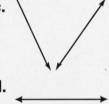

   a. 16 cubic units   **c.** 6 cubic units
   b. 8 cubic units   **d.** 4 cubic units

MACMILLAN / McGRAW-HILL

45. Measure this toy spoon to the nearest $\frac{1}{2}$ inch.

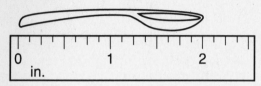

a. $1\frac{1}{2}$ in.   **c.** $2\frac{1}{2}$ in.
b. 2 in.   **d.** 3 in.

46. What is the area?

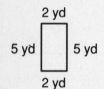

2 yd
5 yd   5 yd
2 yd

a. 20 square yd
b. 14 square yd
c. 10 square yd
d. 7 square yd

47. Which is the best estimate for the mass of a tricycle?

a. 100 mg   **c.** 10 kg
b. 10 g   **d.** 100 kg

48. What is the temperature shown?

a. ⁻10°F
b. 10°F
c. 70°F
d. 75°F

49. Which is the best estimate for the weight of a ten-year-old child?

a. 7 oz   **c.** 70 oz
b. 7 lb   **d.** 70 lb

50. Find the perimeter.

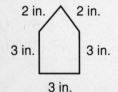

2 in.   2 in.
3 in.   3 in.
3 in.

a. 11 in.
b. 13 in.
c. 26 in.
d. not given

51. Predict how many times the spinner will land on ◆ in 15 spins.

a. 1   **b.** 3   **c.** 10   **d.** 15

52. There are 4 blue cubes, 3 white cubes, and 2 red cubes in a bag. What is the probability of picking a white cube?

a. $\frac{4}{7}$ **b.** $\frac{3}{7}$ **c.** $\frac{2}{9}$ **d.** $\frac{1}{3}$

Use the bar graph to answer Questions 53 and 54.

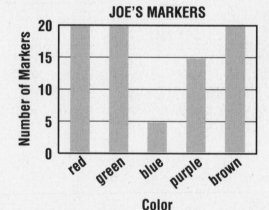

JOE'S MARKERS

53. How many green markers does Joe have?

a. 5   **b.** 10   **c.** 15   **d.** 20

54. Joe has the least number of which color marker?

a. purple   **c.** brown
b. green   **d.** blue

MACMILLAN / McGRAW-HILL

Use the set of numbers to answer Questions 55 and 56.

82, 73, 54, 63

55. What is the range?

a. 73   c. 54
b. 68   d. not given

56. What is the average?

a. 68   b. 73   c. 82   d. 272

Use the graph to answer Questions 57 and 58.

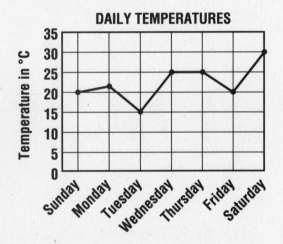

DAILY TEMPERATURES

57. Which day had the lowest temperature?

a. Sunday
b. Monday
c. Tuesday
d. Wednesday

58. What was the temperature on Wednesday?

a. 30°C   c. 20°C
b. 25°C   d. 15°C

Use the grid to answer Questions 59 and 60.

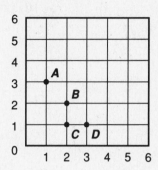

59. The ordered pair for point _D_ is _____.

a. (1, 3)   c. (2, 2)
b. (2, 1)   d. (3, 1)

60. Which letter is at the point (2, 1)?

a. _A_   b. _B_   c. _C_   d. _D_

61. Kay rode 12 blocks on her bike. Her brother rode 16 blocks. Uncle Jim rode more blocks than either of the children. What else do you need to know to find how many more blocks Uncle Jim rode than Kay and her brother?

a. the name of the city
b. how many blocks Uncle Jim rode
c. the name of Kay's brother
d. how many uncles Kay has

62. Use number sense.

Lucas and Dave want to mow 4 lawns in one afternoon. They each mow $1\frac{3}{4}$ lawns. Did they meet their goal?

a. Yes.   b. No.

63. Bryan has 350 pennies. Maria has 90 pennies. Which number sentence should you use to find how many more pennies Bryan has than Maria?

a. 350 + 90 = ■

b. 350 × 90 = ■

c. 350 ÷ 90 = ■

d. 350 − 90 = ■

64. Howie buys 4 cans of juice for $.60 each and 2 boxes of cereal for $2.00 each. How much change should he get from a $10 bill?

a. $.80   **c.** $6.40

b. $3.60   **d.** $9.20

65. In the dance recital, students plan to wear red, green, or white tights with black, white, or red costumes. How many different combinations can each student make?

a. 3   **b.** 5   **c.** 6   **d.** 9

66. Jani is buying groceries for her mother. She buys napkins for $2.25, butter for $1.89, meat for $6.69, and juice for $2.89. Is $15.00 enough to pay for these items?

a. Yes.   **b.** No.

67. The Stone River is 456 km long. It flows into the Cascade River, which is 839 km long. What is the total length of the two rivers combined?

a. 383 km   **c.** 1,295 km

b. 1,200 km   **d.** 1,751 km

68. There are 51 people at the picnic. If each picnic table holds 6 people, how many tables will be needed to seat everyone?

a. 21   **b.** 9   **c.** 8   **d.** 7

69. Wallace needs to sell $30.00 worth of raffle tickets to raise money for the school orchestra. He collects $19.75 on Monday and $11.25 on Tuesday. Has he collected enough money?

a. Yes.   **b.** No.

70. Find the pattern to solve.

Hogan's Fishing Store gives away 2 free hooks for every 8 lures sold, 4 hooks for every 16 lures sold, and 6 hooks for every 24 lures sold. Mr. Tryee buys 48 lures. How many hooks does he receive?

a. 8   **b.** 12   **c.** 30   **d.** 40

71. Sean has 86 baseball cards. Then James gives him 112 cards. How many more cards does Sean need to have 300 cards in his collection?

a. 26   **b.** 102   **c.** 198   **d.** 498

72. A newspaper prints 2,045 copies of its Friday edition and 3,963 copies of its weekend edition. The owner wants to know how many copies were printed in all. Which is the most reasonable answer?

a. 600   **c.** 4,208

b. 3,008   **d.** 6,008

MACMILLAN / McGRAW-HILL

73. Felipe went to the movies 20 times last year. He spent $4 each time. Which number sentence should you use to find how much he spent in all?

a. $20 \times \$4 = $ ▧

b. $20 + \$4 = $ ▧

c. $20 - \$4 = $ ▧

d. $20 \div \$4 = $ ▧

Use the diagram to answer Questions 74 and 75.

Tree Diagram	List
van — red	red van
van — blue	blue van
2-door — red	red 2-door
2-door — blue	blue 2-door
4-door — red	▧
4-door — blue	▧
station wagon — ▧	▧
station wagon — ▧	▧

74. Mr. Elias wants to buy a new car. He has a choice of a van, a 2-door sedan, a 4-door sedan, or a station wagon. All four kinds of cars come in either red or blue. How many choices does Mr. Elias have?

a. 16   **b.** 8   **c.** 4   **d.** 2

75. If Mr. Elias decides that he wants either a van or a station wagon, how many choices does he have?

a. 16   **b.** 8   **c.** 4   **d.** 2

MACMILLAN / McGRAW-HILL

Name _____

Macmillan/McGraw-Hill **Chapter 1 Test**
Mathematics

Grade 4
Form A

Choose the letter of your answer.

1. What is the value of 6 in the number 856,202,000?
a. 600,000
b. 6,000,000
c. 60,000,000
d. 600,000,000

2. Round 7,839 to the nearest hundred.
a. 8,000
b. 7,900
c. 7,840
d. 7,800

3. Which amount is greatest?
a. $32.70
b. $32.67
c. $32.59
d. $32.19

4. How much is 2 five-dollar bills, 1 quarter, and 3 pennies?
a. $2.28
b. $5.40
c. $10.28
d. not given

5. Round 94 to the nearest ten.
a. 90
b. 95
c. 99
d. 100

6. Which 3 coins make 40¢?
a. 2 dimes, 1 nickel
b. 1 quarter, 1 dime, 1 penny
c. 1 quarter, 1 dime, 1 nickel
d. not given

7. What is 100 less than 364,713?
a. 264,713
b. 354,713
c. 364,613
d. 364,703

8. Compare. 62,091 ● 6,289
a. >
b. <
c. =

9. Round 3,579 to the nearest thousand.
a. 3,000
b. 3,500
c. 3,600
d. 4,000

10. Which number is least?
a. 978
b. 789
c. 897
d. 798

11. Round $3.78 to the nearest ten cents.
a. $3.70
b. $3.75
c. $3.80
d. $4.00

12. What number is 1 hundred 3 tens 1 one?
a. 131
b. 331
c. 1,030
d. 100,301

13. Order from greatest to least.
$86.09, $87.27, $86.35
a. $87.27, $86.35, $86.09
b. $86.09, $87.27, $86.35
c. $86.35, $86.09, $87.27
d. $86.09, $86.35, $87.27

14. Cost: $.65 Given: $1.00 Change?
a. 5 dimes, 1 nickel
b. 1 half dollar, 3 nickels
c. 1 quarter, 1 dime
d. not given

15. Which is two hundred twenty-five?
a. 205
b. 225
c. 20,025
d. 200,205

Name _____

16. Find the amount.

a. $6.00
b. $5.92
c. $5.72
d. not given

Use the table to answer Questions 17–20.

Store	Roses	Tulips	Daisies
	Price		
Sue's Flowers	$2.50	$1.75	$.50
Bud and Bulb	$3.00	$1.85	$.50
Town Flowers	$3.50	■	$.50
Blooms, Inc.	$4.00	$1.85	$1.00

17. At Sue's Flowers a daisy costs ___
a. $.50
b. $.75
c. $1.50
d. $1.75

18. What is most likely the price of a tulip at Town Flowers?
a. $3.50
b. $2.50
c. $1.85
d. $1.00

19. Which store sells the most expensive roses?
a. Sue's Flowers
b. Bud and Bulb
c. Town Flowers
d. Blooms, Inc.

20. Which store sells the least expensive tulip?
a. Sue's Flowers
b. Bud and Bulb
c. Town Flowers
d. Blooms, Inc.

21. Tomas is buying a kite that costs $7.45. He wants to give the clerk the exact amount using the fewest bills and coins. Which bills and coins should Tomas use?
a. 1 five-dollar bill, 1 one-dollar bill, 4 dimes, and 1 nickel
b. 1 five-dollar bill, 2 one-dollar bills, 1 quarter, and 2 dimes
c. 1 five-dollar bill, 2 one-dollar bills, and 1 quarter
d. 7 one-dollar bills, 1 quarter, and 5 nickels

22. The hardware store placed an order for 1,575 nails. What is this number to the nearest hundred?
a. 700
b. 1,000
c. 1,500
d. 1,600

23. Use number sense.
If every seat is taken, about how many people are in a car?
a. about 1
b. about 5
c. about 30
d. about 200

24. Mr. Dougan has collected 2,693 baseball cards. What is this number in expanded form?
a. 200 + 60 + 9 + 3
b. 2,000 + 900 + 60 + 3
c. 2,000 + 600 + 90 + 3
d. 20,000 + 6,000 + 900 + 30

25. Use number sense.
Jane buys a pad of notebook paper. About how many sheets of paper are in the pad?
a. about 2
b. about 100
c. about 5,000
d. about 12,000

STOP

Name
Macmillan/McGraw-Hill   **Chapter 1 Test**
Mathematics

Grade 4
Form B
Page 1

Choose the letter of your answer.

1. What is the value of 9 in the number 942,618,000?
   a. 900,000 c. 90,000,000
   b. 9,000,000 **d.** 900,000,000

2. Round 356 to the nearest hundred.
   a. 400 b. 360 c. 350 d. 300

3. Which number is greatest?
   a. 486 b. 648 c. 468 **d.** 684

4. How much is 3 one-dollar bills, 2 dimes, and 3 nickels?
   a. $3.25 c. $4.30
   b. $3.35 d. not given

5. Round $7.55 to the nearest ten cents.
   a. $8.00 c. $7.50
   b. $7.60 d. $7.00

6. Which 3 coins make 45¢?
   a. 1 quarter, 1 dime, 1 penny
   b. 1 quarter, 1 dime, 1 nickel
   c. 1 quarter, 2 dimes
   d. not given

7. Which number is 100 less than 781,319?
   a. 681,319 c. 780,319
   b. 771,319 **d.** 781,219

8. Compare. 51,102 ● 51,021
   a. > b. < c. =

9. Round 2,469 to the nearest thousand.
   a. 2,000 c. 2,500
   b. 2,400 d. 3,000

10. Which amount is least?
    a. $3.19 **c.** $2.89
    b. $3.27 d. $3.00

11. Round $81.43 to the nearest dollar.
    a. $82.00 **c.** $81.00
    b. $81.50 d. $80.00

12. What number is 2 hundreds 4 tens 3 ones?
    a. 243 c. 2,043
    b. 342 d. 200,403

13. Order from greatest to least.
    $63.87, $63.79, $64.01
    a. $63.79, $63.87, $64.01
    b. $63.79, $64.01, $63.87
    c. $64.01, $63.87, $63.79
    d. $63.87, $63.79, $64.01

14. Cost: $1.30 Given: $2.00 Change?
    a. 3 quarters, 1 dime
    b. 1 half dollar, 3 nickels
    c. 2 quarters, 2 dimes
    d. not given

15. Which is six hundred sixty-nine?
    a. 609 c. 6,069
    b. 669 d. 600,609

---

16. Find the amount.

    a. $51.46 **c.** $5.46
    b. $5.71 d. not given

Use the table to answer Questions 17–20.

Store	Fine-Point	Medium-Point	Bold-Point
The Art Shop	137	96	305
Sam's Supply	135	280	81
City Stationer	120	200	105
Write Place	132	88	212

17. How many bold-point pens did Write Place sell?
    a. 212 b. 105 c. 96 d. 72

18. Which store sold the fewest fine-point pens?
    a. The Art Shop **c.** City Stationer
    b. Sam's Supply d. Write Place

19. How many medium-point pens did Sam's Supply sell?
    a. 81 b. 120 c. 200 **d.** 280

20. Which store sold more than 300 bold-point pens?
    a. The Art Shop c. City Stationer
    b. Sam's Supply d. Write Place

[STOP]

21. Emily has two bills and two coins, just enough to pay the exact amount for a pen that costs $2.60. Which bills and coins does Emily have?
    a. 2 one-dollar bills and 2 dimes
    b. 1 five-dollar bill, 1 one-dollar bill, and 2 dimes
    c. 2 one-dollar bills, 1 half dollar, and 1 dime
    d. 2 one-dollar bills, 2 quarters

22. The Sew Good Sewing Shop sold 21,559 spools of thread last year. What is this number to the nearest thousand?
    a. 20,000 **c.** 22,000
    b. 21,000 d. 23,000

23. Use number sense.
    If every seat is taken, about how many people are in a taxi?
    a. about 300 **c.** about 6
    b. about 50 d. about 1

24. Last week 4,250 people went to the movie theater at the mall. What is this number in expanded form?
    a. 40,000 + 2,000 + 50
    b. 4,000 + 200 + 50
    c. 4,000 + 200 + 5
    d. 400 + 20 + 5

25. Use number sense.
    Elizabeth buys a pack of pens. About how many pens are in the pack?
    a. about 1 c. about 3,000
    b. about 20 d. about 80,000

Name

Macmillan/McGraw-Hill   **Chapter 1 Test**   Grade 4
Mathematics   Form C

Mark your answer.

1. Write the value of 6 in the number 856,202,000.

   6,000,000

2. Round 7,839 to the nearest hundred.

   7,800

3. Ring the amount that is greatest.

   (\$32.70)   \$32.59
   \$32.67   \$32.19

4. How much is 2 five-dollar bills, 1 quarter, and 3 pennies?

   \$10.28

5. Round 94 to the nearest ten.

   90

6. Which 3 coins make 40¢?

   1 quarter, 1 dime, 1 nickel

7. What is 100 less than 364,713?

   364,613

8. Compare. Write >, <, or =.

   62,091 **>** 6,289

9. Round 3,579 to the nearest thousand.

   4,000

10. Ring the number that is least.

    978   **(789)**   897   798

11. Round \$3.78 to the nearest ten cents.

    \$3.80

12. What number is 1 hundred 3 tens 1 one?

    131

13. Order from greatest to least.
    \$86.09, \$87.27, \$86.35

    \$87.27, \$86.35, \$86.09

14. Cost: \$.65 Given: \$1.00
    What two coins make change?

    1 quarter, 1 dime

15. Write two hundred twenty-five as a number.

    225

MACMILLAN/McGRAW-HILL

Name

16. Write the amount.

    \$5.67

Use the table to answer Questions 17–20.

Store	Price		
	Roses	Tulips	Daisies
Sue's Flowers	\$2.50	\$1.75	\$.50
Bud and Bulb	\$3.00	\$1.85	\$.50
Town Flowers	\$3.50	▪	\$.50
Blooms, Inc.	\$4.00	\$1.85	\$1.00

17. At Sue's Flowers a daisy costs ____.

    \$.50

18. What is most likely the price of a tulip at Town Flowers?

    accept \$1.75 – \$1.85

19. Which store sells the most expensive roses?

    Blooms, Inc.

20. Which store sells the least expensive tulip?

    Sue's Flowers

21. Tomas is buying a kite that costs \$7.45. He wants to give the clerk the exact amount using the fewest bills and coins. Which bills and coins should Tomas use?

    1 \$5, 2 \$1, 1 quarter, and 2 dimes

22. The hardware store placed an order for 1,575 nails. Write this number to the nearest hundred.

    1,600

23. Use number sense.
    If every seat in a car is taken, about how many people are in the car?

    accept 2 – 9

24. Mr. Dougan has collected 2,693 baseball cards. Write this number in expanded form.

    2,000 + 600 + 90 + 3

25. Use number sense.
    Jane buys a pad of notebook paper. Are there about 2 sheets, 100 sheets, 5,000 sheets, or 12,000 sheets of paper in the pad?

    about 100 sheets

(STOP)

MACMILLAN/McGRAW-HILL

Name

Macmillan/McGraw-Hill Mathematics

Chapter 2 Test

Grade 4
Form A

Choose the letter of your answer.

1. 9 + 6
   a. 3 (b.) 15 c. 16 d. 54

2. What is the length of the goldfish?

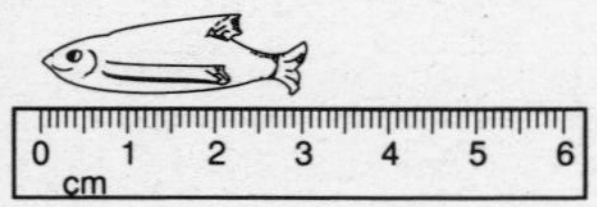

   (a.) 3 cm c. 10 cm
   b. 4 cm d. 30 cm

3. 6 + 7 = ■ + 6
   a. 13 c. 6
   (b.) 7 d. not given

4. 5 + 0
   a. 0
   b. 10
   c. 50
   (d.) not given

5. 4 + 3 + 2 + 8
   a. 12 b. 15 (c.) 17 d. 18

6. How wide is the stamp?

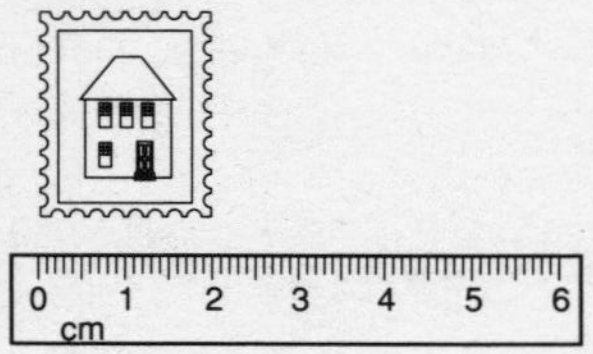

   a. 1 cm c. 3 cm
   (b.) 2 cm d. 4 cm

7. 4 − 0
   a. 0
   (b.) 4
   c. 8
   d. not given

8. 2 + 3 = ■ + 2
   (a.) 3 c. 9
   b. 5 d. not given

9. The length of a banana is about ________.
   a. 20 km (c.) 20 cm
   b. 20 m d. 20 dm

10. 10 − 3
   a. 3
   b. 6
   (c.) 7
   d. 13

11. How long is the bolt?

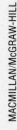

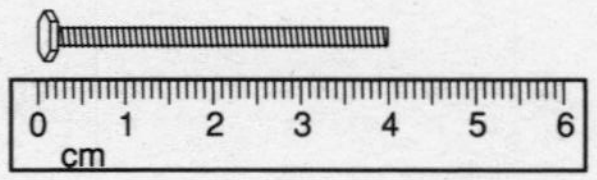

   a. 3 cm c. 5 cm
   (b.) 4 cm d. 6 cm

12. 3 + 9
   a. 6 (b.) 12 c. 27 d. 39

13. 12 − 4
   a. 0
   (b.) 8
   c. 10
   d. 14

Name

14. 7 + 1 = ■ + 7
   (a.) 1 c. 7
   b. 5 d. not given

15. Which is the best unit to measure the length of a pencil?
   a. dm c. m
   (b.) cm d. km

16. Which is the best unit to measure the length of a car?
   a. cm b. dm (c.) m d. km

17. 18 − 9
   a. 8
   (b.) 9
   c. 10
   d. 27

18. 11 − 3
   a. 3 b. 7 (c.) 8 d. 113

19. About how wide is the door to your classroom?
   (a.) about 1 meter
   b. about 1 kilometer
   c. about 1 centimeter
   d. about 1 decimeter

20. 5 + 2
   a. 52
   b. 10
   (c.) 7
   d. 3

21. 7 + 8
   a. 1 (b.) 15 c. 16 d. 78

22. What is the difference between 17 and 8?
   a. 6 (b.) 9 c. 11 d. 25

Use the bar graph to answer Questions 23–27.

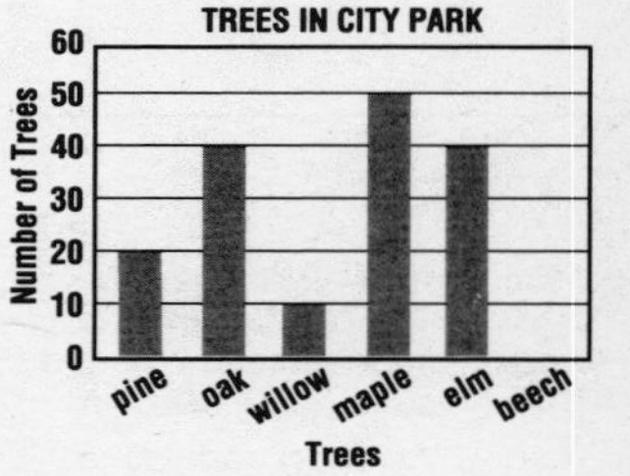

23. How many pine trees are there in City Park?
   (a.) 20 b. 30 c. 40 d. 50

24. There are more pine trees than ________.
   a. oak trees c. elm trees
   (b.) willow trees d. maple trees

25. In City Park there is an equal number of oak trees and ________.
   a. willow trees (c.) elm trees
   b. pine trees d. maple trees

26. How many beech trees are there in City Park?
   a. 160 b. 60 c. 16 (d.) 0

27. There are the greatest number of which kind of tree in City Park?
   a. pine trees (c.) maple trees
   b. oak trees d. elm trees

Name _____

28. What is the length of the paper clip?

- **a.** 1 cm
- **b.** 4 cm
- **c.** 5 cm
- **d.** 6 cm

29. Mr. Garcia bought suntan lotion for $4.98, a bag of ice for $.89, and a pair of sunglasses. What else do you need to know to find out how much he spent in all?
- **a.** the name of the store
- **b.** the type of suntan lotion he bought
- **c.** the temperature outside
- **d.** the price of the sunglasses

30. Karen had 9 beads. She gave 3 beads to Susan. How many beads did Karen have left?
- **a.** 0
- **b.** 3
- **c.** 6
- **d.** 12

31. Use number sense.
If the waiting room at the doctor's office is full, about how many people are in the waiting room?
- **a.** about 2
- **b.** about 25
- **c.** about 300
- **d.** about 5,000

STOP

Page 3

32. Cindy rode 2 km to the store. Then she rode 3 km to the bank. Then she rode 5 km back to her house. How far did she ride?
- **a.** 20 km
- **b.** 10 km
- **c.** 5 km
- **d.** 0 km

33. Mr. Chambers has a square field that measures 18 m on each side. The field has a square pasture in the middle that is 3 m from the edge of the field on all sides. What is the measurement of one side of the pasture in the middle?
- **a.** 15 m
- **b.** 12 m
- **c.** 6 m
- **d.** 3 m

Macmillan/McGraw-Hill, MATHEMATICS IN ACTION
Grade 4, Chapter 2, Form A

Name _____

14. 9 + 5 = ▢ + 9
  a. 5   **c.** 14
  b. 9   **d.** not given

15. Which is the best unit to measure the length of your thumb?
  a. dm   **c.** m
  b. cm   **d.** km

16. Which is the best unit to measure the length of a truck?
  a. cm **b.** dm **c.** m **d.** km

17.   16
    − 8
  a. 24 **b.** 12 **c.** 8 **d.** 0

18. 12 − 4
  a. 16 **b.** 8 **c.** 7 **d.** 4

19. To measure the distance between two cities, the best unit to use is ___
  a. meters   **c.** centimeters
  b. decimeters **d.** kilometers

20.   7
    + 5
  a. 2 **b.** 11 **c.** 12 **d.** 35

21. 9 + 8
  a. 1 **b.** 17 **c.** 72 **d.** 98

22. What is the difference between 15 and 7?
  a. 8 **b.** 9 **c.** 12 **d.** 22

Use the bar graph to answer Questions 23–27.

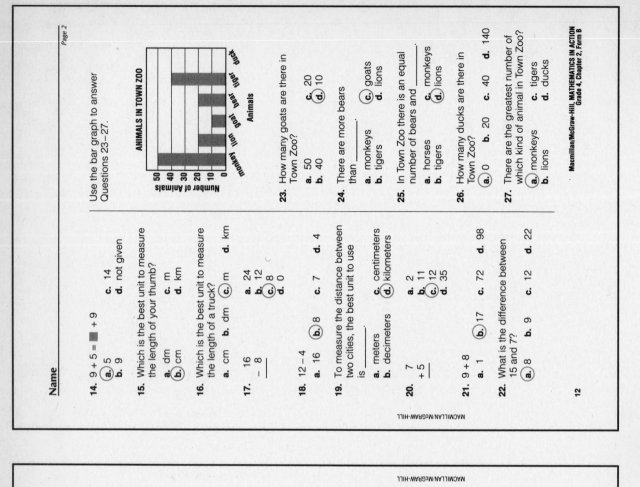

ANIMALS IN TOWN ZOO

23. How many goats are there in Town Zoo?
  a. 50 **c.** 20
  b. 40 **d.** 10

24. There are more bears than ___.
  a. monkeys **c.** goats
  b. tigers **d.** lions

25. In Town Zoo there is an equal number of bears and ___.
  a. horses **c.** monkeys
  b. tigers **d.** lions

26. How many ducks are there in Town Zoo?
  a. 0 **b.** 20 **c.** 40 **d.** 140

27. There are the greatest number of which kind of animal in Town Zoo?
  a. monkeys **c.** tigers
  b. lions **d.** ducks

Name _____

Macmillan/McGraw-Hill   Grade 4
Mathematics   Form B

Chapter 2 Test

Choose the letter of your answer.

1.   9
    + 4
  a. 94 **c.** 13
  b. 14 **d.** 5

2. What is the length of the caterpillar?
  a. 1 cm **c.** 30 cm
  b. 4 cm **d.** 40 cm

3. 5 + 6 = ▢ + 5
  a. 11 **c.** 6
  b. 7 **d.** not given

4.   3
    + 0
  a. 0 **c.** 6
  b. 3 **d.** not given

5. 8 + 3 + 1 + 3
  a. 16 **b.** 15 **c.** 9 **d.** 1

6. How long is the eraser?
  a. 2 cm **c.** 4 cm
  b. 3 cm **d.** 5 cm

7.   2
    − 0
  a. 0 **c.** 4
  b. 2 **d.** not given

8. 4 + 7 = ▢ + 4
  a. 4 **c.** 11
  b. 6 **d.** not given

9. The length of a pencil is about ___
  a. 15 cm **c.** 15 m
  b. 15 dm **d.** 15 km

10.   10
    − 2
  a. 2 **c.** 9
  b. 8 **d.** 12

11. How long is the hair clip?
  a. 2 cm **c.** 4 cm
  b. 3 cm **d.** 5 cm

12. 2 + 9
  a. 29 **b.** 18 **c.** 12 **d.** 11

13.   14
    − 5
  a. 29 **b.** 19 **c.** 9 **d.** 8

Name _____

Page 3

28. What is the length of the nail?

a. 6 cm   **c.** 50 cm
b. 10 cm   **d.** 60 cm

(STOP)

29. Marnie buys shampoo for $2.59, a hairbrush for $1.99, and toothpaste. What else do you need to know to find out how much she spends in all?

a. the price of the shampoo
b. the price of the toothpaste
c. what kind of shampoo she buys
d. what kind of toothpaste she buys

30. Lori has 7 blocks. She gives 4 blocks to Mark. How many blocks does Lori have now?

a. 3   **b.** 4   **c.** 7   **d.** 11

31. Use number sense.
If every seat in the train car is full, about how many people are in the train car?

a. about 5   **c.** about 900
b. about 100   **d.** about 25,000

32. Gloria drove 4 km to the zoo. Then she drove 2 km to the park. Then she drove 6 km home. How far did Gloria drive in all?

a. 0 km   **c.** 6 km
b. 2 km   **d.** 12 km

33. Mrs. Nolan has a square garden that measures 10 m on each side. The garden has a square plot in the middle that is 2 m from the edge of the garden on all sides. What is the measurement of one side of the plot in the middle?

a. 2 m   **c.** 6 m
b. 4 m   **d.** 8 m

TM55

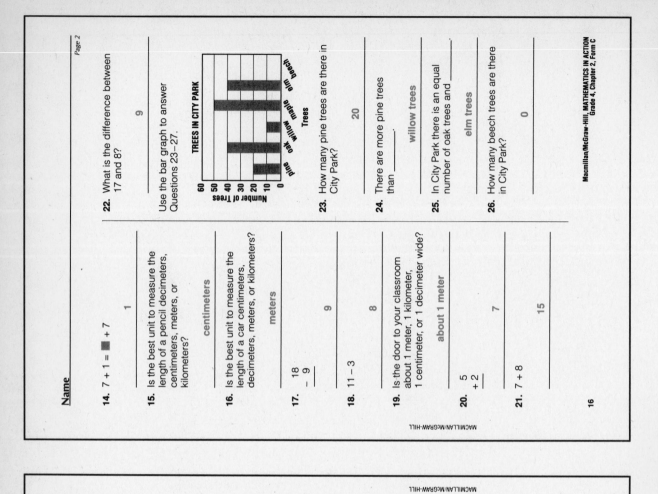

Name _____

Macmillan/McGraw-Hill
Mathematics

Grade 4
Form C

Page 1

Chapter 2 Test

Mark your answer.

1. 9
   + 6

   15

7. 4
   – 0

   4

2. What is the length of the goldfish?

   3 cm

8. 2 + 3 = ▪ + 2

   3

3. 6 + 7 = ▪ + 6

   7

9. Is the length of a banana about 20 kilometers, 20 meters, 20 centimeters, or 20 decimeters?

   about 20 centimeters

4. 5
   + 0

   5

10. 10
    – 3

    7

5. 4 + 3 + 2 + 8

   17

11. How long is the bolt?

   7

6. How wide is the stamp?

   2 cm

12. 3 + 9

   12

13. 12
    – 4

    8

Name _____

Page 2

14. 7 + 1 = ▪ + 7

   1

22. What is the difference between 17 and 8?

   9

15. Is the best unit to measure the length of a pencil decimeters, centimeters, meters, or kilometers?

   centimeters

Use the bar graph to answer Questions 23–27.

TREES IN CITY PARK

23. How many pine trees are there in City Park?

   20

16. Is the best unit to measure the length of a car centimeters, decimeters, meters, or kilometers?

   meters

24. There are more pine trees than _____ willow trees

17. 18
    – 9

    9

25. In City Park there is an equal number of oak trees and _____ elm trees

   7

18. 11 – 3

   8

26. How many beech trees are there in City Park?

   0

19. Is the door to your classroom about 1 meter, 1 kilometer, 1 centimeter, or 1 decimeter wide?

   about 1 meter

20. 5
    + 2

    7

21. 7 + 8

   15

Name _____

27. There are the greatest number of which kind of tree in City Park?

maple trees

28. What is the length of the paper clip?

```
 cm  0   1   2   3   4   5   6
```

5 cm

🛑 STOP

29. Mr. Garcia bought suntan lotion for $4.98, a bag of ice for $.89, and a pair of sunglasses. What else do you need to know to find out how much he spent in all?

the price of the sunglasses

30. Karen had 9 beads. She gave 3 beads to Susan. How many beads did Karen have left?

6

31. Use number sense.
If the waiting room at the doctor's office is full, are there about 2 people, 25 people, 300 people, or 5,000 people in the waiting room?

about 25 people

32. Cindy rode 2 kilometers to the store. Then she rode 3 kilometers to the bank. Then she rode 5 kilometers back to her house. How far did she ride?

10 kilometers

33. Mr. Chambers has a square field that measures 18 meters on each side. The field has a square pasture in the middle that is 3 meters from the edge of the field on all sides. What is the measurement of one side of the pasture in the middle?

12 meters

Macmillan/McGraw-Hill, MATHEMATICS IN ACTION
Grade 4, Chapter 2, Form C

15. What is the best estimate of 9,243 − 4,018?
a. 200
b. 500
c. 5,000
d. 6,000

16. 526 − 19
a. 507
b. 514
c. 517
d. 545

17.
$$\begin{array}{r} 2,946 \\ 1,072 \\ +\ 348 \end{array}$$
a. 3,356
b. 4,256
c. 4,366
d. not given

18. Find the perimeter.

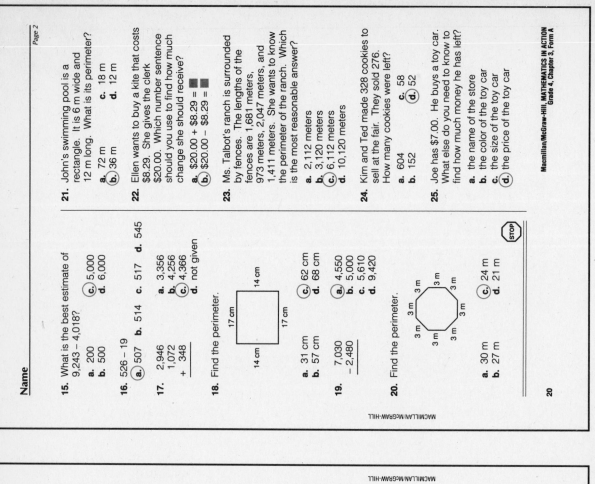

[rectangle: 17 cm, 14 cm, 17 cm, 14 cm]
a. 31 cm
b. 57 cm
c. 62 cm
d. 68 cm

19.
$$\begin{array}{r} 7,030 \\ -\ 2,480 \end{array}$$
a. 4,550
b. 5,000
c. 5,610
d. 9,420

20. Find the perimeter.

[octagon: 3 m each side]
a. 30 m
b. 27 m
c. 24 m
d. 21 m

21. John's swimming pool is a rectangle. It is 6 m wide and 12 m long. What is its perimeter?
a. 72 m
b. 36 m
c. 18 m
d. 12 m

22. Ellen wants to buy a kite that costs $8.29. She gives the clerk $20.00. Which number sentence should you use to find how much change she should receive?
a. $20.00 + $8.29 = ■■
b. $20.00 − $8.29 = ■■

23. Ms. Talbot's ranch is surrounded by fences. The lengths of the fences are 1,681 meters, 973 meters, 2,047 meters, and 1,411 meters. She wants to know the perimeter of the ranch. Which is the most reasonable answer?
a. 2,112 meters
b. 3,120 meters
c. 6,112 meters
d. 10,120 meters

24. Kim and Ted made 328 cookies to sell at the fair. They sold 276. How many cookies were left?
a. 604
b. 152
c. 58
d. 52

25. Joe has $7.00. He buys a toy car. What else do you need to know to find how much money he has left?
a. the name of the store
b. the color of the toy car
c. the size of the toy car
d. the price of the toy car

STOP

Macmillan/McGraw-Hill, **MATHEMATICS IN ACTION**
Grade 4, Chapter 3, Form A

MACMILLAN/McGRAW-HILL

Chapter 3 Test

Grade 4
Form A
Page 1

Choose the letter of your answer.

1. What is the best estimate of 2,072 + 1,386?
a. 10,000
b. 5,000
c. 3,000
d. 2,000

2. $72.15 + $99.07
a. $171.22
b. $161.22
c. $19.52
d. not given

3.
$$\begin{array}{r} 4,978 \\ -\ 2,763 \end{array}$$
a. 2,215
b. 2,341
c. 2,515
d. 7,741

4. Estimate.
$74.65 + $.24 + $25.32
a. $150.00
b. $100.00
c. $80.00
d. $70.00

5. Find the perimeter.

[triangle: 8 cm, 8 cm, 12 cm]
a. 10 cm
b. 20 cm
c. 25 cm
d. 28 cm

6.
$$\begin{array}{r} 342 \\ 29 \\ +\ 14 \end{array}$$
a. 374
b. 383
c. 385
d. not given

7. What is the best estimate of 4,321 − 2,215?
a. 1,000
b. 2,000
c. 3,000
d. 4,000

8.
$$\begin{array}{r} \$76.29 \\ -\ 59.15 \end{array}$$
a. $135.44
b. $27.24
c. $19.14
d. $17.14

9. 2,867 + 6,731
a. 9,598
b. 8,598
c. 3,864
d. not given

10. Find the perimeter.

[square: 6 m]
a. 36 m
b. 24 m
c. 18 m
d. 12 m

11. Estimate by rounding.
$4.32 + $6.89 + $4.99
a. $14.00
b. $15.00
c. $16.00
d. $17.00

12. $100.00 − $10.24
a. $79.76
b. $89.76
c. $89.86
d. $99.06

13.
$$\begin{array}{r} 2,500 \\ 1,000 \\ 700 \\ +\ 300 \end{array}$$
a. 5,200
b. 4,700
c. 3,500
d. not given

14. Find the perimeter.

[triangle: 8 cm, 6 cm, 9 cm, 15 cm]
a. 32 cm
b. 35 cm
c. 38 cm
d. 46 cm

Macmillan/McGraw-Hill, **MATHEMATICS IN ACTION**
Grade 4, Chapter 3, Form A   CMS Test ID 124031

MACMILLAN/McGRAW-HILL

TM58

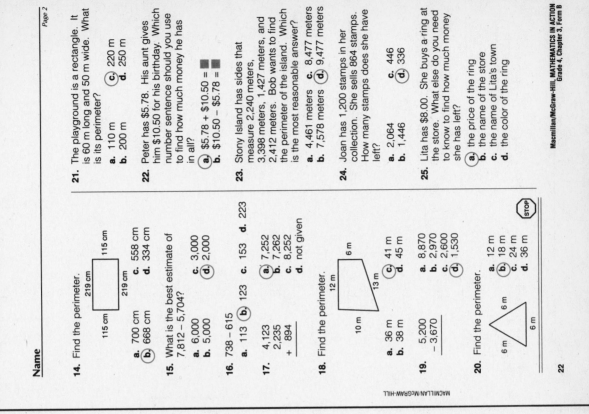

MACMILLAN/McGRAW-HILL

Name _____

Macmillan/McGraw-Hill · Mathematics

Grade 4
Form B

Chapter 3 Test

Page 1

Choose the letter of your answer.

1. What is the best estimate of 3,551 + 3,337?
   a. 8,000
   b. 7,000
   c. 5,000
   d. 1,000

2. $24.32 + $87.46
   a. $111.78
   b. $111.88
   c. $112.76
   d. not given

3. 7,128
   − 4,015
   _____
   a. 2,813
   b. 3,013
   c. 3,113
   d. 11,143

4. Estimate.
   $19.83 + $6.08 + $24.18
   a. $20.00
   b. $40.00
   c. $50.00
   d. $60.00

5. Find the perimeter.
   16 cm
   9 cm
   22 cm
   c. 43 cm
   d. 45 cm
   a. 47 cm
   b. 50 cm

6. 4,528
    110
   +   7
   _____
   a. 4,645
   b. 4,644
   c. 4,536
   d. not given

7. What is the best estimate of 9,215 − 4,328?
   a. 500
   b. 3,000
   c. 4,000
   d. 5,000

8. $36.50
   − 22.98
   _____
   a. $12.52
   b. $13.42
   c. $13.52
   d. $23.12

9. 3,632 + 4,536
   a. 7,569
   b. 8,268
   c. 9,218
   d. not given

10. Find the perimeter.
    120 m
    63 m   63 m
    120 m
    a. 183 m
    b. 366 m
    c. 386 m
    d. 449 m

11. Estimate by rounding.
    $21.36 + $5.79 + $9.38
    a. $34.00
    b. $35.00
    c. $36.00
    d. $41.00

12. $36.27 − $17.95
    a. $17.32
    b. $17.52
    c. $18.32
    d. $18.35

13. 9,000
     2,060
       840
    + 300
    _____
    a. 12,200
    b. 12,010
    c. 11,300
    d. not given

Macmillan/McGraw-Hill, MATHEMATICS IN ACTION
Grade 4, Chapter 3, Form B   CMS Test ID 124032

21

Name _____

Page 2

MACMILLAN/McGRAW-HILL

14. Find the perimeter.
    115 cm
    219 cm   219 cm
    115 cm
    a. 700 cm
    b. 668 cm
    c. 558 cm
    d. 334 cm

15. What is the best estimate of 7,812 − 5,704?
    a. 6,000
    b. 5,000
    c. 3,000
    d. 2,000

16. 738 − 615
    a. 113
    b. 123
    c. 153
    d. 223

17. 4,123
     2,235
    + 894
    _____
    a. 7,252
    b. 7,262
    c. 8,252
    d. not given

18. Find the perimeter.
    12 m
    10 m   6 m
           13 m
    a. 36 m
    b. 38 m
    c. 41 m
    d. 45 m

19. 5,200
    − 3,670
    _____
    a. 8,870
    b. 2,970
    c. 2,600
    d. 1,530

20. Find the perimeter.
    6 m
    6 m   6 m
    a. 12 m
    b. 18 m
    c. 24 m
    d. 36 m

21. The playground is a rectangle. It is 60 m long and 50 m wide. What is its perimeter?
    a. 110 m
    b. 200 m
    c. 220 m
    d. 250 m

22. Peter has $5.78. His aunt gives him $10.50 for his birthday. Which number sentence should you use to find how much money he has in all?
    a. $5.78 + $10.50 =
    b. $10.50 − $5.78 =

23. Stony Island has sides that measure 2,240 meters, 3,398 meters, 1,427 meters, and 2,412 meters. Bob wants to find the perimeter of the island. Which is the most reasonable answer?
    a. 4,461 meters
    b. 7,578 meters
    c. 8,477 meters
    d. 9,477 meters

24. Joan has 1,200 stamps in her collection. She sells 864 stamps. How many stamps does she have left?
    a. 2,064
    b. 1,446
    c. 446
    d. 336

25. Lita has $8.00. She buys a ring at the store. What else do you need to know to find how much money she has left?
    a. the price of the ring
    b. the name of the store
    c. the name of Lita's town
    d. the color of the ring

STOP

Macmillan/McGraw-Hill, MATHEMATICS IN ACTION
Grade 4, Chapter 3, Form B

22

TM59

Chapter 3 Test

Mark your answer.

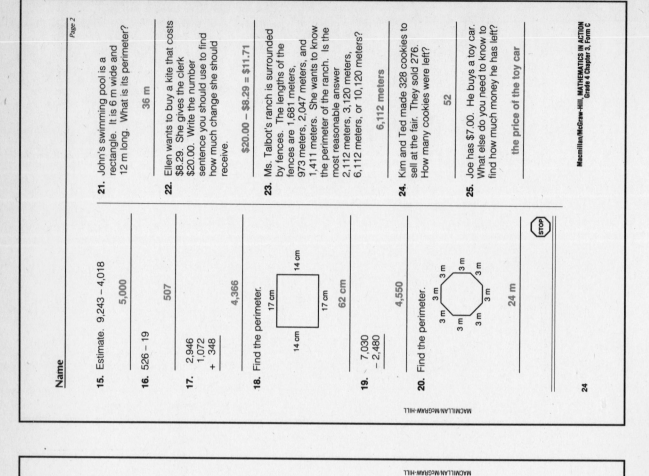

1. Estimate. 2,072 + 1,386

   3,000

2. $72.15 + $99.07

   $171.22

3. 4,978 − 2,763

   2,215

4. Estimate.

   $74.65 + $.24 + $25.32

   accept $90 − $100

5. Find the perimeter.

   (triangle: 8 cm, 8 cm, 12 cm)

   28 cm

6. 342
   29
   + 14

   385

7. Estimate. 4,321 − 2,215

   2,000

8. $76.29 − $59.15

   $17.14

9. 2,867 + 6,731

   9,598

10. Find the perimeter.

    (square: 6 m, 6 m, 6 m, 6 m)

    24 m

11. Estimate by rounding.

    $4.32 + $6.89 + $4.99

    $16.00

12. $100.00 − $10.24

    $89.76

13. 2,500
    1,000
    700
    + 300

    4,500

14. Find the perimeter.

    (triangle: 8 cm, 6 cm, 9 cm, 15 cm)

    38 cm

---

15. Estimate. 9,243 − 4,018

    5,000

16. 526 − 19

    507

17. 2,946
    1,072
    + 348

    4,366

18. Find the perimeter.

    (rectangle: 17 cm, 14 cm, 17 cm, 14 cm)

    62 cm

19. 7,030
    − 2,480

    4,550

20. Find the perimeter.

    (octagon: 3 m each side)

    24 m

21. John's swimming pool is a rectangle. It is 6 m wide and 12 m long. What is its perimeter?

    36 m

22. Ellen wants to buy a kite that costs $8.29. She gives the clerk $20.00. Write the number sentence you should use to find how much change she should receive.

    $20.00 − $8.29 = $11.71

23. Ms. Talbot's ranch is surrounded by fences. The lengths of the fences are 1,681 meters, 973 meters, 2,047 meters, and 1,411 meters. She wants to know the perimeter of the ranch. Is the most reasonable answer 2,112 meters, 3,120 meters, 6,112 meters, or 10,120 meters?

    6,112 meters

24. Kim and Ted made 328 cookies to sell at the fair. They sold 276. How many cookies were left?

    52

25. Joe has $7.00. He buys a toy car. What else do you need to know to find how much money he has left?

    the price of the toy car

STOP

Macmillan/McGraw-Hill
Mathematics

Chapter 4 Test

Grade 4
Form A
Page 1

Choose the letter of your answer.

1. About how long is a movie?
   a. about 2 hours
   b. about 2 minutes
   c. about 200 seconds
   d. about 20 minutes

2. Which is the best estimate for the mass of a bicycle?
   a. 15 mL   c. 15 kg
   b. 5 g   d. 5 L

3. On a good day for ice-skating, the temperature would be _____.
   a. 212°C
   b. 100°C
   c. 32°C
   d. -5°C

4. The time shown is _____.
   a. 7:25
   b. 6:25
   c. 6:05
   d. 5:30

5. Which is the best estimate for the temperature on a warm, sunny day?
   a. -10°C
   b. 0°C
   c. 5°C
   d. 25°C

6. The capacity of a kitchen sink is about _____.
   a. 10 mL   c. 100 L
   b. 10 L   d. 1 mL

7. What is the temperature shown?

   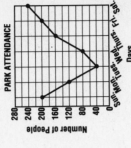

   a. 10°C
   b. 25°C
   c. 30°C
   d. 40°C

8. What time is 40 min after 7:10?
   a. 6:30
   b. 7:40
   c. 7:50
   d. 11:10

9. Which is the best estimate for the mass of a fourth-grade student?
   a. 31 g   c. 31 kg
   b. 310 g   d. 310 kg

10. The capacity of a cereal bowl is about _____.
    a. 250 mL   c. 250 L
    b. 1 L   d. 1 mL

11. How much time passes between 3:10 P.M. and 3:52 P.M.?
    a. 62 minutes
    b. 42 minutes
    c. 40 minutes
    d. 12 minutes

12. You usually need a jacket when the temperature outside is _____.
    a. 5°C
    b. 25°C
    c. 30°C
    d. 40°C

Page 2

Use the grid to answer Questions 13–16.

13. Which letter is at the point (4, 4)?
    a. V   c. X
    b. W   d. not given

14. The ordered pair for point Z is _____.
    a. (1, 4)
    b. (4, 1)
    c. (5, 5)
    d. not given

15. Which letter is at the point (3, 2)?
    a. W
    b. X
    c. Y
    d. not given

16. The ordered pair for point W is _____.
    a. (1, 1)
    b. (2, 2)
    c. (3, 2)
    d. not given

Use the graph to answer Questions 17–20.

PARK ATTENDANCE

17. On which day were the most people at the park?
    a. Tuesday
    b. Saturday
    c. Sunday
    d. Friday

18. How many people were at the park on Wednesday?
    a. 80   c. 160
    b. 120   d. 200

19. On which day were the fewest people at the park?
    a. Saturday
    b. Friday
    c. Thursday
    d. Tuesday

20. How many people were at the park on Thursday?
    a. 40   c. 160
    b. 120   d. 240

STOP

21. At 12 noon the temperature was 28°C. By 5:00 P.M. the temperature was 3° lower. At 9:00 P.M. it was 21°C. How much did the temperature change between 5:00 P.M. and 9:00 P.M.?

a. 7°C   **c.** 3°C
b. 4°C   **d.** 1°C

22. Al and Nick got to the park at 3:30 P.M. Their parents picked them up at 4:45 P.M. How long were the boys at the park?

a. 15 min   **c.** 1 h 15 min
b. 45 min   **d.** 1 h 45 min

23. Jan is cleaning her yard. She spends 1 hour raking leaves. She then takes about 45 minutes to pick up sticks and sweep the sidewalk. About how long does she take to clean the yard?

a. about 2 hours
b. about 1 hour
c. about 45 minutes
d. about 30 minutes

24. Otis has 459 old coins. He sells 128 coins and buys 205 stamps. How many coins does he have left?

a. 536   **c.** 254
b. 331   **d.** 128

25. Mrs. Howe buys a book for $13.73. She gives the clerk $20.00. Which number sentence should you use to find how much change she should receive?

a. $20.00 – $13.73 = ▦ ▦
b. $20.00 + $13.73 = ▦ ▦

Macmillan/McGraw-Hill, MATHEMATICS IN ACTION
Grade 4, Chapter 4, Form A

Name

Macmillan/McGraw-Hill   **Chapter 4 Test**
Mathematics   Grade 4
Form B
Page 1

Choose the letter of your answer.

1. About how long does it take to sing a song?
   - a. about 3 seconds
   - **b. about 3 minutes**
   - c. about 3 hours
   - d. about 30 hours

2. Which is the best estimate for the mass of a large television?
   - **a. 20 kg**
   - b. 2 g
   - c. 20 mL
   - d. 2 L

3. At what temperature would ice cream probably start melting?
   - a. -20°C
   - b. -10°C
   - c. 0°C
   - **d. 10°C**

4. What time does the clock show?
   - a. 4:20
   - b. 4:25
   - **c. 5:20**
   - d. 5:40

5. Which is the best estimate for the temperature on a cold, snowy day?
   - **a. -5°C**
   - b. 5°C
   - c. 20°C
   - d. 50°C

6. The capacity of a water glass is about ___
   - a. 250 L
   - b. 25 L
   - c. 25 mL
   - **d. 250 mL**

7. What is the temperature shown?
   - a. 15°C
   - b. 0°C
   - **c. -10°C**
   - d. -20°C

8. What time is 30 min before 5:15?
   - a. 6:15
   - b. 5:45
   - **c. 4:45**
   - d. 4:30

9. Which is the best estimate for the mass of a nine-year-old child?
   - a. 10 kg
   - **b. 25 kg**
   - c. 25 g
   - d. 90 g

10. The capacity of a cooking pot is about ___
    - **a. 1 L**
    - b. 25 mL
    - c. 2 mL
    - d. 50 L

11. How much time passes between 2:25 P.M. and 2:57 P.M.?
    - a. 25 minutes
    - b. 28 minutes
    - **c. 32 minutes**
    - d. 82 minutes

12. You can usually wear shorts when the temperature outside is ___
    - a. 0°C
    - b. 5°C
    - c. 10°C
    - **d. 30°C**

Name

Use the grid to answer Questions 13–16.

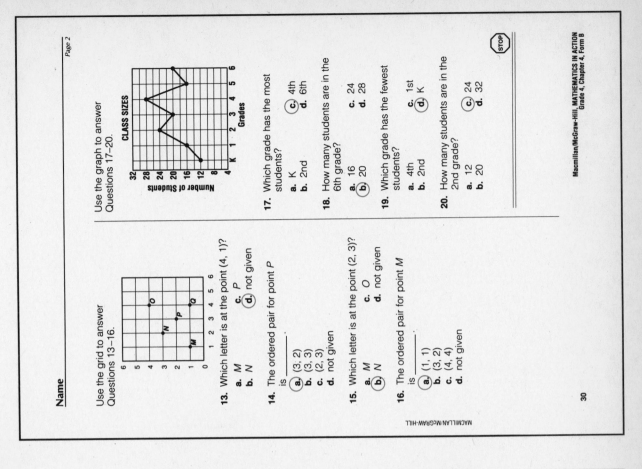

13. Which letter is at the point (4, 1)?
    - a. M
    - b. N
    - c. P
    - **d. not given**

14. The ordered pair for point P is ___
    - **a. (3, 2)**
    - b. (3, 3)
    - c. (2, 3)
    - d. not given

15. Which letter is at the point (2, 3)?
    - a. M
    - **b. N**
    - c. O
    - d. not given

16. The ordered pair for point M is ___
    - **a. (1, 1)**
    - b. (4, 2)
    - c. (4, 4)
    - d. not given

Use the graph to answer Questions 17–20.

CLASS SIZES

17. Which grade has the most students?
    - a. K
    - b. 2nd
    - c. 4th
    - d. 6th

18. How many students are in the 6th grade?
    - a. 16
    - **b. 20**
    - c. 24
    - d. 28

19. Which grade has the fewest students?
    - a. 4th
    - b. 2nd
    - c. 1st
    - **d. K**

20. How many students are in the 2nd grade?
    - a. 12
    - b. 20
    - c. 24
    - d. 32

STOP

TM63

Name ____________________

21. At 7:00 A.M. the temperature was 24°C. By 12 noon it was 2° higher. At 3:00 P.M. it was 29°C. How much did the temperature change between 12 noon and 3:00 P.M.?

a. 2°C　　**c.** 4°C
(b.) 3°C　　**d.** 6°C

22. The movie started at 6:30 P.M. It ended at 8:15 P.M. How long was the movie?

a. 2 h 15 min　　**c.** 1 h 15 min
(b.) 1 h 45 min　　**d.** 45 min

23. Rhonda is painting the living room. She takes 2 hours to paint the walls and about 40 minutes to paint the ceiling. About how long does she take to paint the living room?

a. about 20 minutes
b. about 40 minutes
c. about 2 hours
(d.) about 3 hours

24. The baker makes 212 loaves of bread and 434 muffins. He sells 186 muffins. How many muffins are left?

a. 26　　**(c.)** 248
b. 146　　**d.** 398

25. Ernie buys a hammer and nails for $23.27. He gives the clerk $25.00. Which number sentence should you use to find how much change he should receive?

(a.) $25.00 − $23.27 = ■
b. $25.00 + $23.27 = ■

MACMILLAN/McGRAW-HILL

MACMILLAN/McGRAW-HILL

Name

Use the grid to answer Questions 13–16.

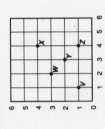

13. Which letter is at the point (4, 4)?

X

14. The ordered pair for point Z is _____.

(4, 1)

15. Which letter is at the point (3, 2)?

Y

16. The ordered pair for point W is _____.

(2, 3)

Use the graph to answer Questions 17–20.

PARK ATTENDANCE

Number of People — 280 240 200 160 120 80 40 0

Days — Sun. Mon. Tue. Wed. Thurs. Fri. Sat.

17. On which day were the most people at the park?

Saturday

18. How many people were at the park on Wednesday?

80

19. On which day were the fewest people at the park?

Tuesday

20. How many people were at the park on Thursday?

160

STOP

Name

Macmillan/McGraw-Hill
Mathematics

Chapter 4 Test

Grade 4
Form C

Mark your answer.

1. Is the length of a movie about 2 hours, 2 minutes, 200 seconds, or 20 minutes?

about 2 hours

2. Is the best estimate for the mass of a bicycle 15 milliliters, 5 grams, 15 kilograms, or 5 liters?

15 kilograms

3. On a good day for ice-skating, would the temperature be 212°C, 100°C, 32°C, or -5°C?

-5°C

4. The time shown is _____.

6:25

5. Is the best estimate for the temperature on a warm, sunny day -10°C, 0°C, 5°C, or 25°C?

25°C

6. Is the capacity of a kitchen sink about 10 milliliters, 10 liters, 100 liters, or 1 milliliter?

about 10 liters

7. What is the temperature shown?

40°C

8. What time is 40 minutes after 7:10?

7:50

9. Is the best estimate for the mass of a fourth-grade student 31 grams, 310 grams, 31 kilograms, or 310 kilograms?

31 kilograms

10. Is the capacity of a cereal bowl about 250 liters, 1 liter, 250 milliliters, or 1 milliliter?

about 250 milliliters

11. How much time passes between 3:10 P.M. and 3:52 P.M.?

42 minutes

12. Do you usually need a jacket when the temperature outside is 5°C, 25°C, 30°C, or 40°C?

5°C

Name _____

21. At 12 noon the temperature was 28°C. By 5:00 P.M. the temperature was 3° lower. At 9:00 P.M. it was 21°C. How much did the temperature change between 5:00 P.M. and 9:00 P.M.?

_____

4°C

22. Al and Nick got to the park at 3:30 P.M. Their parents picked them up at 4:45 P.M. How long were the boys at the park?

_____

1 hour 15 minutes

23. Jan is cleaning her yard. She spends 1 hour raking leaves. She then takes about 45 minutes to pick up sticks and sweep the sidewalk. In hours, about how long does she take to clean the yard?

_____

about 2 hours

24. Otis has 459 old coins. He sells 128 coins and buys 205 stamps. How many coins does he have left?

_____

331

25. Mrs. Howe buys a book for $13.73. She gives the clerk $20.00. Write the number sentence you should use to find how much change she should receive.

_____

$20.00 − $13.73 = $6.27

Macmillan/McGraw-Hill, MATHEMATICS IN ACTION
Grade 4, Chapter 4, Form C

35

TM66

Name _____

Macmillan/McGraw-Hill
Mathematics

Chapter 5 Test

Grade 4
Form A

Page 1

Choose the letter of your answer.

1. 2)‾16‾
   - **a.** 2
   - **b.** 6
   - **c.** 8
   - **d.** not given

2. Find the area.

   3 m — 4 m / 4 m — 3 m
   - **a.** 7 square m
   - **b.** 12 square m
   - **c.** 14 square m
   - **d.** 24 square m

3. Which of the following has only even numbers?
   - **a.** 3, 12, 24, 27
   - **b.** 7, 9, 18, 24
   - **c.** 3, 11, 13, 24
   - **d.** 12, 24, 36, 48

4. 4 × ▮ = 36
   - **a.** 3
   - **b.** 9
   - **c.** 15
   - **d.** 18

5. 0 + 5
   - **a.** 0
   - **b.** 1
   - **c.** 5
   - **d.** 10

6. 2 × 7
   - **a.** 21
   - **b.** 14
   - **c.** 10
   - **d.** not given

7. What is the area of a square with 7-cm sides?
   - **a.** 52 square cm
   - **b.** 49 square cm
   - **c.** 28 square cm
   - **d.** 14 square cm

8. Which number is prime?
   - **a.** 49
   - **b.** 36
   - **c.** 15
   - **d.** 3

9. 9)‾81‾
   - **a.** 9
   - **b.** 12
   - **c.** 18
   - **d.** not given

10. Which numbers are all factors of 36?
    - **a.** 1, 8, 9, 36
    - **b.** 4, 6, 9, 36
    - **c.** 5, 6, 8, 9
    - **d.** 1, 4, 6, 7

11. (3 × 3) × ▮ = 3 × (3 × 7)
    - **a.** 2
    - **b.** 3
    - **c.** 7
    - **d.** 21

12. 6 ÷ 3
    - **a.** 4
    - **b.** 3
    - **c.** 1
    - **d.** not given

13. What is the area of a rectangle 8 cm long and 2 cm wide?
    - **a.** 16 square cm
    - **b.** 15 square cm
    - **c.** 12 square cm
    - **d.** 10 square cm

14. Which number is composite?
    - **a.** 1
    - **b.** 2
    - **c.** 19
    - **d.** 21

15. 5 × 8
    - **a.** 13
    - **b.** 40
    - **c.** 48
    - **d.** not given

Name _____

Page 2

16. 18 ÷ ▮ = 9
    - **a.** 2
    - **b.** 5
    - **c.** 7
    - **d.** 10

17. 5)‾25‾
    - **a.** 15
    - **b.** 7
    - **c.** 5
    - **d.** not given

18. 7 × 0
    - **a.** 0
    - **b.** 1
    - **c.** 3
    - **d.** 7

19. Find the area in square centimeters.

    - **a.** 6 square cm
    - **b.** 8 square cm
    - **c.** 9 square cm
    - **d.** 12 square cm

20. Which numbers are all multiples of 5?
    - **a.** 5, 7, 13, 18
    - **b.** 5, 15, 25, 40
    - **c.** 5, 10, 15, 18
    - **d.** 10, 12, 20, 36

21. 3 × 7
    - **a.** 21
    - **b.** 18
    - **c.** 7
    - **d.** not given

22. 48 ÷ 8
    - **a.** 12
    - **b.** 9
    - **c.** 8
    - **d.** 6

23. Which of the following has only odd numbers?
    - **a.** 8, 13, 21, 24
    - **b.** 15, 19, 23, 27
    - **c.** 3, 11, 14, 21
    - **d.** 13, 15, 18, 24

24. 7 × 9
    - **a.** 63
    - **b.** 54
    - **c.** 36
    - **d.** 16

Use the pictograph to answer Questions 25 – 28.

TAXIS IN LONGVIEW CITY

City Taxis	🚕🚕🚕🚕🚕🚕🚕
ABC Taxis	🚕🚕🚕🚕🚕🚕
Acme Taxi Co.	🚕🚕🚕🚕
Harry's Taxis	🚕

🚕 = 50 taxis

25. How many taxis does ABC Taxis own?
    - **a.** 50
    - **b.** 60
    - **c.** 150
    - **d.** 225

26. What is each 🚕 worth?
    - **a.** 200 taxis
    - **b.** 150 taxis
    - **c.** 100 taxis
    - **d.** 50 taxis

27. How many taxis does City Taxis own?
    - **a.** 150
    - **b.** 200
    - **c.** 350
    - **d.** 450

28. How many more taxis does Acme Taxi Co. own than Harry's Taxis?
    - **a.** 50
    - **b.** 75
    - **c.** 100
    - **d.** 200

STOP

TM67

29. James has 45 model planes. He puts them on shelves that hold 9 planes each. Which number sentence should you use to find how many shelves he will fill with the planes?

a. $45 \times 9 =$
b. $45 + 9 =$
c. $45 \div 9 =$
d. $45 - 9 =$

30. What is the area of a rectangular strip of paper 9 cm long and 2 cm wide?

a. 11 square cm
b. 18 square cm
c. 20 square cm
d. 29 square cm

31. A new movie is playing at the Palace Theater. The first show is at 1:30. The second show is at 3:45. The third show is at 6:00. If the pattern continues, at what time is the fifth show?

a. 9:30
b. 9:45
c. 10:15
d. 10:30

32. Mr. Gomez wants to divide the class into 3 equal lines. There are 27 children in the class. How many children should be in each line?

a. 24
b. 9
c. 7
d. 5

33. Tanya mailed 5 cards yesterday. She mailed 8 cards today. She received 4 cards. How many cards did she mail in all?

a. 4
b. 9
c. 13
d. 17

Macmillan/McGraw-Hill, MATHEMATICS IN ACTION
Grade 4, Chapter 5, Form A

Name

Chapter 5 Test

Choose the letter of your answer.

1. 3)15
- **a.** 3
- **b.** 5 *(circled)*
- **c.** 45
- **d.** not given

2. Find the area.

9 mm × 9 mm square
- **a.** 81 square mm *(circled)*
- **b.** 40.5 square mm
- **c.** 36 square mm
- **d.** 9 square mm

3. Which of the following has only odd numbers?
- **a.** 1, 3, 7, 8
- **b.** 3, 7, 13, 32
- **c.** 3, 7, 9, 13 *(circled)*
- **d.** 2, 5, 7, 9

4. 5 × ▓ = 45
- **a.** 10
- **b.** 9 *(circled)*
- **c.** 5
- **d.** 4

5. 0 + 14
- **a.** 14
- **b.** 7
- **c.** 1
- **d.** 0 *(circled)*

6. 3 × 6
- **a.** 18 *(circled)*
- **b.** 12
- **c.** 9
- **d.** not given

7. What is the area of a rectangle 5 cm long and 2 cm wide?
- **a.** 3 square cm
- **b.** 7 square cm
- **c.** 10 square cm *(circled)*
- **d.** 14 square cm

8. Which number is prime?
- **a.** 5 *(circled)*
- **b.** 9
- **c.** 10
- **d.** 14

9. 7)42
- **a.** 7
- **b.** 6 *(circled)*
- **c.** 3
- **d.** not given

10. Which numbers are all factors of 24?
- **a.** 1, 3, 8, 24 *(circled)*
- **b.** 1, 4, 6, 7
- **c.** 2, 6, 8, 9
- **d.** 3, 6, 7, 24

11. (8 × 3) × 3 = 8 × (3 × ▓)
- **a.** 72
- **b.** 24
- **c.** 6
- **d.** 3 *(circled)*

12. 8 ÷ 2
- **a.** 2
- **b.** 4 *(circled)*
- **c.** 16
- **d.** not given

13. What is the area of a square with 3-cm sides?
- **a.** 3 square cm
- **b.** 9 square cm *(circled)*
- **c.** 18 square cm
- **d.** 81 square cm

14. Which number is composite?
- **a.** 36 *(circled)*
- **b.** 13
- **c.** 7
- **d.** 3

15. 7 × 8
- **a.** 15
- **b.** 49
- **c.** 64
- **d.** not given *(circled)*

Macmillan/McGraw-Hill, MATHEMATICS IN ACTION
Grade 4, Chapter 5, Form B   CMS Test ID 124052

Name

16. ▓ ÷ 4 = 4
- **a.** 3
- **b.** 8
- **c.** 16 *(circled)*
- **d.** 36

17. 6)30
- **a.** 10
- **b.** 6
- **c.** 4
- **d.** not given *(circled)*

18. 5 × 0
- **a.** 10
- **b.** 5
- **c.** 1
- **d.** 0 *(circled)*

19. Find the area in square centimeters.
- **a.** 9 square cm *(circled)*
- **b.** 12 square cm
- **c.** 15 square cm
- **d.** 25 square cm

20. Which numbers are all multiples of 7?
- **a.** 1, 7, 14, 21
- **b.** 7, 14, 20, 28
- **c.** 7, 21, 28, 56 *(circled)*
- **d.** 21, 28, 36, 42

21. 6 × 9
- **a.** 48
- **b.** 54 *(circled)*
- **c.** 72
- **d.** not given

22. 36 ÷ 9
- **a.** 9
- **b.** 5
- **c.** 4 *(circled)*
- **d.** 3

23. Which of the following has only even numbers?
- **a.** 2, 4, 6, 9
- **b.** 4, 10, 12, 15
- **c.** 6, 10, 13, 18
- **d.** 4, 8, 12, 22 *(circled)*

24. 4 × 7
- **a.** 11
- **b.** 16
- **c.** 21
- **d.** 28 *(circled)*

Use the pictograph to answer Questions 25–28.

DAILY MILK PRODUCTION IN THE U.S.

Wisconsin	🐄🐄🐄🐄🐄
Minnesota	🐄🐄🐄
California	🐄🐄🐄🐄
New York	🐄🐄

🐄 = 1,000 gallons

25. Which two states produce about the same amount of milk?
- **a.** Wisconsin and New York
- **b.** California and Minnesota *(circled)*
- **c.** California and New York
- **d.** New York and Minnesota

26. What is each 🐄 worth?
- **a.** 50 gal
- **b.** 100 gal
- **c.** 1,000 gal *(circled)*
- **d.** 2,500 gal

27. How much milk is produced daily in New York?
- **a.** 1,000 gal
- **b.** 2,000 gal *(circled)*
- **c.** 3,500 gal
- **d.** 4,000 gal

28. How much more milk is produced in Wisconsin than in California?
- **a.** 2,000 gal
- **b.** 1,500 gal
- **c.** 1,000 gal *(circled)*
- **d.** 500 gal

STOP

Macmillan/McGraw-Hill, MATHEMATICS IN ACTION
Grade 4, Chapter 5, Form B

29. Theresa has 21 toy cars. She puts them in baskets that hold 7 toy cars each. Which number sentence should you use to find how many baskets she will fill with the toy cars?

a. 21 + 7 = ▨
b. 21 × 7 = ▨
c. 21 + 7 = ▨
d. 21 − 7 = ▨

30. What is the area of a rectangular bookmark 4 cm wide and 9 cm long?

a. 5 square cm
b. 13 square cm
c. 26 square cm
d. 36 square cm

31. Nancy stacks 7 rows of cans in a pattern for a store display. She puts 31 cans on the bottom row, 27 cans in the row above that, and 23 cans in the next row. How many cans will be in the top row?

a. 3
b. 4
c. 7
d. 9

32. There are 54 students riding in 6 vans. If there is an equal number of students in each van, how many students are in each van?

a. 10
b. 9
c. 8
d. 6

33. Nat read 9 books last month. He read 6 books this month. He saw 3 movies this month. How many books did he read in all?

a. 15
b. 18
c. 27
d. 54

Name _____

Macmillan/McGraw-Hill
Mathematics

Chapter 5 Test

Grade 4
Form C

Mark your answer.

1. 2)16   8

2. Find the area.

   [square: 4 m × 3 m]

   12 square m

3. Ring the even numbers.

   3, 11, (12), (24), 27, (36)

4. 4 × ▦ = 36   9

5. 0 + 5   0

6. 2 × 7   14

7. What is the area of a square with 7-cm sides?

   49 square cm

8. Is 49, 36, 15, or 3 a prime number?   3

9. 9)81   9

10. Ring the factors of 36.

    (4), 5, (6), 8, (9), (36)

11. (3 × 3) × ▦ = 3 × (3 × 7)   7

12. 6 ÷ 3   2

13. What is the area of a rectangle 8 cm long and 2 cm wide?

    16 square cm

14. Is 1, 2, 19, or 21 a composite number?   21

15. 5 × 8   40

16. 18 ÷ ▦ = 9   2

Macmillan/McGraw-Hill, MATHEMATICS IN ACTION
Grade 4, Chapter 5, Form C

Name _____

17. 5)25   5

18. 7 × 0   0

19. Find the area in square centimeters.

    [grid]

    6 square cm

20. Ring the multiples of 5.

    3, (5), 12, (15), 18, (25)

21. 3 × 7   21

22. 48 ÷ 8   6

23. Ring the odd numbers.

    (3), 8, (11), 12, 14, (15)

24. 7 × 9   63

TAXIS IN LONGVIEW CITY

Use the pictograph to answer Questions 25 - 28.

City Taxis	🚕🚕🚕🚕
ABC Taxis	🚕🚕🚕
Acme Taxi Co.	🚕
Harry's Taxis	🚕

🚕 = 50 taxis

25. How many taxis does ABC Taxis own?   150

26. What is each 🚕 worth?   **50 taxis**

27. How many taxis does City Taxis own?   200

28. How many more taxis does Acme Taxi Co. own than Harry's Taxis?   50

(STOP)

Macmillan/McGraw-Hill, MATHEMATICS IN ACTION
Grade 4, Chapter 5, Form C

29. James has 45 model planes. He puts them on shelves that hold 9 planes each. Write the number sentence that you should use to find how many shelves he will fill with the planes.

45 ÷ 9 = 5

30. What is the area of a rectangular strip of paper 9 cm long and 2 cm wide?

18 square cm

31. A new movie is playing at the Palace Theater. The first show is at 1:30. The second show is at 3:45. The third show is at 6:00. If the pattern continues, at what time is the fifth show?

10:30

32. Mr. Gomez wants to divide the class into 3 equal lines. There are 27 children in the class. How many children should be in each line?

9

33. Tanya mailed 5 cards yesterday. She mailed 8 cards today. She received 4 cards. How many cards did she mail in all?

13

Macmillan/McGraw-Hill, **MATHEMATICS IN ACTION**
Grade 4, Chapter 5, Form C

47

MACMILLAN/McGRAW-HILL

TM72

Chapter 6 Test

Name
Macmillan/McGraw-Hill
Mathematics

Grade 4
Form A
Page 1

Choose the letter of your answer.

1. 4 × 100
a. 400   c. 40
b. 104   d. not given

2. Estimate by rounding.
  5 × 62
a. 20   c. 200
b. 30   d. 300

3. 3 × 927
a. 2,781   c. 2,761
b. 2,771   d. 2,751

4. $5.33
  × 2
a. $10.06   c. $10.66
b. $10.55   d. $10.99

5. 60
  × 6
a. 30   c. 300
b. 36   d. not given

6. About how much is 3 × $42?
a. about $70   c. about $700
b. about $120   d. about $1,200

7. 6 × 89
a. 534   c. 474
b. 484   d. 194

8. 4 × $4.95
a. $16.60   c. $19.80
b. $17.39   d. $22.00

9. 7 × 80
a. 56   c. 5,600
b. 560   d. not given

10. Estimate by using the front digits.
  2 × 285
a. 300   c. 500
b. 400   d. 600

11. 708
  × 4
a. 2,332   c. 2,812
b. 2,802   d. 2,832

12. $.80
  × 2
a. $.16   c. $16.00
b. $1.60   d. $160.00

13. 8 × 9,000
a. 720   c. 72,000
b. 7,200   d. not given

14. Estimate by rounding.
  9 × 2,023
a. 700   c. 7,000
b. 1,800   d. 18,000

15. 5 × 698
a. 3,620   c. 3,090
b. 3,490   d. 3,050

16. 8 × $4.70
a. $32.60   c. $36.58
b. $33.58   d. $37.60

Name

Page 2

17. 300
  × 5
a. 1,500   c. 15
b. 150   d. not given

18. About how much is 5 × $3.95?
a. about $20.00   c. about $2.00
b. about $15.00   d. about $1.50

19. 821
  × 7
a. 6,547   c. 5,647
b. 5,747   d. 4,947

20. $7.89
  × 6
a. $47.34   c. $42.84
b. $46.95   d. $42.04

STOP

21. In a baseball game, Ernie and Tanya made 12 hits. Tanya got twice as many hits as Ernie did. How many hits did Ernie make?
a. 12   c. 5
b. 8   d. 4

22. Jim has some shells he wants to glue onto a board. He puts 14 shells in each of 4 rows. How many shells does he have?
a. 56   c. 18
b. 46   d. 14

23. The fourth-grade students wanted to raise $75.00 for the library. They held a car wash to raise the money. They made $48.50 on Saturday and $31.89 on Sunday. Did the students reach their goal?
a. Yes.   b. No.

24. Jeanne has 19 pieces of string. She puts 8 beads on each string. About how many beads does she have in all? Use rounding.
a. about 250
b. about 160
c. about 100
d. about 50

25. Each row in the auditorium has 9 seats. There are 36 students in Mr. Marquez's class. Which number sentence should you use to find how many rows they will fill in the auditorium?
a. 36 × 9 =
b. 36 ÷ 9 =
c. 36 + 9 =
d. 36 − 9 =

TM73

Name
Macmillan/McGraw-Hill
Mathematics

Grade 4
Form B
Page 1

Chapter 6 Test

Choose the letter of your answer.

1. 3 × 600
   - a. 18
   - b. 180
   - **c. 1,800**
   - d. not given

2. Estimate by rounding.
   5 × 38
   - a. 500
   - **b. 200**
   - c. 50
   - d. 20

3. 2 × 755
   - a. 1,400
   - b. 1,410
   - c. 1,500
   - **d. 1,510**

4. $8.49
   × 7
   - **a. $59.43**
   - b. $58.96
   - c. $56.83
   - d. $56.23

5. 30
   × 9
   - **a. 270**
   - b. 210
   - c. 21
   - d. not given

6. About how much is 4 × $21?
   - a. about $1,500
   - b. about $800
   - c. about $150
   - **d. about $80**

7. 3 × 59
   - a. 222
   - b. 217
   - **c. 177**
   - d. 157

8. 9 × $5.08
   - a. $45.02
   - b. $45.17
   - **c. $45.72**
   - d. $54.72

9. 6 × 70
   - a. 42,000
   - b. 4,200
   - **c. 420**
   - d. not given

10. Estimate by using the front digits.
    4 × 312
    - a. 120
    - b. 900
    - c. 1,100
    - **d. 1,200**

11. 634
    × 7
    - **a. 4,438**
    - b. 4,238
    - c. 4,231
    - d. 4,218

12. $.50
    × 3
    - a. $150.00
    - b. $15.00
    - **c. $1.50**
    - d. $.15

13. 2 × 5,000
    - a. 1,000
    - b. 100
    - c. 10
    - **d. not given**

14. Estimate by rounding.
    8 × 3,011
    - **a. 24,000**
    - b. 16,000
    - c. 2,400
    - d. 1,600

15. 6 × 452
    - a. 2,402
    - b. 2,412
    - **c. 2,712**
    - d. 2,718

16. 8 × $6.30
    - a. $48.40
    - b. $49.10
    - c. $50.10
    - **d. $50.40**

17. 100
    × 5
    - a. 5,000
    - **b. 500**
    - c. 50
    - d. not given

18. About how much is 4 × $9.89?
    - a. about $3.60
    - b. about $4.00
    - c. about $20.00
    - **d. about $40.00**

19. 990
    × 6
    - **a. 5,940**
    - b. 5,720
    - c. 5,440
    - d. 4,850

20. $5.68
    × 9
    - a. $45.42
    - b. $50.42
    - **c. $51.12**
    - d. $51.21

21. Sondra and Clarence read 24 books. Clarence read 3 times as many books as Sondra read. How many books did Clarence read?
    - a. 6
    - **b. 18**
    - c. 21
    - d. 72

22. Mike is planting vegetables. He puts 25 plants in each of 6 rows. How many plants does he have?
    - a. 200
    - **b. 150**
    - c. 31
    - d. 4

23. The fourth-grade students held a bake sale to raise $50.00 for their class trip. The students made $39.15 on Saturday and $21.60 on Sunday. Did they make enough money?
    - **a. Yes.**
    - b. No.

24. Seth makes 17 stacks of baseball cards. There are 9 cards in each stack. About how many cards does Seth have in all? Use rounding.
    - a. about 250
    - **b. about 170**
    - c. about 30
    - d. about 2

25. There are 25 children at soccer practice. The coach wants to make 5 teams. Which number sentence should you use to find how many children will be on each team?
    - **a. 25 ÷ 5 =**
    - b. 25 + 5 =
    - c. 25 × 5 =
    - d. 25 − 5 =

STOP

Name

Macmillan/McGraw-Hill
Mathematics

Grade 4
Form C
Page 1

Chapter 6 Test

Mark your answer.

1. 4 × 100

   400

9. 7 × 80

   560

2. Estimate by rounding.
   5 × 62

   300

10. Estimate by using the front digits.
    2 × 285

    400

3. 3 × 927

   2,781

11. 708
    × 4

    2,832

4. $5.33
   ×   2

   $10.66

12. $.80
    ×   2

    $1.60

5. 60
   × 6

   360

13. 8 × 9,000

    72,000

6. About how much is 3 × $42?

   about $120

14. Estimate by rounding.
    9 × 2,023

    18,000

7. 6 × 89

   534

15. 5 × 698

    3,490

8. 4 × $4.95

   $19.80

16. 8 × $4.70

    $37.60

Name

Page 2

17. 300
    ×   5

    1,500

23. The fourth-grade students wanted to raise $75.00 for the library. They held a car wash to raise the money. They made $48.50 on Saturday and $31.89 on Sunday. Did the students reach their goal?

    Yes.

18. About how much is 5 × $3.95?

    accept $15 – $20

24. Jeanne has 19 pieces of string. She puts 8 beads on each string. About how many beads does she have in all? Use rounding.

    about 160

19. 821
    ×   7

    5,747

25. Each row in the auditorium has 9 seats. There are 36 students in Mr. Marquez's class. Write a number sentence to find how many rows the students will fill in the auditorium.

    36 ÷ 9 = 4

20. $7.89
    ×   6

    $47.34

21. In a baseball game, Ernie and Tanya made 12 hits. Tanya got twice as many hits as Ernie did. How many hits did Ernie make?

    4

22. Jim has some shells he wants to glue onto a board. He puts 14 shells in each of 4 rows. How many shells does he have?

    56

STOP

Left Page

Name

Macmillan/McGraw-Hill
Mathematics

Grade 4
Form A

Page 1

Chapter 7 Test

Choose the letter of your answer.

1. 60 ÷ 2
   - **a.** 3
   - **(b.)** 30
   - **c.** 120
   - **d.** 1,200

2. Which is the best estimate of 3,892 + 9?
   - **a.** greater than 1,000
   - **(b.)** greater than 400
   - **c.** less than 300
   - **d.** less than 200

3. 800 ÷ 4
   - **a.** 2
   - **b.** 40
   - **(c.)** 200
   - **d.** 400

4. Which is the best estimate of 2,513 + 6?
   - **a.** less than 300
   - **b.** between 300 and 400
   - **(c.)** between 400 and 500
   - **d.** greater than 500

5. 65 ÷ 9
   - **a.** 6 R3
   - **b.** 17
   - **c.** 70
   - **(d.)** not given

6. 5)509
   - **a.** 11 R4
   - **(b.)** 101 R4
   - **c.** 110
   - **d.** not given

7. 560 ÷ 7
   - **a.** 8
   - **(b.)** 80
   - **c.** 800
   - **d.** 8,000

8. 47 ÷ 3
   - **(a.)** 15
   - **b.** 15 R2
   - **c.** 16 R1
   - **d.** not given

9. Estimate by using compatible numbers. $50.00 ÷ 6
   - **a.** $.80
   - **b.** $1.00
   - **(c.)** $8.00
   - **d.** $10.00

10. 8)$7.44
    - **(a.)** $.93
    - **b.** $9.30
    - **c.** $93.00
    - **d.** not given

11. About how much is 271 ÷ 4?
    - **a.** about 100
    - **b.** about 90
    - **(c.)** about 70
    - **d.** about 7

12. 4)362
    - **a.** 9 R2
    - **(b.)** 90 R2
    - **c.** 92
    - **d.** not given

13. 4,500 ÷ 9
    - **a.** 5,000
    - **(b.)** 500
    - **c.** 50
    - **d.** 5

14. Estimate by rounding. 4,213 ÷ 5
    - **a.** 80
    - **b.** 90
    - **(c.)** 800
    - **d.** 9,000

15. 9,000 ÷ 3
    - **(a.)** 3,000
    - **b.** 360
    - **c.** 300
    - **d.** 36

Right Page

Use the set of numbers to answer Questions 16 and 17.

103; 92; 95; 100; 115

16. What is the average?
    - **a.** 92
    - **b.** 95
    - **c.** 100
    - **(d.)** 101

17. What is the median?
    - **(a.)** 100
    - **b.** 95
    - **c.** 92
    - **d.** 16

Use the set of numbers to answer Questions 18–20.

32; 26; 38; 40; 34

18. What is the average?
    - **a.** 136
    - **b.** 40
    - **(c.)** 34
    - **d.** 32

19. What is the median?
    - **a.** 35
    - **(b.)** 34
    - **c.** 32
    - **d.** 26

20. What is the range?
    - **a.** 8
    - **(b.)** 14
    - **c.** 26
    - **d.** 34

STOP

21. Seth is selling candles for his softball team. He sells 12 on Monday, 20 on Tuesday, 14 on Friday, and 30 on Saturday. What is the average number of candles he sells each day?
    - **a.** 18
    - **(b.)** 19
    - **c.** 22
    - **d.** 30

22. A can of 3 tennis balls costs $4.59. What is the cost of each tennis ball?
    - **a.** $.15
    - **b.** $1.50
    - **c.** $1.53
    - **d.** $13.77

23. Laura made 84 posters for the fair in two days. She made twice as many on Saturday as she did on Sunday. How many posters did Laura make on Sunday?
    - **a.** 64
    - **b.** 56
    - **(c.)** 28
    - **d.** 14

24. There are 23 children in line for the roller coaster. If 5 children can sit in each car, how many cars will be needed?
    - **a.** 3
    - **b.** 4
    - **(c.)** 5
    - **d.** 6

25. Complete and use the table to answer the question.

One apple, one pear, and one orange are on the table. Mark, Kim, and Todd each pick one of the fruits. Mark does not pick the apple or the pear. Kim does not pick the pear. Who picks the apple?

	Orange	Apple	Pear
Mark		no	no
Kim		no	no
Todd			

- **(a.)** Kim
- **b.** Todd
- **c.** Mark

Name

Macmillan/McGraw-Hill   **Chapter 7 Test**   Grade 4
Mathematics   Form B

Choose the letter of your answer.

1. 80 ÷ 2
   a. 4   c. 160
   b. 40   d. 1,600

2. Which is the best estimate of 449 ÷ 7?
   a. less than 30
   b. less than 60
   c. greater than 60
   d. greater than 80

3. 900 ÷ 3
   a. 300   c. 30
   b. 90   d. 9

4. Which is the best estimate of 2,641 ÷ 9?
   a. less than 200
   b. between 200 and 300
   c. between 300 and 400
   d. greater than 400

5. 49 ÷ 8
   a. 5 R3   c. 16
   b. 6 R1   d. 60

6. 3)‾605
   a. 202   c. 21 R2
   b. 201 R2   d. not given

7. 350 ÷ 7
   a. 5,000   c. 50
   b. 500   d. 5

8. 74 ÷ 5
   a. 10 R3   c. 14 R4
   b. 13 R4   d. not given

9. Estimate by using compatible numbers. $27.00 ÷ 4
   a. $.05   c. $5.00
   b. $.70   d. $7.00

10. 9)‾$5.22
    a. $.58   c. $58.00
    b. $5.80   d. not given

11. About how much is 365 ÷ 5?
    a. about 70   c. about 700
    b. about 90   d. about 800

12. 6)‾543
    a. 9 R3   c. 93
    b. 92   d. not given

13. 6,000 ÷ 3
    a. 2   c. 200
    b. 20   d. 2,000

14. Estimate by rounding. 5,641 ÷ 3
    a. 6,000   c. 2,000
    b. 4,000   d. 200

15. 2,400 ÷ 6
    a. 4,000   c. 40
    b. 400   d. 4

Name

Use the set of numbers to answer Questions 16 and 17.

115; 84; 92; 101; 123

16. What is the average?
    a. 84   b. 103   c. 123   d. 515

17. What is the median?
    a. 123   b. 103   c. 101   d. 39

Use the set of numbers to answer Questions 18–20.

32; 41; 52; 35; 40

18. What is the average?
    a. 160   b. 52   c. 41   d. 40

19. What is the median?
    a. 38   b. 40   c. 41   d. 52

20. What is the range?
    a. 3   b. 17   c. 20   d. 32

(STOP)

21. During the first quarter of the game, the basketball team scores 23 points. The team scores 31 points in the second quarter, 18 points in the third quarter, and 40 points in the fourth quarter. What is the average number of points the team scores in a quarter?
    a. 22   b. 27   c. 28   d. 40

22. A bag of 7 apples costs $2.59. What is the cost of each apple?
    a. $.37   c. $18.13
    b. $3.70   d. $18.79

23. The twins made $27.30 selling lemonade last weekend. They made twice as much on Sunday as they did on Saturday. How much did they make on Sunday?
    a. $4.55   c. $27.30
    b. $18.20   d. $50.00

24. There are 25 children waiting for the bus. If 3 children can sit in each seat, how many seats will be needed?
    a. 10   b. 9   c. 8   d. 6

25. Complete and use the table to answer the question.
The children leave one blue, one green, and one red bike in the driveway. Jen's bike is not red or blue. Nick's bike is not blue. Who has the red bike?

	Red	Blue	Green
Nick		no	
Jen	no	no	
Julie			

    a. Nick   b. Julie   c. Jen

Page 1 (left)

Chapter 7 Test

Mark your answer.

1. $60 \div 2$

   30

2. Which is the best estimate of $3,892 \div 9$? Ring your answer.

   greater than 1,000
   (greater than 400)
   less than 300
   less than 200

3. $800 \div 4$

   200

4. Which is the best estimate of $2,513 \div 6$? Ring your answer.

   less than 300
   between 300 and 400
   (between 400 and 500)
   greater than 500

5. $65 \div 9$

   7 R2

6. $5\overline{)509}$

   101 R4

7. $560 \div 7$

   80

8. $47 \div 3$

   15 R2

9. Estimate by using compatible numbers.

   $50.00 \div 6$

   $8.00

10. $8\overline{)\$7.44}$

    $.93

11. About how much is $271 \div 4$?

    accept 70–75

12. $4\overline{)362}$

    90 R2

13. $4,500 \div 9$

    500

14. Estimate by rounding.

    $4,213 \div 5$

    800

15. $9,000 \div 3$

    3,000

Page 2 (right)

Use the set of numbers to answer Questions 16 and 17.

103; 92; 95; 100; 115

16. What is the average?

    101

17. What is the median?

    100

Use the set of numbers to answer Questions 18–20.

32; 26; 38; 40; 34

18. What is the average?

    34

19. What is the median?

    34

20. What is the range?

    14

21. Seth is selling candles for his softball team. He sells 12 on Monday, 20 on Tuesday, 14 on Friday, and 30 on Saturday. What is the average number of candles he sells each day?

    19

22. A can of 3 tennis balls costs $4.59. What is the cost of each tennis ball?

    $1.53

23. Laura made 84 posters for the fair in two days. She made twice as many on Saturday as she did on Sunday. How many posters did Laura make on Sunday?

    28

24. There are 23 children in line for the roller coaster. If 5 children can sit in each car, how many cars will be needed?

    5

25. Complete and use the table to answer the question.

    One apple, one pear, and one orange are on the table. Mark, Kim, and Todd each pick one of the fruits. Mark does not pick the apple or the pear. Kim does not pick the pear. Who picks the apple?

	Orange	Apple	Pear
Mark		no	no
Kim			no
Todd			

    Kim

(STOP)

Name

Macmillan/McGraw-Hill
Mathematics

Chapter 8 Test

Grade 4
Form A

Choose the letter of your answer.

1. Which describes the figure? 
   a. angle RS   c. ray SR
   b. line RS (circled)   d. plane RS

2. Which word describes this figure? 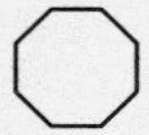
   a. square
   b. pentagon
   c. hexagon
   d. octagon (circled)

3. What is the volume of the figure? 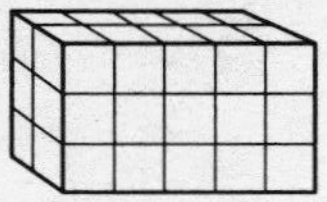
   a. 5 cubic units
   b. 10 cubic units
   c. 25 cubic units
   d. not given (circled)

4. Which figure is symmetrical?
   a. 
   b.
   c. (circled)
   d.

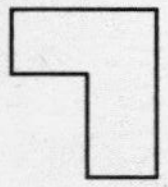

5. Is the figure the result of a flip, slide, or turn?
   a. flip (circled)   b. slide   c. turn 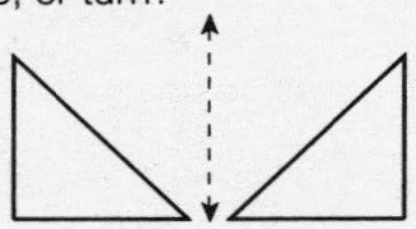

6. Which two figures are congruent?
   a. 
   c. (circled) 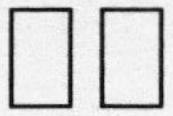
   b. 
   d.

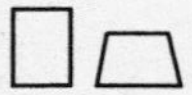

7. What is the volume of this figure?
   a. 30 cubic units 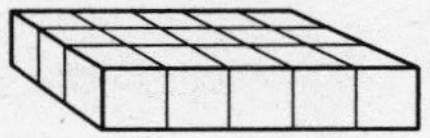
   b. 15 cubic units (circled)
   c. 12 cubic units
   d. not given

8. How many sides does a hexagon have?
   a. 3   b. 4   c. 5   d. 6 (circled)

Macmillan/McGraw-Hill, MATHEMATICS IN ACTION
Grade 4, Chapter 8, Form A   CMS Test ID 124081

Name

9. Which figure shows ray $\overrightarrow{PQ}$?
   a. (circled) 
   c. 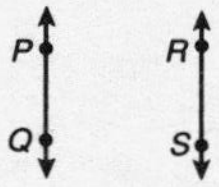
   b. 
   d.

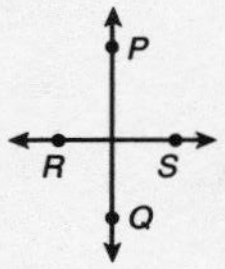

10. Which describes the figure?
    a. plane QRS 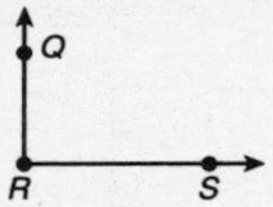
    b. $\overline{EG}$
    c. $\angle QRS$ (circled)
    d. $\overrightarrow{QR} \parallel \overrightarrow{RS}$

11. Which pair of figures shows a slide?
    a. (circled)
    b. 
    c.
    d.

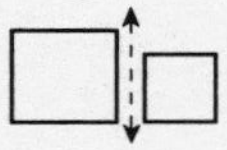

12. Which is a line of symmetry in this figure?
    a. a 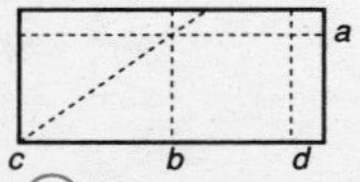
    b. b (circled)
    c. c
    d. d

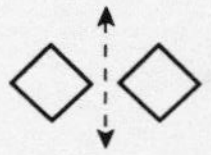

Use the figure below to answer Questions 13 and 14.

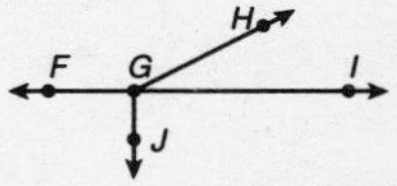

13. Which angle is a right angle?
    a. ∠HGI
    b. ∠FGI
    c. ∠JGI (circled)
    d. ∠FGH

14. Find the angle that is greater than a right angle.
    a. ∠FGJ
    b. ∠FGH (circled)
    c. ∠HGI
    d. ∠JGI

Use the figures below to answer Questions 15 and 16.

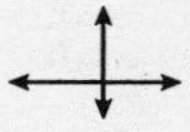

15. Which figure shows two parallel lines?
    a. A   b. B   c. C (circled)   d. D

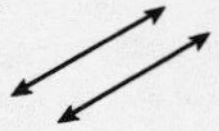

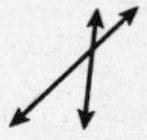

16. Which figure shows two perpendicular lines?
    a. A (circled)   b. B   c. C   d. D

Macmillan/McGraw-Hill, MATHEMATICS IN ACTION
Grade 4, Chapter 8, Form A

26. Find the volume of a rectangular prism 6 units long, 3 units wide, and 2 units high.
   a. 11 cubic units
   b. 20 cubic units
   c. 36 cubic units
   d. not given

27. Find the volume of a cube with sides 4 units long.
   a. 64 cubic units
   b. 16 cubic units
   c. 12 cubic units
   d. not given

28. Find the volume.

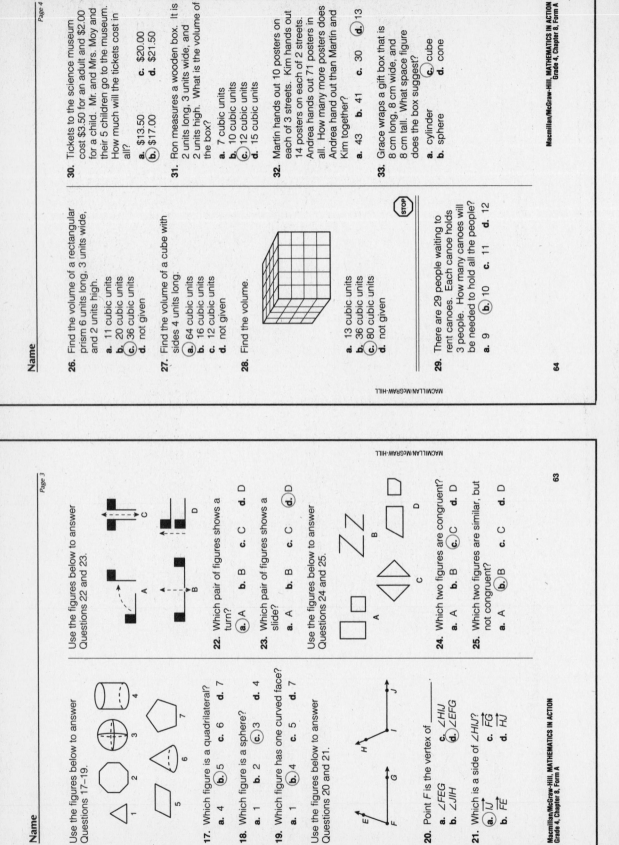

   a. 13 cubic units
   b. 36 cubic units
   c. 80 cubic units
   d. not given

29. There are 29 people waiting to rent canoes. Each canoe holds 3 people. How many canoes will be needed to hold all the people?
   a. 9   **b.** 10   c. 11   d. 12

30. Tickets to the science museum cost $3.50 for an adult and $2.00 for a child. Mr. and Mrs. Moy and their 5 children go to the museum. How much will the tickets cost in all?
   a. $13.50   c. $20.00
   b. $17.00   d. $21.50

31. Ron measures a wooden box. It is 2 units long, 3 units wide, and 2 units high. What is the volume of the box?
   a. 7 cubic units
   b. 10 cubic units
   c. 12 cubic units
   d. 15 cubic units

32. Martin hands out 10 posters on each of 3 streets. Kim hands out 14 posters on each of 2 streets. Andrea hands out 71 posters in all. How many more posters does Andrea hand out than Martin and Kim together?
   a. 43   b. 41   c. 30   **d.** 13

33. Grace wraps a gift box that is 8 cm long, 8 cm wide, and 8 cm tall. What space figure does the box suggest?
   a. cylinder   **c.** cube
   b. sphere   d. cone

Use the figures below to answer Questions 17–19.

17. Which figure is a quadrilateral?
   a. 4   **b.** 5   c. 6   d. 7

18. Which figure is a sphere?
   a. 1   b. 2   **c.** 3   d. 4

19. Which figure has one curved face?
   a. 1   **b.** 4   c. 5   d. 7

Use the figures below to answer Questions 20 and 21.

20. Point F is the vertex of
   a. ∠FEG   c. ∠HIJ
   b. ∠JIH   **d.** ∠EFG

21. Which is a side of ∠HIJ?
   a. $\overrightarrow{IJ}$ c. $\overrightarrow{FG}$
   b. $\overrightarrow{FE}$ d. $\overrightarrow{HJ}$

Use the figures below to answer Questions 22 and 23.

22. Which pair of figures shows a turn?
   a. A   b. B   c. C   d. D

23. Which pair of figures shows a slide?
   a. A   b. B   c. C   **d.** D

Use the figures below to answer Questions 24 and 25.

24. Which two figures are congruent?
   a. A   b. B   **c.** C   d. D

25. Which two figures are similar, but not congruent?
   a. A   **b.** B   c. C   d. D

Name _____

Macmillan/McGraw-Hill
Mathematics

Chapter 8 Test

Grade 4
Form B

Choose the letter of your answer.

1. Which describes the figure?

   a. angle YZ
   b. line ZY
   c. ray YZ
   d. plane XY

2. Which word describes this figure?

   a. pentagon
   b. octagon
   c. quadrilateral
   d. decagon

3. What is the volume of the figure?

   a. 24 cubic units
   b. 20 cubic units
   c. 12 cubic units
   d. not given

4. Which figure is symmetrical?

   a.
   b.
   c.
   d.

5. Is the figure the result of a slide, flip, or turn?

   a. slide
   b. flip
   c. turn

6. Which two figures are congruent?

   a.
   b.
   c.
   d.

7. What is the volume of this figure?

   a. 19 cubic units
   b. 15 cubic units
   c. 12 cubic units
   d. not given

8. How many sides does a pentagon have?

   a. 10
   b. 8
   c. 6
   d. 5

Name _____

9. Which figure shows line LM?

   a.
   b.
   c.
   d.

10. Which describes the figure?

    a. EG
    b. EF ‖ FG
    c. plane EFG
    d. ∠EFG

11. Which pair of figures shows a slide?

    a.
    b.
    c.
    d.

12. Which is the line of symmetry in this figure?

    a. a
    b. b
    c. c
    d. d

Use the figure below to answer Questions 13 and 14.

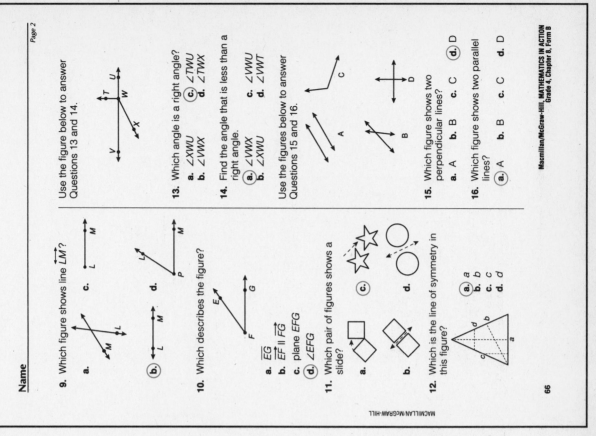

13. Which angle is a right angle?

    a. ∠XWU
    b. ∠VWX
    c. ∠TWU
    d. ∠TWX

14. Find the angle that is less than a right angle.

    a. ∠VWX
    b. ∠XWU
    c. ∠VWU
    d. ∠VWT

Use the figures below to answer Questions 15 and 16.

15. Which figure shows two perpendicular lines?

    a. A
    b. B
    c. C
    d. D

16. Which figure shows two parallel lines?

    a. A
    b. B
    c. C
    d. D

26. Find the volume of a rectangular prism 5 units long, 3 units wide, and 1 unit high.
   a. 9 cubic units
   b. 15 cubic units
   c. 16 cubic units
   d. not given

27. Find the volume of a cube with sides 5 units long.
   a. 15 cubic units
   b. 25 cubic units
   c. 125 cubic units
   d. not given

28. Find the volume.

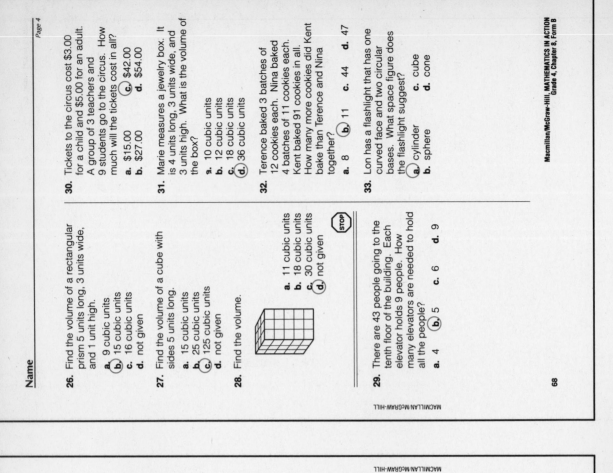

   a. 11 cubic units
   b. 18 cubic units
   c. 30 cubic units
   d. not given

29. There are 43 people going to the tenth floor of the building. Each elevator holds 9 people. How many elevators are needed to hold all the people?
   a. 4
   b. 5
   c. 6
   d. 9

STOP

30. Tickets to the circus cost $3.00 for a child and $5.00 for an adult. A group of 3 teachers and 9 students go to the circus. How much will the tickets cost in all?
   a. $15.00
   b. $27.00
   c. $42.00
   d. $54.00

31. Marie measures a jewelry box. It is 4 units long, 3 units wide, and 3 units high. What is the volume of the box?
   a. 10 cubic units
   b. 12 cubic units
   c. 18 cubic units
   d. 36 cubic units

32. Terence baked 3 batches of 12 cookies each. Nina baked 4 batches of 11 cookies each. Kent baked 91 cookies in all. How many more cookies did Kent bake than Terence and Nina together?
   a. 8
   b. 11
   c. 44
   d. 47

33. Lon has a flashlight that has one curved face and two circular bases. What space figure does the flashlight suggest?
   a. cylinder
   b. sphere
   c. cube
   d. cone

Macmillan/McGraw-Hill, MATHEMATICS IN ACTION
Grade 4, Chapter 8, Form B

Use the figures below to answer Questions 17–19.

17. Which figure is a triangle?
   a. 1   b. 2   c. 5   d. 6

18. Which figure is a cone?
   a. 1   b. 2   c. 3   d. 4

19. Which figure has two flat faces?
   a. 1   b. 3   c. 5   d. 7

Use the figures below to answer Questions 20 and 21.

20. Which is a side of ∠IJK?
   a. $\overrightarrow{ML}$
   b. $\overrightarrow{JK}$
   c. $\overrightarrow{IK}$
   d. $\overrightarrow{MN}$

21. Which point is the vertex of ∠LMN?
   a. N
   b. J
   c. L
   d. M

Use the figures below to answer Questions 22 and 23.

22. Which pair of figures shows a slide?
   a. A   b. B   c. C   d. D

23. Which pair of figures shows a turn?
   a. A   b. B   c. C   d. D

Use the figures below to answer Questions 24 and 25.

24. Which two figures are similar, but not congruent?
   a. A   b. B   c. C   d. D

25. Which two figures are congruent?
   a. A   b. B   c. C   d. D

Macmillan/McGraw-Hill, MATHEMATICS IN ACTION
Grade 4, Chapter 8, Form B

Chapter 8 Test

Name
Macmillan/McGraw-Hill
Mathematics

Grade 4
Form C
Page 1

Mark your answer.

1. Write the name of the figure.

line *RS* ($\overrightarrow{RS}$)

2. Name the figure.

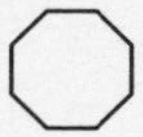

octagon

3. What is the volume of the figure?

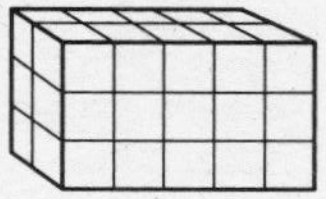

30 cubic units

4. Ring the figure that is symmetrical.

5. Is the figure the result of a flip, slide, or turn?

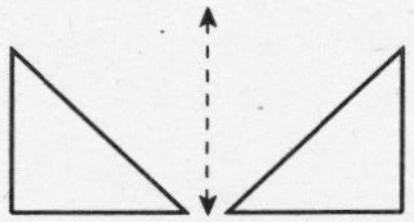

flip

6. Ring the pair of congruent figures.

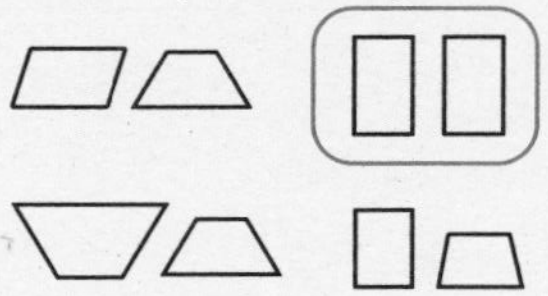

7. What is the volume of this figure?

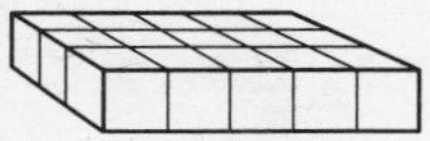

15 cubic units

8. How many sides does a hexagon have?

6

Macmillan/McGraw-Hill, MATHEMATICS IN ACTION
Grade 4, Chapter 8, Form C

---

9. Ring the figure that shows ray $\overrightarrow{PQ}$.

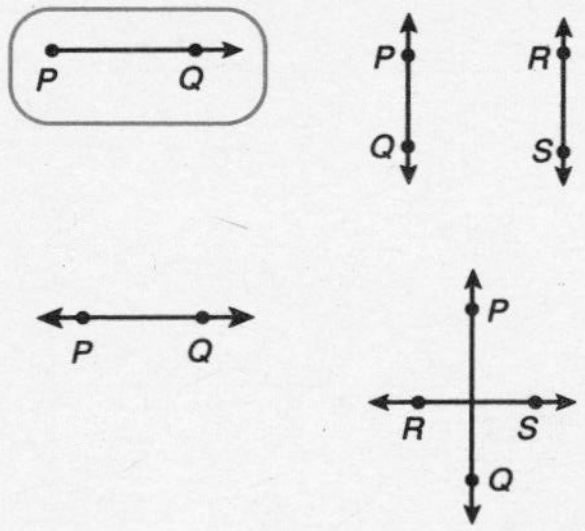

10. Write the name of the figure.

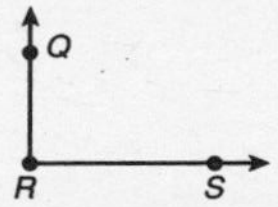

∠QRS (angle QRS)

11. Ring the pair of figures that shows a slide.

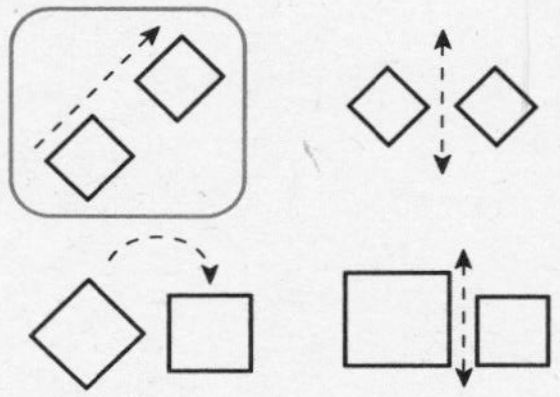

12. Which is a line of symmetry in this figure?

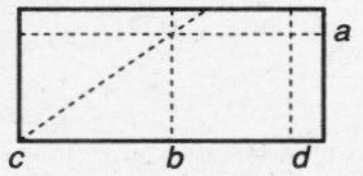

Use the figure below to answer Questions 13 and 14.

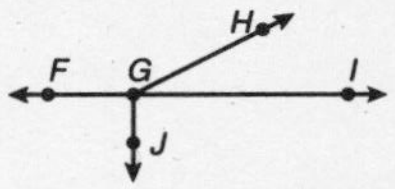

13. Which angle is a right angle?
accept ∠JGI or ∠FGJ
(angle JGI or angle FGJ)

14. Find the angle that is greater than a right angle.
accept ∠FGH or ∠JGH
(angle FGH or angle JGH)

Use the figures below to answer Questions 15 and 16.

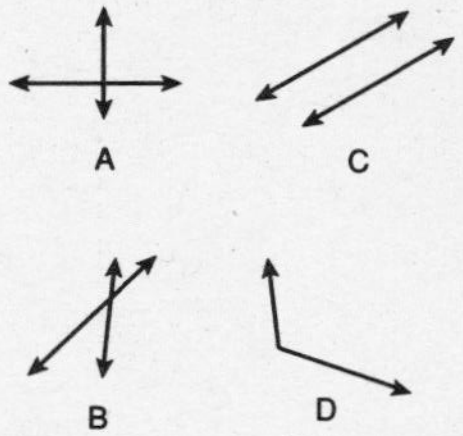

15. Which figure shows two parallel lines?

C

16. Which figure shows two perpendicular lines?

A

Macmillan/McGraw-Hill, MATHEMATICS IN ACTION
Grade 4, Chapter 8, Form C

Name

Use the figures below to answer
Questions 17–19.

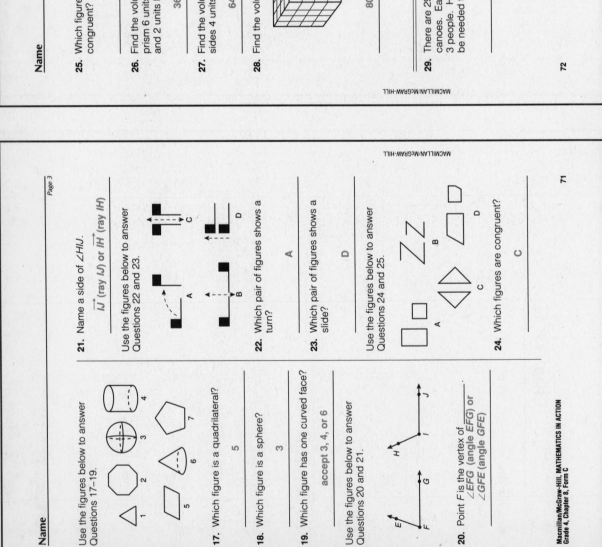

1. (triangle) 2. (octagon) 3. (sphere) 4. (cylinder)

5. (quadrilateral) 6. (cone) 7. (pentagon)

17. Which figure is a quadrilateral?

5

18. Which figure is a sphere?

3

19. Which figure has one curved face?

accept 3, 4, or 6

Use the figures below to answer
Questions 20 and 21.

20. Point *F* is the vertex of
∠*EFG* (angle *EFG*) or
∠*GFE* (angle *GFE*)

21. Name a side of ∠*HIJ*.

$\overrightarrow{IJ}$ (ray *IJ*) or $\overrightarrow{IH}$ (ray *IH*)

Use the figures below to answer
Questions 22 and 23.

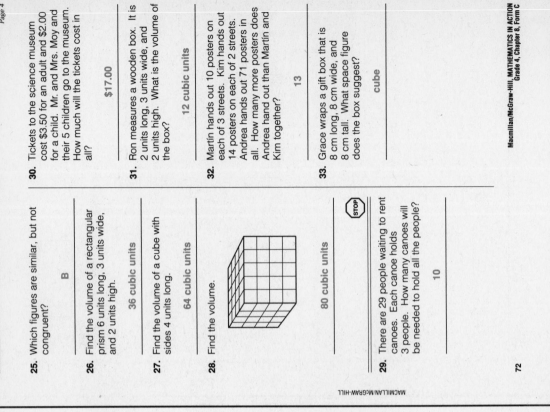

22. Which pair of figures shows a
turn?

A

23. Which pair of figures shows a
slide?

D

Use the figures below to answer
Questions 24 and 25.

24. Which figures are congruent?

C

Name

25. Which figures are similar, but not
congruent?

B

26. Find the volume of a rectangular
prism 6 units long, 3 units wide,
and 2 units high.

36 cubic units

27. Find the volume of a cube with
sides 4 units long.

64 cubic units

28. Find the volume.

80 cubic units

29. There are 29 people waiting to rent
canoes. Each canoe holds
3 people. How many canoes will
be needed to hold all the people?

10

(STOP)

30. Tickets to the science museum
cost $3.50 for an adult and $2.00
for a child. Mr. and Mrs. Moy and
their 5 children go to the museum.
How much will the tickets cost in
all?

$17.00

31. Ron measures a wooden box. It is
2 units long, 3 units wide, and
2 units high. What is the volume of
the box?

12 cubic units

32. Martin hands out 10 posters on
each of 3 streets. Kim hands out
14 posters on each of 2 streets.
Andrea hands out 71 posters in
all. How many more posters does
Andrea hand out than Martin and
Kim together?

13

33. Grace wraps a gift box that is
8 cm long, 8 cm wide, and
8 cm tall. What space figure
does the box suggest?

cube

TM84

Choose the letter of your answer.

1. What fraction is shaded?

   a. $\frac{2}{9}$ b. $\frac{2}{7}$ c. $\frac{7}{2}$ d. $\frac{9}{2}$

2. Which fraction is equivalent to $\frac{3}{6}$?

   a. $\frac{3}{12}$ b. $\frac{1}{3}$ c. $\frac{6}{12}$ d. $\frac{6}{3}$

3. What is $\frac{17}{5}$ in simplest form?

   a. $2\frac{3}{5}$ c. $5\frac{2}{3}$

   b. $3\frac{2}{5}$ d. not given

4. Which number is greatest?

   a. 1 c. $1\frac{7}{12}$

   b. $1\frac{2}{12}$ d. $\frac{4}{9}$

5. About how tall is a horse?

   a. about 6 miles
   b. about 6 yards
   c. about 6 feet
   d. about 6 inches

6. Complete. $\frac{2}{7} = \frac{?}{21}$

   a. 3 b. 6 c. 8 d. 10

7. Which is two and one-half?

   a. $1\frac{2}{5}$ c. $2\frac{1}{2}$

   b. $2\frac{1}{3}$ d. not given

8. Compare. $3\frac{1}{5}$ ● $3\frac{3}{5}$

   a. > b. < c. =

9. Measure this small pencil to the nearest inch.

   a. 1 inch c. 3 inches
   b. 2 inches d. 4 inches

10. What part of the set is shaded?

    a. $\frac{5}{12}$ c. $\frac{5}{7}$

    b. $\frac{7}{12}$ d. $\frac{7}{5}$

11. What is $\frac{15}{5}$ in simplest form?

    a. 3 c. 10

    b. 5 d. not given

12. Which number is least?

    a. $2\frac{1}{2}$ c. $2\frac{5}{8}$

    b. $3\frac{1}{4}$ d. $3\frac{1}{5}$

13. Which is the best estimate for the length of a fork?

    a. 8 feet c. 8 miles
    b. 8 inches d. 8 yards

14. What is $\frac{3}{8}$ of the set?

    a. 3 b. 4 c. 5 d. 6

MACMILLAN/McGRAW-HILL

---

15. What is $\frac{4}{12}$ in simplest form?

    a. $\frac{1}{8}$ b. $\frac{1}{4}$ c. $\frac{1}{3}$ d. $\frac{12}{4}$

16. Compare. $5\frac{5}{9}$ ● $5\frac{2}{18}$

    a. > b. < c. =

17. Measure this line segment to the nearest $\frac{1}{2}$ inch.

    a. $\frac{1}{2}$ inch c. 2 inches
    b. $1\frac{1}{2}$ inches d. $2\frac{1}{2}$ inches

18. What is $\frac{4}{5}$ of 15?

    a. 4 b. 8 c. 12 d. 16

19. What is $\frac{12}{16}$ in simplest form?

    a. $\frac{1}{4}$ b. $\frac{1}{2}$ c. $\frac{1}{3}$ d. $\frac{3}{4}$

20. What is $\frac{14}{3}$ in simplest form?

    a. $2\frac{3}{4}$ c. $4\frac{2}{3}$

    b. $3\frac{3}{4}$ d. not given

21. Miguel asked 8 of his friends to choose their favorite sport. Football was chosen by 2 friends, soccer by 3 friends, tennis by 2 friends, and lacrosse by 1 friend. What fraction of Miguel's friends chose soccer?

    a. $\frac{2}{8}$ b. $\frac{3}{8}$ c. $\frac{4}{8}$ d. $\frac{5}{8}$

22. Carol read 3 times as many books as Tom. Pete read 3 more books than Tom. Sally read 2 fewer books than Pete. Sally read 7 books. How many books did Carol read?

    a. 18 b. 15 c. 9 d. 6

23. Henry collected 437 baseball cards. His grandfather gave him 148 more cards. Henry gave 74 cards to his friend Joyce. How many baseball cards did Henry have left?

    a. 289 b. 366 c. 511 d. 733

24. Annette made 24 sandwiches. She wants to take $\frac{2}{3}$ of them to her class. How many should she take?

    a. 2 b. 8 c. 12 d. 16

25. Use number sense.
    Helena wants to make 2 skirts in sewing class. She will need $2\frac{1}{4}$ yards of fabric for each skirt. She has 5 yards of fabric. Does she have enough fabric?

    a. Yes. b. No.

STOP

MACMILLAN/McGRAW-HILL

TM85

Page 1

Name

Macmillan/McGraw-Hill
Mathematics

Chapter 9 Test

Grade 4
Form B

Choose the letter of your answer.

1. What fraction is shaded?

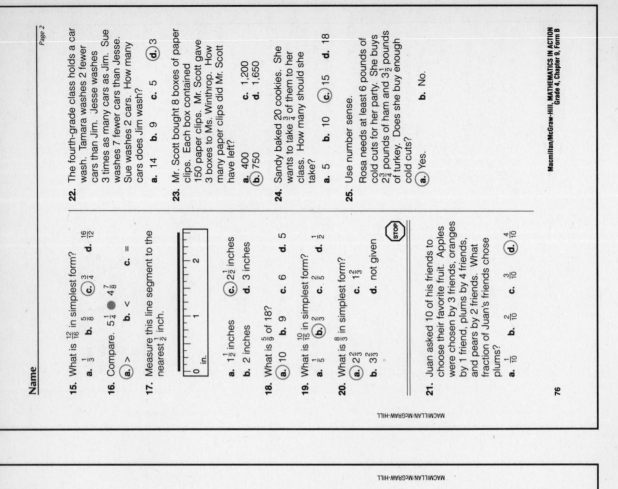

a. $\frac{3}{5}$ b. $\frac{3}{8}$ c. $\frac{5}{8}$ d. $\frac{5}{3}$

2. Which fraction is equivalent to $\frac{4}{7}$?

a. $\frac{7}{14}$ b. $\frac{8}{14}$ c. $\frac{8}{7}$ d. $\frac{7}{4}$

3. What is $\frac{19}{7}$ in simplest form?

a. $2\frac{5}{7}$ b. $5\frac{5}{7}$ c. $7\frac{5}{2}$ d. not given

4. Which number is greatest?

a. $3\frac{2}{9}$ b. $\frac{8}{12}$ c. $4\frac{1}{2}$ d. $\frac{10}{16}$

5. About how tall is a sheep?

a. about 3 inches
b. about 3 feet
c. about 3 yards
d. about 3 miles

6. Complete. $\frac{7}{8} = \frac{14}{\blacksquare}$

a. 2   b. 16   c. 21   d. 24

7. Which is three and four-fifths?

a. $4\frac{3}{5}$ b. $3\frac{5}{4}$ c. $\frac{4}{5}$ d. not given

8. Compare. $3\frac{2}{7}$ ● $3\frac{3}{14}$

a. >   b. <   c. =

9. Measure this toothpick to the nearest inch.

a. 4 inches   b. 3 inches   c. 2 inches   d. 1 inch

10. What part of the set is shaded?

a. $\frac{1}{6}$ b. $\frac{1}{5}$ c. $\frac{5}{6}$ d. $\frac{5}{1}$

11. What is $\frac{20}{4}$ in simplest form?

a. 3   b. 10   c. 16   d. not given

12. Which number is least?

a. $1\frac{8}{9}$ b. $2\frac{6}{10}$ c. $1\frac{7}{9}$ d. $4\frac{1}{9}$

13. Which is the best estimate for the length of a spoon?

a. 6 feet   b. 6 inches   c. 6 miles   d. 6 yards

14. What is $\frac{5}{12}$ of the set?

a. 5   b. 6   c. 9   d. 10

MACMILLAN/McGRAW-HILL

Page 2

Name

15. What is $\frac{12}{16}$ in simplest form?

a. $\frac{1}{3}$ b. $\frac{5}{8}$ c. $\frac{3}{4}$ d. $\frac{16}{12}$

16. Compare. $5\frac{1}{4}$ ● $4\frac{7}{8}$

a. >   b. <   c. =

17. Measure this line segment to the nearest $\frac{1}{2}$ inch.

a. $1\frac{1}{2}$ inches   b. 2 inches   c. $2\frac{1}{2}$ inches   d. 3 inches

18. What is $\frac{5}{9}$ of 18?

a. 10   b. 9   c. 6   d. 5

19. What is $\frac{10}{15}$ in simplest form?

a. $\frac{1}{5}$ b. $\frac{2}{3}$ c. $\frac{2}{5}$ d. $\frac{1}{2}$

20. What is $\frac{8}{3}$ in simplest form?

a. $2\frac{2}{3}$ b. $3\frac{2}{3}$ c. $1\frac{2}{3}$ d. not given

STOP

21. Juan asked 10 of his friends to choose their favorite fruit. Apples were chosen by 3 friends, oranges by 1 friend, plums by 4 friends, and pears by 2 friends. What fraction of Juan's friends chose plums?

a. $\frac{1}{10}$ b. $\frac{2}{10}$ c. $\frac{3}{10}$ d. $\frac{4}{10}$

22. The fourth-grade class holds a car wash. Tamara washes 2 fewer cars than Jim. Jesse washes 3 times as many cars as Jim. Sue washes 7 fewer cars than Jesse. Sue washes 2 cars. How many cars does Jim wash?

a. 14   b. 9   c. 5   d. 3

23. Mr. Scott bought 8 boxes of paper clips. Each box contained 150 paper clips. Mr. Scott gave 3 boxes to Ms. Winthrop. How many paper clips did Mr. Scott have left?

a. 400   b. 750   c. 1,200   d. 1,650

24. Sandy baked 20 cookies. She wants to take $\frac{3}{4}$ of them to her class. How many should she take?

a. 5   b. 10   c. 15   d. 18

25. Use number sense. Rosa needs at least 6 pounds of cold cuts for her party. She buys $2\frac{3}{4}$ pounds of ham and $3\frac{1}{2}$ pounds of turkey. Does she buy enough cold cuts?

a. Yes.   b. No.

MACMILLAN/McGRAW-HILL

Name _____

Macmillan/McGraw-Hill **Chapter 9 Test**
Mathematics

Grade 4
Form C

Mark your answer.

1. Write a fraction for the part is shaded.

$\frac{2}{9}$

2. Ring the fraction that is equivalent to $\frac{3}{6}$.

$\frac{3}{12}$ $\frac{1}{3}$ $\left(\frac{6}{12}\right)$ $\frac{6}{3}$

3. What is $\frac{17}{5}$ in simplest form?

$3\frac{2}{5}$

4. Order $1\frac{2}{12}$, $\frac{4}{9}$, and $1\frac{7}{12}$ from greatest to least.

$1\frac{7}{12}$, $1\frac{2}{12}$, $\frac{4}{9}$

5. Is the best estimate for the height of a horse 6 miles, 6 yards, 6 feet, or 6 inches?

6 feet

6. Complete. $\frac{2}{7} = \frac{\blacksquare}{21}$

6

7. Write the number for two and one-half.

$2\frac{1}{2}$

8. Compare. Write >, <, or =.

$3\frac{1}{5}$ ● $3\frac{3}{5}$

<

9. Measure this small pencil to the nearest inch.

2 inches

10. Write a fraction for the part of the set that is shaded.

$\frac{7}{12}$

11. What is $\frac{15}{5}$ in simplest form?

3

12. Order $3\frac{1}{4}$, $3\frac{1}{5}$, and $2\frac{5}{8}$ from least to greatest.

$2\frac{5}{8}$, $3\frac{1}{5}$, $3\frac{1}{4}$

13. Estimate the length of a fork.

accept 5 – 9 inches

Name _____

14. What is $\frac{3}{8}$ of the set?

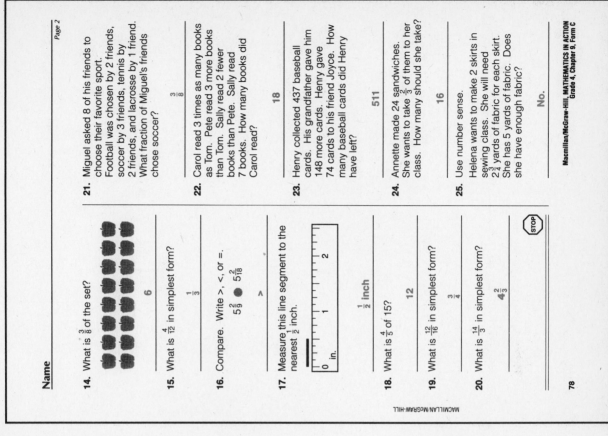

6

15. What is $\frac{4}{12}$ in simplest form?

$\frac{1}{3}$

16. Compare. Write >, <, or =.

$5\frac{2}{9}$ ● $5\frac{2}{18}$

>

17. Measure this line segment to the nearest $\frac{1}{2}$ inch.

$\frac{1}{2}$ inch

18. What is $\frac{4}{5}$ of 15?

12

19. What is $\frac{12}{16}$ in simplest form?

$\frac{3}{4}$

20. What is $\frac{14}{3}$ in simplest form?

$4\frac{2}{3}$

21. Miguel asked 8 of his friends to choose their favorite sport. Football was chosen by 2 friends, soccer by 3 friends, tennis by 2 friends, and lacrosse by 1 friend. What fraction of Miguel's friends chose soccer?

$\frac{3}{8}$

22. Carol read 3 times as many books as Tom. Pete read 3 more books than Tom. Sally read 2 fewer books than Pete. Sally read 7 books. How many books did Carol read?

18

23. Henry collected 437 baseball cards. His grandfather gave him 148 more cards. Henry gave 74 cards to his friend Joyce. How many baseball cards did Henry have left?

511

24. Annette made 24 sandwiches. She wants to take $\frac{2}{3}$ of them to her class. How many should she take?

16

25. Use number sense. Helena wants to make 2 skirts in sewing class. She will need $2\frac{3}{4}$ yards of fabric for each skirt. She has 5 yards of fabric. Does she have enough fabric?

No.

(STOP)

Name

Macmillan/McGraw-Hill

Mathematics

Grade 4
Form A
Page 1

Chapter 10 Test

Choose the letter of your answer.

1. $\frac{3}{5} + \frac{1}{5}$
   a. $\frac{2}{5}$
   b. $\frac{3}{10}$
   c. $\frac{4}{5}$
   d. not given

2. What is $\frac{5}{6} - \frac{1}{6}$ in simplest form?
   a. $\frac{2}{3}$
   b. $\frac{4}{5}$
   c. 1
   d. 4

3. What is the area of the figure?

   (6 ft by 3 ft)
   a. 3 square ft
   b. 9 square ft
   c. 18 square ft
   d. 32 square ft

4. Which is the best unit to measure the capacity of a jelly jar?
   a. cup
   b. pint
   c. quart
   d. gallon

5. Which is the most reasonable estimate for the temperature of a glass of cold juice?
   a. 40°F
   b. 55°F
   c. 60°F
   d. 75°F

6. $\frac{5}{9} + \frac{2}{9}$
   a. $\frac{1}{3}$
   b. $\frac{3}{2}$
   c. $\frac{7}{9}$
   d. not given

7. What is $\frac{6}{7} - \frac{2}{7}$ in simplest form?
   a. $\frac{4}{14}$
   b. $\frac{4}{7}$
   c. $\frac{4}{7}$
   d. $1\frac{1}{7}$

8. What is the perimeter of the figure?

   (2 in., 4 in., 2 in., 3 in., 4 in.)
   a. 13 in.
   b. 15 in.
   c. 19 in.
   d. 30 in.

9. About how much does a car weigh?
   a. about 35 oz
   b. about 35 lb
   c. about 350 oz
   d. about 3,500 lb

10. What is the temperature?

    (thermometer)
    a. -12°F
    b. 22°F
    c. 35°F
    d. 47°F

11. What is $\frac{2}{10} + \frac{3}{10}$ in simplest form?
    a. $\frac{1}{10}$
    b. $\frac{1}{2}$
    c. $\frac{2}{3}$
    d. not given

12. What is $\frac{11}{12} - \frac{7}{12}$ in simplest form?
    a. 4
    b. $1\frac{1}{2}$
    c. $\frac{5}{12}$
    d. $\frac{1}{3}$

13. What is the area of the figure?

    (4 yd square)
    a. 64 square yd
    b. 16 square yd
    c. 8 square yd
    d. 4 square yd

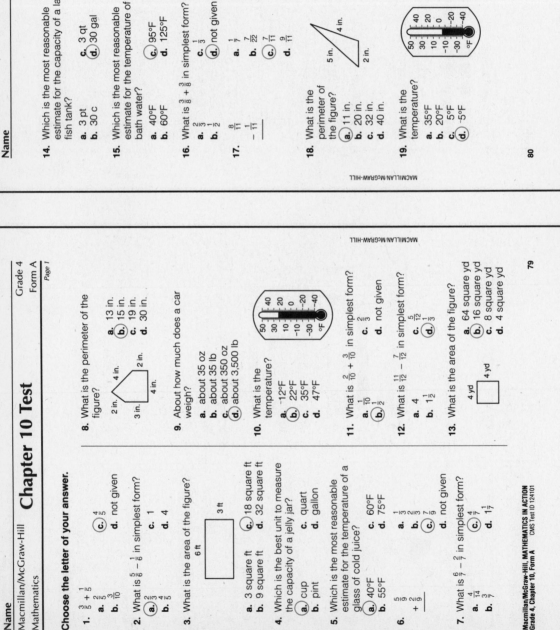

---

14. Which is the most reasonable estimate for the capacity of a large fish tank?
    a. 3 pt
    b. 30 c
    c. 3 qt
    d. 30 gal

15. Which is the most reasonable estimate for the temperature of bath water?
    a. 40°F
    b. 60°F
    c. 95°F
    d. 125°F

16. What is $\frac{3}{8} + \frac{3}{8}$ in simplest form?
    a. $\frac{2}{3}$
    b. $\frac{1}{2}$
    c. $\frac{1}{3}$
    d. not given

17. $\frac{8}{11} - \frac{1}{11}$
    a. $\frac{1}{7}$
    b. $\frac{7}{22}$
    c. $\frac{7}{11}$
    d. $\frac{9}{11}$

18. What is the perimeter of the figure?

    (triangle 5 in., 4 in., 2 in.)
    a. 11 in.
    b. 20 in.
    c. 32 in.
    d. 40 in.

19. What is the temperature?

    a. 35°F
    b. 20°F
    c. 5°F
    d. -5°F

20. Which is the best estimate for the weight of an orange?
    a. 14 oz
    b. 14 lb
    c. 4 oz
    d. 4 lb

    STOP

21. Melinda has a vegetable garden. She planted twice as many beans as cucumbers. She planted 7 more cucumbers than carrots. She planted 40 beans. How many carrots did she plant?
    a. 54
    b. 27
    c. 13
    d. 8

22. Samuel has 327 pennies, 211 nickels, and 159 dimes. How many coins does he have in all?
    a. 116
    b. 370
    c. 588
    d. 697

23. Mrs. Rico buys $\frac{7}{8}$ yd of lace. She sews $\frac{5}{8}$ yd onto a dress. How much lace does she have left?
    a. $\frac{1}{8}$ yd
    b. $\frac{1}{4}$ yd
    c. $\frac{3}{8}$ yd
    d. $\frac{1}{2}$ yd

24. Use number sense.

    Mr. Connell wants to wash the second floor windows of his house. His $11\frac{1}{2}$-ft ladder is too short to reach the windows. Should he get an $11\frac{1}{4}$-ft ladder or an $11\frac{5}{8}$-ft ladder?
    a. $11\frac{1}{4}$-ft ladder
    b. $11\frac{5}{8}$-ft ladder

25. Lea has a square garden that measures 7 yards on each side. What is the area of the garden?
    a. 14 square yd
    b. 21 square yd
    c. 49 square yd
    d. 98 square yd

TM88

Name _____

Chapter 10 Test

Grade 4
Form B

Page 1

Choose the letter of your answer.

1. $\frac{4}{9} + \frac{1}{9}$
   a. $\frac{5}{9}$
   b. $\frac{1}{3}$
   c. $\frac{5}{18}$
   d. not given

2. What is $\frac{7}{8} - \frac{3}{8}$ in simplest form?
   a. $\frac{1}{4}$
   b. $\frac{1}{2}$
   c. $\frac{5}{8}$
   d. $1\frac{1}{4}$

3. What is the area of the figure?
   [3 in. square]
   a. 81 square in.
   b. 12 square in.
   c. 9 square in.
   d. 6 square in.

4. Which is the best unit to measure the capacity of a washing machine?
   a. gallon
   b. quart
   c. pint
   d. cup

5. Which is the most reasonable estimate for the temperature of a cup of hot coffee?
   a. -10°F
   b. 40°F
   c. 75°F
   d. 120°F

6. $\frac{2}{5}$
   $+\frac{1}{5}$
   a. $2\frac{1}{25}$
   b. $1\frac{1}{5}$
   c. $\frac{3}{5}$
   d. not given

7. What is $\frac{5}{8} - \frac{3}{8}$ in simplest form?
   a. $\frac{1}{4}$
   b. $\frac{3}{8}$
   c. $\frac{3}{4}$
   d. $1\frac{1}{8}$

8. What is the perimeter of the figure?
   [triangle: 5 ft, 3 ft, 6 ft]
   a. 11 ft
   b. 14 ft
   c. 28 ft
   d. 90 ft

9. About how much does a pencil weigh?
   a. about 1 oz
   b. about 1 lb
   c. about 10 lb
   d. about 100 oz

10. What is the temperature?
    [thermometer]
    a. -10°F
    b. 10°F
    c. 25°F
    d. 50°F

11. What is $\frac{7}{12} + \frac{1}{12}$ in simplest form?
    a. $\frac{1}{8}$
    b. $\frac{1}{4}$
    c. $\frac{1}{2}$
    d. not given

12. What is $\frac{5}{11} - \frac{2}{11}$ in simplest form?
    a. $\frac{3}{11}$
    b. $\frac{7}{22}$
    c. $\frac{7}{11}$
    d. 3

13. What is the area of the figure?
    [rectangle: 5 yd by 2 yd]
    a. 20 square yd
    b. 14 square yd
    c. 10 square yd
    d. 7 square yd

Name _____

Page 2

14. Which is the most reasonable estimate for the capacity of a Thermos bottle?
    a. 8 c
    b. 8 pt
    c. 80 qt
    d. 8 gal

15. Which is the best estimate for the temperature of snow?
    a. 25°F
    b. 40°F
    c. 55°F
    d. 70°F

16. What is $\frac{1}{8} + \frac{1}{8}$ in simplest form?
    a. 1
    b. $\frac{1}{2}$
    c. $\frac{1}{4}$
    d. not given

17. $\frac{7}{10}$
    $-\frac{4}{10}$
    a. $1\frac{1}{10}$
    b. $\frac{11}{20}$
    c. $\frac{1}{2}$
    d. $\frac{3}{10}$

18. What is the perimeter of the figure?
    [hexagon: 2 in. sides]
    a. 10 in.
    b. 12 in.
    c. 24 in.
    d. 64 in.

19. What is the temperature?
    [thermometer]
    a. -5°F
    b. 12°F
    c. 25°F
    d. 40°F

20. Which is the best estimate for the weight of a school bus?
    a. 200 oz
    b. 200 lb
    c. 20,000 oz
    d. 20,000 lb
    STOP

21. Jay is buying art supplies. A paint tube costs $2.79. A paintbrush costs $6.00. A pad of special paper costs $9.59. Jay needs 5 paint tubes, 2 brushes, and 1 pad of paper. Will $25.00 be enough to pay for these items?
    a. Yes.
    b. No.

22. Calvin has 446 red tiles, 318 blue tiles, and 120 green tiles. How many tiles does he have in all?
    a. 884
    b. 750
    c. 568
    d. 87

23. Mr. Girard buys $\frac{3}{4}$ yd of canvas. He uses $\frac{1}{4}$ yd to repair a tent. How much canvas does he have left?
    a. $\frac{1}{8}$ yd
    b. $\frac{1}{4}$ yd
    c. $\frac{1}{2}$ yd
    d. 1 yd

24. Use number sense.
    Sarah needs to tie up a large box. A $9\frac{1}{4}$-ft piece of twine is not long enough. Should she use a $9\frac{1}{2}$-ft or a $9\frac{1}{8}$-ft piece of twine?
    a. $9\frac{1}{2}$-ft piece of twine
    b. $9\frac{1}{8}$-ft piece of twine

25. A rectangular swimming pool measures 8 yards by 10 yards. What is the area of the pool?
    a. 160 square yd
    b. 80 square yd
    c. 36 square yd
    d. 18 square yd

Name

Macmillan/McGraw-Hill
Mathematics

Grade 4
Form C
Page 1

Chapter 10 Test

Mark your answer.

1. $\frac{3}{5} + \frac{1}{5}$

$\frac{4}{5}$

2. What is $\frac{5}{6} - \frac{1}{6}$ in simplest form?

$\frac{2}{3}$

3. What is the area of the figure?

3 ft

6 ft

18 square ft

4. Is a cup, a pint, a quart, or a gallon the best unit to measure the capacity of a jelly jar?

a cup

5. Ring the most reasonable estimate for the temperature of a glass of cold juice.

40°F   60°F
55°F   75°F

6. $\begin{array}{r} \frac{5}{9} \\ + \frac{2}{9} \\ \hline \end{array}$

$\frac{7}{9}$

7. What is $\frac{6}{7} - \frac{2}{7}$ in simplest form?

$\frac{4}{7}$

8. What is the perimeter of the figure?

2 in.   4 in.
2 in.
3 in.   4 in.

15 in.

9. Is the best estimate of a car's weight 35 oz, 35 lb, 350 oz, or 3,500 lb?

3,500 lb

10. What is the temperature?

22°F

11. What is $\frac{2}{10} + \frac{3}{10}$ in simplest form?

$\frac{1}{2}$

12. What is $\frac{11}{12} - \frac{7}{12}$ in simplest form?

$\frac{1}{3}$

13. What is the area of the figure?

4 yd

4 yd

16 square yd

Macmillan/McGraw-Hill, MATHEMATICS IN ACTION
Grade 4, Chapter 10, Form C

MACMILLAN/McGRAW-HILL

Name

Page 2

14. Is the most reasonable estimate for the capacity of a large fish tank 3 pints, 30 cups, 3 quarts, or 30 gallons?

30 gallons

15. Ring the most reasonable estimate for the temperature of bath water.

40°F   95°F
60°F   125°F

16. What is $\frac{3}{8} + \frac{3}{8}$ in simplest form?

$\frac{3}{4}$

17. $\begin{array}{r} \frac{8}{11} \\ - \frac{1}{11} \\ \hline \end{array}$

$\frac{7}{11}$

18. What is the perimeter of the figure?

5 in.   4 in.
2 in.

11 in.

19. What is the temperature?

–5°F

20. Is the best estimate for the weight of an orange 14 oz, 14 lb, 4 oz, or 4 lb?

4 oz

STOP

21. Melinda has a vegetable garden. She planted twice as many beans as cucumbers. She planted 7 more cucumbers than carrots. She planted 40 beans. How many carrots did she plant?

13

22. Samuel has 327 pennies, 211 nickels, and 159 dimes. How many coins does he have in all?

697

23. Mrs. Rico buys $\frac{7}{8}$ yd of lace. She sews $\frac{5}{8}$ yd onto a dress. How much lace does she have left?

$\frac{1}{4}$ yd

24. Use number sense.
Mr. Connell wants to wash the second floor windows of his house. His $11\frac{1}{2}$-ft ladder is too short to reach the windows. Should he get an $11\frac{1}{4}$-ft ladder or an $11\frac{5}{8}$-ft ladder?

$11\frac{5}{8}$-ft ladder

25. Lea has a square garden that measures 7 yards on each side. What is the area of the garden?

49 square yd

Macmillan/McGraw-Hill, MATHEMATICS IN ACTION
Grade 4, Chapter 10, Form C

Name _____

Macmillan/McGraw-Hill **Chapter 11 Test**   Grade 4
Mathematics   Form A

Page 1

Choose the letter of your answer.

1. What is the decimal for $\frac{6}{10}$?
a. 6.0   c. 0.06
(b.) 0.6   d. not given

2. Compare.
   0.45 ⬤ $\frac{45}{100}$
a. >   b. <   (c.) =

3. Estimate by rounding.
   5.12 + 7.79
a. 5   b. 8   c. 12   (d.) 13

4. 4.5 + 2.3
(a.) 6.8   c. 0.68
b. 2.2   d. 0.22

5. A quarter is tossed 150 times. Predict how many times it will land heads up.
a. 150   b. 125   c. 100   (d.) 75

6. Seven hundredths is the word name for _____.
a. 7   (c.) 0.07
b. 1.7   d. not given

7. Compare.
   3.8 ⬤ 8.3
a. >   (b.) <   c. =

8. Estimate. Use the front digits and adjust.
   18.23 − 9.37
a. <8   (b.) <9   c. >9   d. >18

9. 0.9 − 0.5
a. 4.0   (c.) 0.4
b. 1.4   d. 0.04

10. Predict how many times the spinner will land on ▲ in 8 spins.

(a.) 2   b. 4   c. 6   d. 8

11. What is the decimal for $2\frac{3}{10}$?
(a.) 2.3   c. 0.3
b. 1.3   d. not given

12. Compare.
   5.90 ⬤ 5.09
(a.) >   b. <   c. =

13. Which is the best estimate of 6.8 − 5.4?
a. <0   b. >0   (c.) >1   d. >10

14.   0.75
       + 0.81
a. 0.06   b. 0.16   (c.) 1.56   d. 15.6

15. There are 3 blue cubes, 2 red cubes, and 1 green cube in a bag. What is the probability of picking a red cube?
(a.) $\frac{1}{3}$ b. $\frac{1}{2}$ c. $\frac{1}{5}$ d. $\frac{1}{6}$

Macmillan/McGraw-Hill, MATHEMATICS IN ACTION
Grade 4, Chapter 11, Form A   CMS Test ID 124111

85

Name _____

16. Which is nine-tenths?
a. 9.1   c. 1.9
b. 9.01   (d.) not given

17. Which set of numbers is ordered from least to greatest?
(a.) 0.13, 0.3, 3.1   c. 1.3, 0.3, 0.13
b. 5.6, 6.5, 0.65   d. 0.65, 6.5, 5.6

18. Estimate by rounding. 3.7 + 8.9
a. 11   b. 12   (c.) 13   d. 15

19.   12.1
       − 8.25
a. 3.25   b. 3.85   c. 16.15   d. 20.35
(b.) 3.85

20. Predict how many times the spinner will land on R in 12 spins.

a. 12   b. 6   (c.) 4   d. 2

🛑 STOP

21. Roger has $1.79 in his pocket. He has $3.33 in his coin jar. About how much money does he have in all?
a. about $1.00   (c.) about $5.00
b. about $3.00   d. about $7.00

22. Each student in the school play plans to wear a white, black, or red hat with a red or blue scarf. How many different combinations can each student make?
a. 3   b. 4   c. 5   (d.) 6

23. Janna collected 57 seashells. Peter and Steve collected 49 seashells each. Sophie collected 31 seashells. How many seashells did the children collect in all?
a. 96   b. 137   (c.) 186   d. 217

24. Marcia and her mother drive $13\frac{6}{10}$ miles to the store. Which decimal shows how many miles Marcia and her mother drive?
a. 0.13 mi   c. 6.13 mi
b. 1.36 mi   (d.) 13.6 mi

Use the tree diagram to answer Question 25.

Tree Diagram	List
3-speed bike — basket — rack	3-speed—basket 3-speed—rack
5-speed bike — basket — rack	
10-speed bike	

25. Jeb wants to get a new bicycle. He has a choice of a 3-speed, a 5-speed, or a 10-speed bike. All three types come with either a handlebar basket or a rear-wheel rack. How many choices does Jeb have?
(a.) 6   b. 9   c. 12   d. 18

Macmillan/McGraw-Hill, MATHEMATICS IN ACTION
Grade 4, Chapter 11, Form A

86

Page 1 (right side)

Choose the letter of your answer.

1. What is the decimal for $\frac{3}{10}$?
a. 0.03 c. 3.0
b. 1.3 (d.) not given

2. Compare.
2.5 ● 5.2
a. > (b.) < c. =

3. Estimate by rounding.
4.22 + 6.85
a. 63 (b.) 11 c. 10 d. 3

4. 7.6 + 1.3
a. 0.89 c. 6.3
b. 0.63 (d.) 8.9

5. A quarter is tossed 100 times. Predict how many times it will land tails up.
a. 10 b. 20 (c.) 50 d. 100

6. Eight tenths is the word name for _____.
a. 0.08 c. 1.8
(b.) 0.8 d. not given

7. Compare.
0.72 ● $\frac{72}{100}$
a. > b. < (c.) =

8. Estimate. Use the front digits and adjust.
14.13 − 6.33
(a.) < 8 b. > 8 c. < 20 d. > 20

9. 0.8 − 0.2
a. 0.06 c. 1.0
(b.) 0.6 d. 6.0

10. Predict how many times the spinner will land on J in 10 spins.

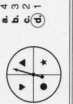

a. 1
b. 2
c. 3
(d.) 4

11. What is the decimal for $8\frac{5}{10}$?
a. 0.58 c. 8.5
b. 0.85 d. not given

12. Compare.
1.40 ● 1.04
(a.) > b. < c. =

13. Which is the best estimate of 5.7 − 4.2?
a. < 0 c. > 1
b. < 1 d. > 10

14. 0.97
+ 0.62
a. 0.95
(b.) 1.59
c. 9.5
d. 15.9

15. There are 4 apples, 2 pears, and 1 orange in a bag. What is the probability of picking a pear?
a. $\frac{1}{7}$ (b.) $\frac{2}{7}$ c. $\frac{2}{5}$ d. $\frac{4}{7}$

Page 2 (top section)

16. Which is three hundredths?
(a.) 0.03 c. 3.00
b. 0.3 d. not given

17. Which set of numbers is ordered from least to greatest?
a. 2.7, 0.27, 0.7 (c.) 0.27, 0.7, 2.7
b. 0.5, 1.5, 0.15 d. 0.15, 1.5, 0.5

18. Estimate by rounding.
6.3 + 4.8
a. 12 (b.) 11 c. 10 d. 9

19. 17.5
− 8.37
a. 25.87
b. 11.27
c. 9.27
(d.) 9.13

20. Predict how many times the spinner will land on ♥ in 4 spins.

a. 4
b. 3
c. 2
(d.) 1

STOP

21. Monica earns $4.85 selling newspapers on Saturday. She earns $7.32 selling newspapers on Sunday. About how much money does she earn in all?
a. about $10.00 c. about $14.00
(b.) about $12.00 d. about $15.00

22. Each clown in the parade plans to wear an orange, green, or purple wig with a black, white, or red hat. How many different combinations can each clown make?
(a.) 9 b. 6 c. 5 d. 4

23. Carol saved 205 pennies. Mitch saved 39 nickels. Henry saved 54 dimes and 146 pennies. How many coins did they save in all?
a. 351 (b.) 444 c. 550 d. 1,086

24. The Lord family drives $23\frac{7}{10}$ miles to the beach. Which decimal shows how many miles the Lord family drives?
a. 0.7 mi (c.) 23.7 mi
b. 2.37 mi d. 70.23 mi

Use the tree diagram to answer Question 25.

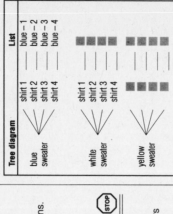

25. Kathy wants to wear a shirt and sweater combination. She has a blue sweater, a white sweater, and a yellow sweater. She has 4 shirts. How many different combinations can she put together?
a. 7 (b.) 12 c. 24 d. 32

Chapter 11 Test

Name
Macmillan/McGraw-Hill
Mathematics

Grade 4
Form C
Page 1

Mark your answer.

1. What is the decimal for $\frac{6}{10}$?

   0.6

2. Compare. Write >, <, or =.

   0.45 ● $\frac{45}{100}$

   =

3. Estimate by rounding.

   5.12 + 7.79

   13

4. 4.5 + 2.3

   6.8

5. A quarter is tossed 150 times. Predict how many times it will land heads up.

   75

6. Seven hundredths is the word name for what decimal?

   0.07

7. Compare. Write >, <, or =.

   3.8 ● 8.3

   <

8. Estimate. Use the front digits and adjust.

   18.23 − 9.37

   <9

9. 0.9 − 0.5

   0.4

10. Predict how many times the spinner will land on ▲ in 8 spins.

    2

11. What is the decimal for $2\frac{3}{10}$?

    2.3

12. Compare. Write >, <, or =.

    5.90 ● 5.09

    >

13. Ring the best estimate of 6.8 − 5.4.

    < 0
    > 0
    (> 1)
    > 10

14. 0.75 + 0.81

    1.56

15. There are 3 blue cubes, 2 red cubes, and 1 green cube in a bag. What is the probability of picking a red cube?

    $\frac{1}{3}$

---

16. Write the decimal for nine-tenths.

    0.9

17. Write in order from least to greatest.

    0.3, 0.13, 3.1

    0.13, 0.3, 3.1

18. Estimate by rounding. 3.7 + 8.9

    13

19. 12.1
    − 8.25

    3.85

20. Predict how many times the spinner will land on R in 12 spins.

    4

21. Roger has $1.79 in his pocket. He has $3.33 in his coin jar. About how much money does he have in all?

    about $5.00

22. Each student in the school play plans to wear a white, black, or red hat with a red or blue scarf. How many different combinations can each student make?

    6

23. Janna collected 57 seashells. Peter and Steve collected 49 seashells each. Sophie collected 31 seashells. How many seashells did the children collect in all?

    186

24. Marcia and her mother drive $13\frac{6}{10}$ miles to the store. Write the decimal that shows how many miles Marcia and her mother drive.

    13.6 mi

Use the tree diagram to answer Question 25.

Tree Diagram		List
3-speed bike	basket \ rack	3-speed—basket
		3-speed—rack
5-speed bike	basket \ rack	
10-speed bike		

25. Jeb wants to get a new bicycle. He has a choice of a 3-speed, a 5-speed, or a 10-speed bike. All three types come with either a handlebar basket or a rear-wheel rack. How many choices does Jeb have?

    6

Chapter 12 Test

Choose the letter of your answer.

1. 20 × 40
   a. 8
   b. 80
   c. 800 ⟲
   d. not given

2. Estimate by using the front digits.
   23 × 56
   a. 100
   b. 120
   c. 1,000 ⟲
   d. 1,200

3. 18 × 97
   a. 1,755
   b. 1,746 ⟲
   c. 1,696
   d. 873

4. 10)500
   a. 5
   b. 50 ⟲
   c. 500
   d. 5,000

5. 25 ÷ 10
   a. 2 R5 ⟲
   b. 2 R15
   c. 10 R5
   d. 20 R10

6. 500 × 40
   a. 200
   b. 2,000
   c. 200,000
   d. not given ⟲

7. Estimate by rounding.
   97 × $68
   a. $700
   b. $7,000 ⟲
   c. $70,000
   d. $700,000

8. 20 ÷ 20
   a. 20
   b. 10
   c. 1 ⟲
   d. 0

9. $24 × 23
   a. $110
   b. $120
   c. $552 ⟲
   d. $561

10. 90)360
    a. 4 ⟲
    b. 40
    c. 270
    d. 400

11. Which is the best estimate of 26 × $84?
    a. $240
    b. $2,400 ⟲
    c. $24,000
    d. $240,000

12. 80 × 9,000
    a. 720,000 ⟲
    b. 72,000
    c. 7,200
    d. not given

13. 42 × $32
    a. $210
    b. $814
    c. $1,234
    d. $1,344 ⟲

14. 800 ÷ 40
    a. 200
    b. 3,200
    c. 200 ⟲
    d. 20

15. 30)525
    a. 2 R25
    b. 17 R15 ⟲
    c. 20 R25
    d. 170 R15

16. 300 × 60
    a. 18,000 ⟲
    b. 1,800
    c. 180
    d. not given

---

17. 69
    × 41
    a. 28
    b. 345
    c. 2,589
    d. 2,829 ⟲

18. Estimate by using the front digits.
    44 × 72
    a. 2,800 ⟲
    b. 3,500
    c. 28,000
    d. 35,000

19. 50)3,000
    a. 6
    b. 60 ⟲
    c. 600
    d. 6,000

20. 120 ÷ 10
    a. 1,200
    b. 110
    c. 30
    d. 12 ⟲

21. Carla wants to collect 600 baseball cards. The cards come in packages of 20. How many packages will she need?
    a. 3
    b. 20
    c. 30 ⟲
    d. 200

22. The Blue Kites baseball team bought 30 new T-shirts. Each T-shirt cost $12. How much did the team spend in all?
    a. $2
    b. $18
    c. $42
    d. $360 ⟲

23. Each student in the rally plans to make a poster with a red or white background and blue or black letters. How many color combinations of background and letters can each student make?
    a. 2
    b. 4 ⟲
    c. 6
    d. 8

24. The school band must sell 500 boxes of fruit. If each member sells 10 boxes, all the fruit will be gone. How many band members are there?
    a. 5
    b. 50 ⟲
    c. 500
    d. 5,000

25. There are 25 classrooms in Brian's school. Each classroom holds 20 desks. Which number sentence should you use to find how many desks there are in all?
    a. 25 + 20 =
    b. 25 – 20 =
    c. 25 × 20 = ⟲
    d. 25 + 20 =

STOP

TM94

Name _____

Macmillan/McGraw-Hill
Mathematics

Chapter 12 Test

Grade 4
Form B

Choose the letter of your answer.

1. 30 × 60
   a. 18
   b. 180
   c. 1,800
   d. not given

2. Estimate by using the front digits.
   35 × 47
   a. 20,000
   b. 2,000
   c. 1,600
   d. 1,200

3. 15 × 79
   a. 474
   b. 1,185
   c. 1,190
   d. 1,194

4. 70)700
   a. 1
   b. 10
   c. 100
   d. 1,000

5. 83 ÷ 10
   a. 8 R3
   b. 8 R13
   c. 10 R3
   d. 10 R13

6. 200 × 50
   a. 10,000
   b. 1,000
   c. 100
   d. not given

7. Estimate by using the front digits.
   43 × $95
   a. $36,000
   b. $4,000
   c. $3,600
   d. $320

8. 40 ÷ 10
   a. 400
   b. 40
   c. 30
   d. 4

9. $53 × 38
   a. $304
   b. $1,594
   c. $1,672
   d. $2,014

10. 80)480
    a. 6
    b. 7
    c. 60
    d. 600

11. Which is the best estimate of 61 × $73?
    a. $420
    b. $480
    c. $4,200
    d. $48,000

12. 70 × 5,000
    a. 35,000
    b. 3,500
    c. 350
    d. not given

13. 54 × $86
    a. $4,644
    b. $4,392
    c. $4,324
    d. $744

14. 600 ÷ 30
    a. 30
    b. 20
    c. 3
    d. 2

15. 20)166
    a. 8 R6
    b. 71 R3
    c. 80 R6
    d. 710 R3

16. 700 × 90
    a. 63,000
    b. 6,300
    c. 630
    d. not given

Name _____

17. 71
    × 65
    a. 45,565
    b. 4,615
    c. 781
    d. 620

18. Estimate by rounding.
    16 × 88
    a. 80
    b. 180
    c. 1,800
    d. 8,000

19. 50)4,000
    a. 8
    b. 80
    c. 800
    d. 8,000

20. 190 ÷ 10
    a. 9
    b. 19
    c. 180
    d. 1,900

21. Sally has 300 stamps. She plans to put them in books that hold 30 stamps each. How many books will she need?
    a. 100
    b. 30
    c. 20
    d. 10

22. The Jets baseball team bought 20 new uniforms this year. Each uniform cost $38. How much did the team spend in all?
    a. $760
    b. $58
    c. $18
    d. $2

23. Each student in the Halloween parade plans to wear orange or black socks with black, white, or gray sneakers. How many color combinations of sneakers and socks can each student make?
    a. 2
    b. 4
    c. 6
    d. 8

24. There are 20 cabins at Connie's summer camp for girls. Each cabin houses 10 girls. How many girls can stay at the camp at one time?
    a. 80
    b. 100
    c. 200
    d. 1,000

25. There are 36 teachers in Claudia's school. Each teacher has 20 students. Which number sentence should you use to find how many students there are in all?
    a. 36 + 20 =
    b. 36 − 20 =
    c. 36 + 20 =
    d. 36 × 20 =

STOP

Page 1

Name
Macmillan/McGraw-Hill
Mathematics

Grade 4
Form C
Page 1

Chapter 12 Test

Mark your answer.

1. 20 × 40

   800

2. Estimate by using the front digits.
   23 × 56

   1,000

3. 18 × 97

   1,746

4. 10)500

   50

5. 25 ÷ 10

   2 R5

6. 500
   × 40

   20,000

7. Estimate by rounding.
   97 × $68

   $7,000

8. 20 ÷ 20

   1

9. $24
   × 23

   $552

10. 90)360

    4

11. Estimate. 26 × $84

    accept $1,600 – $2,400

12. 80 × 9,000

    720,000

13. 42 × $32

    $1,344

14. 800 ÷ 40

    20

15. 30)525

    17 R15

16. 300
    × 60

    18,000

Page 2

17. 69
    × 41

    2,829

18. Estimate by using the front digits.
    44 × 72

    2,800

19. 50)3,000

    60

20. 120 ÷ 10

    12

STOP

21. Carla wants to collect 600 baseball cards. The cards come in packages of 20. How many packages will she need?

    30

22. The Blue Kites baseball team bought 30 new T-shirts. Each T-shirt cost $12. How much did the team spend in all?

    $360

23. Each student in the rally plans to make a poster with a red or white background and blue or black letters. How many color combinations of background and letters can each student make?

    4

24. The school band must sell 500 boxes of fruit. If each member sells 10 boxes, all the fruit will be gone. How many band members are there?

    50

25. There are 25 classrooms in Brian's school. Each classroom holds 20 desks. Write a number sentence to find how many desks there are in all.

    25 × 20 = 500

Name

Choose the letter of your answer.

1. What is the value of 7 in the number 247,102,000?
a. 7,000   **c. 7,000,000**
b. 70,000   d. 700,000,000

2. How much is 1 five-dollar bill, 3 one-dollar bills, 2 quarters, and 1 dime?
a. $5.60   c. $8.99
b. $8.60   d. not given

3. Compare. 34,798 ● 35,100
a. >   **b. <**   c. =

4. Round 892 to the nearest hundred.
a. 800   **c. 900**
b. 850   d. 1,000

5. 9 − 0
a. 0   **b. 9**   c. 10   d. 90

6. Cost: $4.70 Given: $5.00 Change?
a. 3 dimes, 1 nickel
b. 2 dimes, 3 nickels
c. 1 quarter, 1 dime
d. 1 quarter, 1 nickel

7. Which amount is greatest?
a. $2.99   c. $2.20
b. $3.00   **d. $3.02**

8. Round $11.47 to the nearest ten cents.
a. $11.00   **c. $11.50**
b. $11.45   d. $11.60

9. Find the perimeter.
[square: 8 cm, 11 cm, 8 cm, 11 cm]
a. 88 cm   c. 29 cm
b. 38 cm   d. not given

10. What is the length of the flower?
[ruler 0–6 cm]
a. 1 cm   c. 5 cm
b. 2 cm   d. 10 cm

11. Find the perimeter.
[triangle: 18 m, 23 m, 12 m]
a. 35 m   **c. 53 m**
b. 48 m   d. 63 m

12. Which is the best unit to measure the length of a river?
a. cm   b. dm   c. m   **d. km**

13. Which is the best unit to measure the length of a house?
a. km   **b. m**   c. dm   d. cm

Name

14. Find the perimeter.
[trapezoid: 9 cm, 15 cm, 7 cm, 20 cm]
a. 28 cm   **c. 51 cm**
b. 44 cm   d. 56 cm

15. What is the length of the bolt?
[ruler 0–6 cm]
a. 1 cm   c. 28 cm
b. 2 cm   d. 200 cm

16. Find the perimeter.
[square: 5 cm each side]
a. 25 cm   c. 18 cm
b. 20 cm   d. 10 cm

17. The length of an envelope is about ___.
a. 22 km   c. 22 dm
b. 22 m   **d. 22 cm**

18. Find the perimeter.
[pentagon: 12 m each side]
a. 60 m   c. 108 m
b. 72 m   d. 144 m

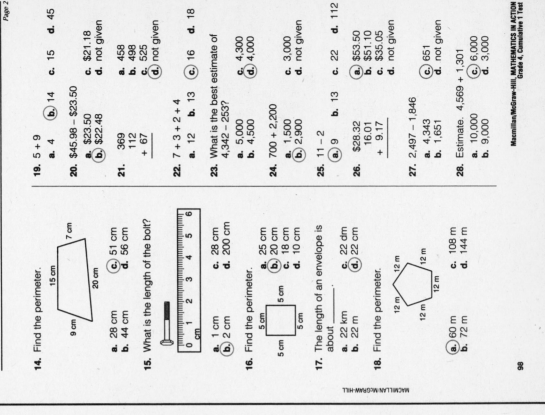

19. 5 + 9
a. 4   **b. 14**   c. 15   d. 45

20. $45.98 − $23.50
a. $23.50   c. $21.18
b. $22.48   d. not given

21. 369
112
+ 67
a. 458   b. 498   c. 525   **d. not given**

22. 7 + 3 + 2 + 4
a. 12   b. 13   **c. 16**   d. 18

23. What is the best estimate of 4,342 − 253?
a. 5,000   c. 4,300
b. 4,500   **d. 4,000**

24. 700 + 2,200
a. 1,500   c. 3,000
b. 2,900   d. not given

25. 11 − 2
a. 9   b. 13   c. 22   d. 112

26. $28.32
16.01
+ 9.17
a. $53.50   c. $35.05
b. $51.10   d. not given

27. 2,497 − 1,846
a. 4,343   **c. 651**
b. 1,651   d. not given

28. Estimate. 4,569 + 1,301
a. 10,000   **c. 6,000**
b. 9,000   d. 3,000

TM97

29. 17
  − 9

a. 7   c. 9
b. 8   d. 10

30. $54.62 + $19.90

a. $74.52   c. $75.62
b. $74.65   d. not given

31. Estimate by rounding.

$8.99 + $1.03 + $4.24

a. $12.00   c. $14.00
b. $13.00   d. $15.00

32. $97.28 − $82.36

a. $14.92   c. $16.89
b. $15.02   d. not given

33. 7,800
  + 700

a. 1,480   c. 14,800
b. 7,700   d. not given

Use the table to answer Questions 34–36.

Store	Price		
	Wrench	Bolt	Nail
Discount Wares	$5.95	$.28	$.08
T & B Hardware	$7.95	$.33	$.03
Nails and Things	$7.50		$.08
Home Works	$9.99	$.33	$.15

34. What is the price of a nail at T & B Hardware?

a. $.01 b. $.03 c. $.15 d. $.28

35. What is the most likely price of a bolt at Nails and Things?

a. $.53   c. $.08
b. $.28   d. $.01

36. Which store sells the most expensive wrench?

a. Discount Wares
b. T & B Hardware
c. Nails and Things
d. Home Works

Use the bar graph to answer Questions 37–40.

TOY CARS IN DICK'S STORE

37. Dick's store has the most of which color toy car?

a. black   c. blue
b. red   d. yellow

38. How many black toy cars are there in Dick's store?

a. 40 b. 30 c. 20 d. 10

39. How many red toy cars are there in Dick's store?

a. 50 b. 30 c. 10 d. 0

40. The store has an equal number of green toy cars and ___ toy cars.

a. red   c. yellow
b. blue   d. black

STOP

---

41. Use number sense.

If Wenona buys 3 notebooks, about how much money will she spend?

a. about $.50   c. about $50.00
b. about $5.00   d. about $100.00

42. Use number sense.

Anita buys one loaf of bread. About how many slices of bread can she cut from one loaf?

a. about 5   c. about 200
b. about 20   d. about 500

43. Jane builds 8 sandcastles at the beach. She puts 2 flags on top of each sandcastle. Then the ocean washes away some of the sandcastles. What information is needed to find how many sandcastles are left?

a. the amount of time Jane takes to build each sandcastle
b. the colors of the flags
c. the number of sandcastles the ocean washes away

44. Use number sense.

If Roy gives a flower to each student in his fourth-grade classroom, about how many flowers will he give out?

a. about 30   c. about 3,000
b. about 300   d. about 30,000

45. Alex spends $2.98 at the store. He gives the clerk $5.00. Which number sentence tells how much change Alex should receive?

a. $5.00 − $2.98 = ▪
b. $5.00 + $2.98 = ▪

46. At the park Karl spent $6.50 on rides, $3.35 on games, and $4.80 on food. Which is the most reasonable answer for how much Karl spent in all?

a. $14.65   c. $146.50
b. $24.65   d. $1,465.00

47. May has $10.00 to buy 25 cookies at the store. What else do you need to know to find if May has enough money for the cookies?

a. the name of the store
b. how large the cookies are
c. how much each cookie costs
d. what the cookies are made of

48. Stan's Juice Stand sold 948 glasses of lemonade and 432 glasses of orange juice. Which number sentence should you use to find how many more glasses of lemonade than orange juice were sold?

a. 948 − 432 = ▪
b. 948 + 432 = ▪

49. Mr. Okiko is building a fence that is 10 meters long. He puts a post at each end and at every 2 meters along the inside of the fence. How many posts are there in all?

a. 4 b. 5 c. 6 d. 7

50. On their vacation the Nash family drove 74 km on Sunday, 117 km on Monday, and 153 km on Tuesday. They want to know how many km they drove in all. Which is the most reasonable answer?

a. 191 km   c. 344 km
b. 270 km   d. 497 km

TM98

Name

Macmillan/McGraw-Hill
Mathematics

Cumulative 2 Test

Grade 4

Choose the letter of your answer.

1. Which number is greatest?
   a. 3,894   c. 3,984
   b. 3,498   d. 3,489

2. Round $15.43 to the nearest ten cents.
   a. $15.50   c. $15.00
   b. $15.40   d. not given

3. 0 + 8
   a. 16   b. 8   c. 1   d. 0

4. Which numbers are all factors of 32?
   a. 2, 4, 6, 8   c. 2, 4, 8, 18
   b. 2, 4, 8, 16   d. 2, 8, 16, 18

5. Which of the following has only even numbers?
   a. 2, 4, 6, 9
   b. 12, 16, 21, 32
   c. 1, 10, 14, 28
   d. 20, 24, 28, 46

6. 5 × 4
   a. 15   c. 25
   b. 20   d. not given

7. Which numbers are all multiples of 9?
   a. 3, 9, 18, 27   c. 9, 18, 27, 36
   b. 9, 18, 27, 32   d. 18, 27, 45, 56

8. Which number is prime?
   a. 35   b. 21   c. 18   d. 11

9. Find the perimeter.
   a. 7 cm   c. 4 cm
   b. 8 cm   d. 3 cm
   d. 12 cm

10. How long is the doll necklace?
    a. 6 cm   c. 4 cm
    b. 5 cm   d. 3 cm

11. What time does the clock show?
    a. 11:10   c. 1:10
    b. 11:50   d. 1:50

12. You can usually go ice-skating outside when the temperature is ____
    a. -10°C   c. 30°C
    b. 20°C   d. 100°C

13. What is the area?
    a. 16 square m   c. 40 square m
    b. 32 square m   d. 64 square m

14. What is the best estimate for the mass of a large dog?
    a. 20 kg   c. 2 g
    b. 20 mg   d. 2 mg

Name

15. How much time passes between 9:05 A.M. and 9:50 A.M.?
    a. 55 minutes   c. 45 minutes
    b. 50 minutes   d. not given

16. What is the temperature shown?
    a. -40°C   c. 10°C
    b. -10°C   d. 40°C

17. What is the area of a rectangle 7 cm long and 5 cm wide?
    a. 12 square cm
    b. 24 square cm
    c. 35 square cm
    d. not given

18. About how long is a school day?
    a. about 6 seconds
    b. about 60 minutes
    c. about 6 hours
    d. about 60 hours

19. 9 + 3
    a. 11   b. 12   c. 13   d. 93

20. What is the best estimate of 5,703 - 2,981?
    a. 1,000   c. 3,000
    b. 2,000   d. 4,000

21. 4,538 + 9,876
    a. 14,414   c. 14,304
    b. 14,314   d. 13,304

22. 5 × 6,000
    a. 30,000   c. 3,000,000
    b. 300,000   d. not given

23. About how much is 7 × $9.89?
    a. about $50.00
    b. about $60.00
    c. about $70.00
    d. about $100.00

24. 3 × 534
    a. 1,502   c. 1,597
    b. 1,592   d. 1,602

25. 2 × $8.55
    a. $17.10   c. $16.77
    b. $17.00   d. not given

26. Estimate by rounding.
    $7.16 + $4.87 + $5.31
    a. $16.00   c. $18.00
    b. $17.00   d. $19.00

27. $87.14
    − 39.85
    a. $58.39   c. $47.39
    b. $58.29   d. $47.29

28. 70
    × 8
    a. 56   c. 56,000
    b. 5,600   d. not given

29. Estimate. 5 × 78
    a. 350   c. 3,500
    b. 400   d. 4,000

30. 112
    × 8
    a. 886
    b. 890
    c. 896
    d. 904

Name

41. Find the pattern to solve.

The night watchman first checks Building A at 12:30. The second time he checks the building is at 1:45. The third time he checks the building is at 3:00. At what time does he check the building for the fifth time?

a. 5:15   c. 5:45
b. 5:30   d. 6:00

42. Lou had 23 toy trains. He received 2 more as gifts. He bought some more. What else do you need to know to find how many toy trains he has now?

a. what city the store is in
b. how many toy trains he bought
c. what color the toy trains are
d. how many cars are in each train

43. Three airport runways measure 613 m, 789 m, and 574 m long. Which is the most reasonable answer for the total length of all three runways?

a. 7,493 m   c. 1,402 m
b. 1,976 m   d. 1,187 m

44. The library had 4,368 books. The library then bought 546 more books. How many books does the library have now?

a. 1,092   c. 4,914
b. 3,822   d. 9,828

45. Draper's Ranch has 435 horses and 552 cows. The ranch sells 143 cows. How many cows does the ranch have now?

a. 292   b. 409   c. 844   d. 987

46. Ed takes $15.63 to the baseball game. He spends $2.27. His mother gives him $5.75 more. How much money does he have now?

a. $3.48   c. $19.11
b. $8.36   d. $23.65

47. Mr. Polk has 736 pieces of wood. He has 8 crates and wants to put an equal amount of wood into each crate. How many pieces of wood should he put in each crate?

a. 92   c. 744
b. 728   d. 5,888

48. Use number sense.

Anna bought 2 cookies. About how much did she spend?

a. about $1
b. about $15
c. about $100
d. about $500

49. Susana and Andy drew 28 pictures. Andy drew 3 times as many pictures as Susana drew. How many pictures did Andy draw?

a. 3   b. 7   c. 14   d. 21

50. Wyatt and Cindy wanted to save $50.00 to buy a radio. Wyatt saved $27.25 and Cindy saved $18.50. Did they save enough money to buy the radio?

a. Yes.   b. No.

Name

31. 5 × $7.01

a. $12.06   c. $35.55
b. $35.05   d. not given

32. 29
× 9

a. 181   c. 261
b. 252   d. 299

33. 4 × $.62

a. $3.10   c. $2.48
b. $2.58   d. not given

Use the bar graph to answer Questions 34–36.

TOM'S FRUIT STAND

34. Tom's Fruit Stand has the least amount of which fruit?

a. cherries   c. apples
b. oranges   d. lemons

35. Tom's Fruit Stand has the same amount of _____.

a. lemons and oranges
b. oranges and bananas
c. apples and lemons
d. cherries and apples

36. How many bananas does Tom's Fruit Stand have?

a. 10   b. 20   c. 30   d. 40

Use the grid to answer Questions 37 and 38.

37. The ordered pair for point *E* is _____.

a. (1, 2)   c. (3, 3)
b. (2, 4)   d. not given

38. Which letter is at the point (2, 2)?

a. *A*   b. *B*   c. *C*   d. *E*

Use the line graph to answer Questions 39 and 40.

SNOWFALL IN CROW VALLEY

39. Which month had the greatest amount of snowfall?

a. January   c. April
b. March   d. May

40. How much snow fell in March?

a. 4 meters   c. 2 meters
b. 3 meters   d. 1 meters

STOP

Name

Macmillan/McGraw-Hill **Cumulative 3 Test** Grade 4
Mathematics

Page 1

Choose the letter of your answer.

1. 7 + 1
a. 6   c. 8
b. 7   d. not given

2. Which numbers are all factors of 60?
a. 0, 2, 3, 9
b. 1, 3, 12, 15
c. 2, 4, 8, 10
d. 3, 10, 12, 24

3. Which number is composite?
a. 61   b. 71   c. 87   d. 97

4. What fraction is shaded?
a. $\frac{3}{7}$ b. $\frac{4}{7}$ c. $\frac{3}{4}$ d. $\frac{4}{3}$

5. Complete. $\frac{7}{10} = \frac{\square}{50}$
a. 14   b. 35   c. 47   d. 70

6. What is $\frac{28}{3}$ in simplest form?
a. $1\frac{3}{9}$ b. $3\frac{1}{9}$ c. $9\frac{1}{3}$ d. not given

7. Which number is greatest?
a. $6\frac{4}{5}$ b. 6   c. $6\frac{5}{7}$ d. $6\frac{3}{4}$

8. What is $\frac{5}{6}$ of 30?
a. 5   b. 15   c. 20   d. 25

9. 6 × 396
a. 1,846   c. 2,346
b. 1,926   d. 2,376

10. 6)$6.42
a. $1.07   c. $17.00
b. $1.70   d. $107.00

11. $34.69 + $9.05
a. $34.64   c. $43.64
b. $34.74   d. not given

12. 8,000 ÷ 4
a. 2,000   c. 32
b. 320   d. 20

13. Which is the best estimate of 205 ÷ 5?
a. 4   c. 400
b. 40   d. 4,000

14. Estimate by rounding. $9.84 - $3.46
a. $6.00   c. $8.00
b. $7.00   d. $13.00

15. 5,302
   - 2,709
a. 2,593   c. 3,603
b. 2,693   d. not given

16. 75
   × 5
a. 130   c. 355
b. 145   d. 375

17. About how much is 3 × $9.89?
a. about $30.00
b. about $36.00
c. about $300.00
d. about $360.00

Name

Page 2

18. 3 × $6.44
a. $9.77   c. $18.32
b. $18.22   d. $19.32

19. 369 ÷ 8
a. 40 R9   c. 46 R1
b. 41 R1   d. 46 R6

20. 630 ÷ 9
a. 7   c. 700
b. 70   d. 7,000

21. Estimate by rounding. 5,149 ÷ 5
a. 100   c. 800
b. 200   d. 1,000

22. 40 × 70
a. 21,000   c. 280
b. 2,800   d. 210

23. 5)83
a. 10 R3   c. 16 R3
b. 13 R3   d. not given

24. Find the perimeter.
6 cm × 6 cm square
a. 36 cm   c. 18 cm
b. 24 cm   d. not given

25. Which is the best estimate for the capacity of a water pitcher?
a. 2 mL   c. 2 L
b. 20 mL   d. 20 L

26. How much time passes between 11:50 A.M. and 1:30 P.M.?
a. 40 min   c. 2 h 40 min
b. 1 h 40 min   d. 25 h 40 min

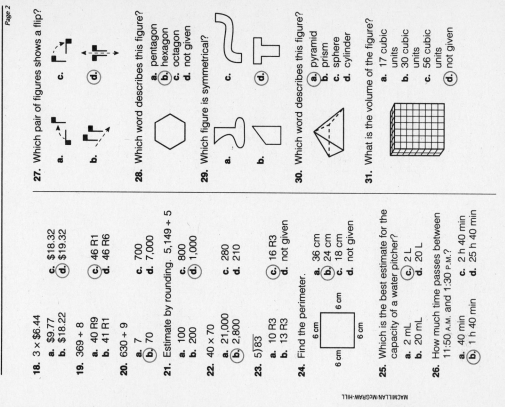

27. Which pair of figures shows a flip?
a.   b.   c.   d.

28. Which word describes this figure?
a. pentagon
b. hexagon
c. octagon
d. not given

29. Which figure is symmetrical?
a.   b.   c.   d.

30. Which word describes this figure?
a. pyramid
b. prism
c. sphere
d. cylinder

31. What is the volume of the figure?
a. 17 cubic units
b. 30 cubic units
c. 56 cubic units
d. not given

TM101

Page 4

Name

42. What is the average?

   a. 160 **b.** 53 **c.** 40 **d.** 32

🛑 STOP

43. The manager of the Tire Hut has 48 tires and 6 racks for the tires. If the manager puts an equal number of tires on each rack, how many tires will be on each rack?

   a. 8 **b.** 42 **c.** 44 **d.** 54

44. Inés and Wally raked 36 yards. Inés raked twice as many yards as Wally raked. How many yards did Inés rake?

   a. 12 **b.** 18 **c.** 24 **d.** 72

45. Mrs. Cleary is putting 134 reports into files. Each file can hold 9 reports. How many files will Mrs. Cleary need?

   a. 9 **b.** 14 **c.** 15 **d.** 21

46. Lindy has 45 stamps. She divides the stamps into 5 equal piles. Then she takes the stamps from the first pile and gives 5 of those stamps to Joan. How many stamps are left in the first pile?

   a. 4 **b.** 5 **c.** 9 **d.** 25

47. Trevor bakes 12 cupcakes. Angela bakes 3 times as many cupcakes as Trevor. Then they sell 16 cupcakes. How many cupcakes are left?

   a. 3 **b.** 20 **c.** 32 **d.** 64

48. Complete and use the table to answer the question.

A ring, a necklace, and a bracelet are in a box. Gina, Mary, and Dawn each pick one of the items. Gina does not pick the ring or the bracelet. Dawn does not pick the ring. Who picks the bracelet?

	ring	bracelet	necklace
Gina	no	no	
Mary			
Dawn		no	

   a. Gina **b.** Mary **c.** Dawn

49. Laverne has twice as many marbles as Don. Terry has 6 more marbles than Don. Elise has 4 fewer marbles than Terry. Elise has 12 marbles. How many marbles does Laverne have?

   a. 4 **b.** 11 **c.** 20 **d.** 24

50. Use number sense.

Addie needs 2 pieces of rope to make a swing. She will need $8\frac{1}{3}$ feet of rope for each piece. She has a piece of rope 17 feet long. Does she have enough rope to make the swing?

   a. Yes. **b.** No.

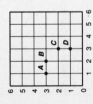

Page 3

Name

32. Which is the best estimate for the length of a fourth-grade student's arm?

   a. 18 inches **c.** 18 yards
   b. 18 feet **d.** 18 miles

Use the diagram to answer Questions 33–35.

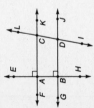

33. Point C is the vertex of ____.

   a. ∠ABD **c.** ∠CDB
   b. ∠EAB **d.** ∠LCK

34. Which two lines are parallel?

   a. $\overleftrightarrow{EH}$ and $\overleftrightarrow{LI}$ **c.** $\overleftrightarrow{FK}$ and $\overleftrightarrow{EH}$
   b. $\overleftrightarrow{GJ}$ and $\overleftrightarrow{FK}$ **d.** not given

35. Which names a line segment in the diagram?

   a. $\overline{BD}$ **c.** ∠LCK
   b. $\overleftrightarrow{EH}$ **d.** $\overleftrightarrow{AF}$

Use the grid to answer Question 36.

36. What is the ordered pair for point B?

   a. (1, 3) **c.** (3, 2)
   b. (2, 3) **d.** not given

Use the pictograph to answer Questions 37–39.

FLOWERS IN LANDVIEW GARDEN

Kind of Flower	Number
Rose	🌼🌼🌼
Tulip	🌼🌼🌼
Poppy	🌼🌼
Daisy	🌼🌼🌼
Lily	🌼

🌼 = 20 flowers

37. Which type of flower is least common at Landview Garden?

   a. rose **c.** daisy
   b. lily **d.** tulip

38. Landview Garden has the same number of which two flowers?

   a. tulip, daisy **c.** daisy, rose
   b. rose, tulip **d.** lily, poppy

39. How many more daisies than poppies are there at Landview Garden?

   a. 2 **b.** 10 **c.** 20 **d.** 40

Use the set of numbers to answer Questions 40–42.

   25, 39, 43, 53

40. What is the median?

   a. 25 **b.** 39 **c.** 41 **d.** 48

41. What is the range?

   a. 53 **b.** 41 **c.** 40 **d.** 28

Name

Macmillan/McGraw-Hill **End-Year Test** Grade 4
Mathematics

Choose the letter of your answer.

1. Which amount is greatest?
   a. $24.52 c. $24.39
   b. $24.48 **d.** $24.61

2. 13
   − 0
   a. 0
   b. 13
   c. 130
   d. not given

3. Which numbers are all factors of 48?
   a. 3, 6, 9, 12 c. 3, 4, 12, 15
   b. 4, 8, 12, 24 d. 1, 2, 3, 5

4. What is $\frac{2}{5}$ of the set?
   a. 2 **b.** 4 c. 5 d. 25

5. Which fraction is equivalent to $\frac{9}{18}$?
   a. $\frac{9}{36}$ b. $\frac{1}{3}$ **c.** $\frac{1}{2}$ d. $\frac{1}{9}$

6. Compare. 1.6 ☐ $1\frac{6}{10}$
   a. > b. < **c.** =

7. Which number is least?
   a. $1\frac{4}{10}$ b. $2\frac{1}{5}$ c. $1\frac{7}{10}$ **d.** $1\frac{3}{10}$

8. What is the decimal for $\frac{43}{100}$?
   a. 0.04 c. 4.3
   b. 0.43 d. not given

9. Compare. 5.2 ☐ 4.9
   a. > b. < c. =

10. What fraction is shaded?
    a. $\frac{1}{3}$ **b.** $\frac{3}{8}$ c. $\frac{1}{2}$ d. $\frac{5}{8}$

11. Estimate by rounding.
    $7.71 + $3.28 + $4.10
    a. $14.00 c. $16.00
    b. $15.00 d. $17.00

12. 2,312 + 4,896
    a. 2,584 c. 7,108
    b. 6,228 **d.** not given

13. 25 ÷ 5
    a. 29 b. 24 c. 10 **d.** 5

14. 60 × 90
    a. 480 **c.** 4,800
    b. 540 d. not given

15. Which is the best estimate of 5 × 803?
    a. 400 **c.** 4,000
    b. 1,300 d. 13,000

16. 3 × $7.00
    a. $21.00 c. $2.10
    b. $18.00 d. not given

17. What is $\frac{4}{9} + \frac{2}{9}$ in simplest form?
    a. $\frac{2}{9}$ b. $\frac{6}{18}$ **c.** $\frac{2}{3}$ d. 6

Name

18. 8)480
    a. 6
    b. 60
    c. 600
    d. 6,000

19. $9.95 ÷ 5
    a. $1.99 c. $49.75
    b. $19.90 d. not given

20. What is $\frac{7}{8} - \frac{3}{8}$ in simplest form?
    a. $\frac{1}{2}$ c. $1\frac{1}{4}$
    b. $\frac{5}{8}$ d. not given

21. 30 × 300
    a. 900,000 **c.** 9,000
    b. 90,000 d. 900

22. Estimate by using the front digits.
    13 × $65
    a. $70 c. $700
    b. $600 d. $6,000

23. 63 × 71
    a. 42,813 c. 639
    b. 4,473 d. not given

24. 50)8,000
    a. 16 **c.** 160
    b. 106 d. 1,060

25. 40)360
    a. 8 **b.** 9 c. 90 d. 120

26. Estimate by rounding.
    2.81 + 1.31
    a. 1 b. 2 **c.** 3 d. 4

27. 9 × 305
    a. 2,705 **c.** 2,745
    b. 2,714 d. 2,835

28. $\frac{5}{7} - \frac{2}{7}$
    a. $\frac{3}{7}$ b. $\frac{1}{2}$ c. $\frac{4}{7}$ d. 3

29. 40 × 5,000
    a. 2,000 **c.** 200,000
    b. 20,000 d. not given

30. Estimate by rounding.
    49 × 66
    a. 2,800 c. 3,500
    b. 3,200 **d.** 4,000

31. $64
    × 12
    a. $768 c. $120
    b. $192 d. $52

32. 2,100 ÷ 30
    a. 700 **b.** 70 c. 30 d. 7

33. 71 ÷ 30
    a. 2 R11 c. 20 R1
    b. 3 R1 d. not given

34. Which is the best estimate of 9.8 − 7.4?
    a. less than 0.2
    b. less than 2
    c. greater than 2
    d. greater than 16

35. How much time passes between 6:15 P.M. and 11:59 P.M.?
    a. 5 h 16 min c. 6 h 16 min
    b. 5 h 44 min d. not given

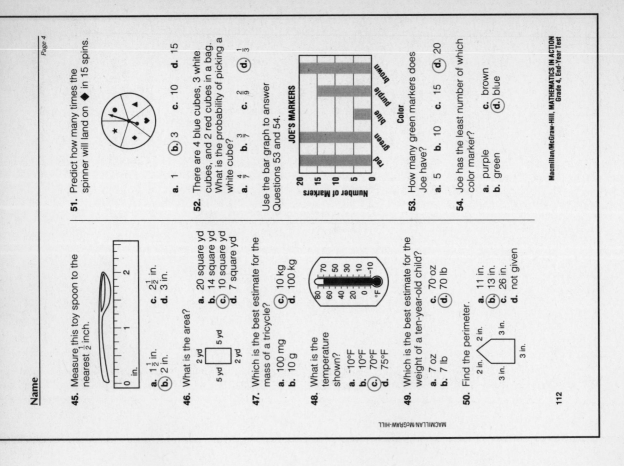

45. Measure this toy spoon to the nearest ½ inch.
a. 1½ in.
b. 2 in.
c. 2½ in.
d. 3 in.

46. What is the area?
2 yd · 5 yd · 5 yd · 2 yd
a. 20 square yd
b. 14 square yd
c. 10 square yd
d. 7 square yd

47. Which is the best estimate for the mass of a tricycle?
a. 100 mg
b. 10 g
c. 10 kg
d. 100 kg

48. What is the temperature shown?
a. -10°F
b. 10°F
c. 70°F
d. 75°F

49. Which is the best estimate for the weight of a ten-year-old child?
a. 7 oz
b. 7 lb
c. 70 oz
d. 70 lb

50. Find the perimeter.
2 in. 2 in. 3 in. 3 in. 3 in.
a. 11 in.
b. 13 in.
c. 26 in.
d. not given

51. Predict how many times the spinner will land on ◆ in 15 spins.
a. 1
b. 3
c. 10
d. 15

52. There are 4 blue cubes, 3 white cubes, and 2 red cubes in a bag. What is the probability of picking a white cube?
a. $\frac{4}{7}$
b. $\frac{3}{7}$
c. $\frac{2}{9}$
d. $\frac{1}{3}$

Use the bar graph to answer Questions 53 and 54.

JOE'S MARKERS

Number of Markers: 0 5 10 15 20
Color: red green blue purple brown

53. How many green markers does Joe have?
a. 5
b. 10
c. 15
d. 20

54. Joe has the least number of which color marker?
a. purple
b. green
c. brown
d. blue

36. You can usually go roller-skating outside when the temperature is
a. 80°C
b. 60°C
c. 30°C
d. -10°C

37. Which is the best estimate of the length of a candle?
a. 10 cm
b. 100 cm
c. 10 m
d. 100 m

38. Which figure shows perpendicular lines?
a.   c.
b.   d.

39. Find the perimeter.
5 ft   6 ft   4 ft
a. 10 ft
b. 11 ft
c. 13 ft
d. not given

40. Which figure is a rectangle?
a.   c.
b.   d.

41. Which angle has point E as a vertex?
a. ∠DEX
b. ∠GHY
c. ∠EHI
d. not given

42. Which pair of figures shows a slide?
a.   c.
b.   d.

43. Which figure is symmetrical?
a.   c.
b.   d.

44. What is the volume of the figure?
a. 16 cubic units
b. 8 cubic units
c. 6 cubic units
d. 4 cubic units

Name

Use the set of numbers to answer Questions 55 and 56.

82, 73, 54, 63

55. What is the range?

a. 73
b. 68
c. 54
d. not given

56. What is the average?

a. 68
b. 73
c. 82
d. 272

Use the graph to answer Questions 57 and 58.

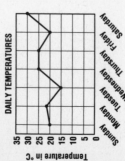

DAILY TEMPERATURES

57. Which day had the lowest temperature?

a. Sunday
b. Monday
c. Tuesday
d. Wednesday

58. What was the temperature on Wednesday?

a. 30°C
b. 25°C
c. 20°C
d. 15°C

Use the grid to answer Questions 59 and 60.

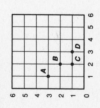

59. The ordered pair for point D is ____.

a. (1, 3)
b. (2, 1)
c. (2, 2)
d. (3, 1)

60. Which letter is at the point (2, 1)?

a. A
b. B
c. C
d. D **STOP**

61. Kay rode 12 blocks on her bike. Her brother rode 16 blocks. Uncle Jim rode more blocks than either of the children. What else do you need to know to find how many more blocks Uncle Jim rode than Kay and her brother?

a. the name of the city
b. how many blocks Uncle Jim rode
c. the name of Kay's brother
d. how many uncles Kay has

62. Use number sense.

Lucas and Dave want to mow 4 lawns in one afternoon. They each mow $1\frac{3}{4}$ lawns. Did they meet their goal?

a. Yes.
b. No.

Name

63. Bryan has 350 pennies. Maria has 90 pennies. Which number sentence should you use to find how many more pennies Bryan has than Maria?

a. 350 + 90 =
b. 350 × 90 =
c. 350 + 90 =
d. 350 − 90 =

64. Howie buys 4 cans of juice for $.60 each and 2 boxes of cereal for $2.00 each. How much change should he get from a $10 bill?

a. $.80
b. $3.60
c. $6.40
d. $9.20

65. In the dance recital, students plan to wear red, green, or white tights with black, white, or red costumes. How many different combinations can each student make?

a. 3
b. 5
c. 6
d. 9

66. Jani is buying groceries for her mother. She buys napkins for $2.25, butter for $1.89, meat for $6.69, and juice for $2.89. Is $15.00 enough to pay for these items?

a. Yes.
b. No.

67. The Stone River is 456 km long. It flows into the Cascade River, which is 839 km long. What is the total length of the two rivers combined?

a. 383 km
b. 1,200 km
c. 1,295 km
d. 1,751 km

68. There are 51 people at the picnic. If each picnic table holds 6 people, how many tables will be needed to seat everyone?

a. 21
b. 9
c. 8
d. 7

69. Wallace needs to sell $30.00 worth of raffle tickets to raise money for the school orchestra. He collects $19.75 on Monday and $11.25 on Tuesday. Has he collected enough money?

a. Yes.
b. No.

70. Find the pattern to solve.

Hogan's Fishing Store gives away 2 free hooks for every 8 lures sold, 4 hooks for every 16 lures sold, and 6 hooks for every 24 lures sold. Mr. Tryee buys 48 lures. How many hooks does he receive?

a. 8
b. 12
c. 30
d. 40

71. Sean has 86 baseball cards. Then James gives him 112 cards. How many more cards does Sean need to have 300 cards in his collection?

a. 26
b. 102
c. 198
d. 498

72. A newspaper prints 2,045 copies of its Friday edition and 3,963 copies of its weekend edition. The owner wants to know how many copies were printed in all. Which is the most reasonable answer?

a. 600
b. 3,008
c. 4,208
d. 6,008

73. Felipe went to the movies 20 times last year. He spent $4 each time. Which number sentence should you use to find how much he spent in all?

   a. $20 \times \$4 = $ ▨
   b. $20 + \$4 = $ ▨
   c. $20 - \$4 = $ ▨
   d. $20 \div \$4 = $ ▨

Use the diagram to answer Questions 74 and 75.

Tree Diagram	List
van — red / blue	red van / blue van
2-door — red / blue	red 2-door / blue 2-door
4-door — red / blue	▨ ▨ ▨ ▨
station wagon — red / blue	▨ ▨ ▨ ▨

74. Mr. Elias wants to buy a new car. He has a choice of a van, a 2-door sedan, a 4-door sedan, or a station wagon. All four kinds of cars come in either red or blue. How many choices does Mr. Elias have?

   a. 16   **b.** 8   **c.** 4   **d.** 2

75. If Mr. Elias decides that he wants either a van or a station wagon, how many choices does he have?

   a. 16   **b.** 8   **c.** 4   **d.** 2

Macmillan/McGraw-Hill, MATHEMATICS IN ACTION
Grade 4, End-Year Test